GEO

NASCAR RACING

The History of NASCAR

by A. R. Schaefer

Consultant:
Betty L. Carlan
Research Librarian
International Motorsports Hall of Fame
Talladega, Alabama

Capstone press

Mankato, Minnesota

Edge Books are published by Capstone Press,
151 Good Counsel Drive, P.O. Box 669, Mankato, Minnesota 56002.
www.capstonepress.com

Library of Congress Cataloging-in-Publication Data
Schaefer, A. R. (Adam Richard), 1976–
    The history of NASCAR / by A.R. Schaefer.
    p. cm.—(Edge Books NASCAR racing)
    Includes bibliographical references and index.
    ISBN 0-7368-3774-4 (hardcover)
    1. Stock car racing—United States—History—Juvenile literature. 2. NASCAR
(Association)—History—Juvenile literature. I. Title. II. Series.
GV1029.9.S74S35 2005
796.72—dc22   2004012840

Summary: Explores the history of NASCAR, including the sport's early years, growing
    popularity, sponsorships, and its most famous drivers.

Editorial Credits
Tom Adamson, editor; Jason Knudson, set designer; Enoch Peterson, book designer;
    Jo Miller, photo researcher; Scott Thoms, photo editor

Photo Credits
AP/Wide World Photos, 15; Ric Feld, 5, 6
Corbis/NewSport/George Tiedemann, 7, 27; Bettmann, 9, 12
Getty Images Inc./Time Life Pictures/Grey Villet, 11; AllSport/Tom Copeland, 17;
    Robert Laberge, 18; Jamie Squire, 19; Chris Stanford, 21; Andy Lyons, 23
Transparencies Inc., cover; Tim O'Dell, 24

Table of Contents

CHAPTER 1

A Dramatic Finish

Some of the greatest NASCAR drivers of all time battled for the lead all afternoon in the 1979 Daytona 500. Dale Earnhardt, Donnie Allison, Cale Yarborough, A. J. Foyt, and Richard Petty were all near the front of the pack at different times. The 120,000 people in the stands cheered.

By the final lap, Donnie Allison held a small lead over Cale Yarborough. Richard Petty and Darrell Waltrip were third and fourth, several seconds behind.

Rounding the second turn, Yarborough tried to pass Allison at the bottom of the track. But Allison got in the way. The cars bumped. The contact sent Yarborough into the grass. His car spun back on the track and into Allison's car. The two cars crashed into the wall in the third turn. Petty and Waltrip zoomed past. Petty won by a car length.

Donnie Allison (#1) and Cale Yarborough (#11) crashed on the last lap of the 1979 Daytona 500.

Learn about:

→ **1979 Daytona 500**
→ **The fight**
→ **A nationwide sport**

Bobby Allison fought with Yarborough after the race.

Back at the crash, Allison's brother Bobby stopped his car. He argued with Yarborough. The three drivers got into a fight as Petty drove into the winner's circle.

This race was the first Daytona 500 broadcast on national TV from start to finish. Millions of viewers loved what they saw. Many people think the 1979 Daytona 500 helped make NASCAR a popular sport.

About NASCAR

The National Association for Stock Car Auto Racing (NASCAR) is now more popular than ever. The three major NASCAR racing series are the Nextel Cup Series, the Busch Series, and the Craftsman Truck Series. Every NASCAR race is on live TV across the country. Even practice and qualifying sessions are shown on national TV.

Nextel Cup races are some of the biggest sporting events in the world. Races in Daytona, Indianapolis, and Charlotte usually have several hundred thousand fans at the track.

Fans pack the stands to watch Nextel Cup races.

CHAPTER 2

The Early Years

When NASCAR started, its popularity was not even close to what it is today. Some race winners made less than $100. Races were run on dirt tracks, mostly in the southern United States. Today, drivers earn millions of dollars. The sport has grown quickly in a short time.

First Years

In 1947, NASCAR formed in Daytona Beach, Florida. Before this time, drivers faced different rules from race to race. NASCAR brought a standard set of rules to the sport.

NASCAR's first season was 1948. Drivers raced modified cars and roadsters in this first season. Modified cars were all different. Drivers made changes to their race cars to make them faster. Roadsters were sporty convertibles.

Modified cars crash in this dirt track race in Daytona Beach in 1953.

Learn about:

→ NASCAR's start

→ Growth of a sport

→ The first Daytona 500

Stock Cars

People also raced stock cars at this time. The first big NASCAR stock car race was in 1949 in Charlotte. Promoters offered $5,000 in prize money. The race was a huge success. Many fans showed up to watch the 225-mile (362-kilometer) race.

Stock cars were different from the modified cars and roadsters. A true stock car is not changed from the way the manufacturer made it. In the late 1940s, stock cars were just like the cars that people bought at car dealerships.

"The driving was more fun than the competition. It didn't make a lot of difference to me where I finished or who won the race as long as I got to run."
—Early NASCAR star Buck Baker, *NASCAR: The Definitive History of America's Sport*

Drivers and fans loved the stock car competitions. NASCAR ran seven more stock car races in 1949. In 1950, NASCAR ran 19 stock car races. That year, the first 500-mile (805-kilometer) stock car race was held in Darlington, South Carolina. NASCAR ran 41 races in the 1951 season.

Darlington became one of NASCAR's elite tracks in the 1950s.

A car spins out during the first Daytona 500 in 1959.

The Daytona 500

A big step for NASCAR was the opening of Daytona International Speedway in 1959. The 2.5-mile (4-kilometer) track was built as a combination of a triangle and an oval. This tri-oval track lets fans see more of the action. Daytona was the fastest track that stock car drivers had ever raced.

The first Daytona 500 was the beginning of a new time in NASCAR racing. The race took place in February 1959. The race had such a close finish that race officials looked at photos for three days before deciding who won. More fans began enjoying NASCAR's fast cars, fast tracks, and exciting races.

"Daytona was bigger and wider than anything we had run on."
—Early NASCAR star Ned Jarrett, *NASCAR: The Definitive History of America's Sport*

CHAPTER 3

Sponsors

NASCAR began to change rapidly. In the 1960s, more fast racetracks opened. Charlotte, Atlanta, Rockingham, Dover, Talladega, and Bristol were new, exciting sites for NASCAR events. The next 10 years were even bigger for the sport.

Sponsorships and TV

During the 1970s, NASCAR saw big changes. Many businesses began sponsoring the sport and the teams. With sponsors, race teams could spend more money on cars and mechanics.

In 1979, people who had never heard of NASCAR had a front-row seat. The TV network CBS showed the complete Daytona 500 live. Viewers loved watching this race that included a wreck, a fight, and an exciting finish.

In the 1970s, sponsorships became important in NASCAR.

Learn about:

→ TV

→ Race weekend

→ The race cars

NASCAR Today

NASCAR's growth continued through the 1980s and 1990s. The sport saw a big increase in money and fans. NASCAR became recognized as a major sports league. Drivers earned more money, cars raced faster, and stands held more fans.

NASCAR is now very different from what it was in its first season in 1948. Today, drivers are well-known. People don't have to be NASCAR fans to have heard the names Jeff Gordon, Dale Earnhardt Jr., and Tony Stewart.

Even though the drivers are celebrities, NASCAR has always been a team sport. The pit crew, mechanics, and crew chief all help a team win races.

"The way the sport is now and how exciting it is, it's really awesome to be a part of it at this time."
—Dale Earnhardt Jr., nascar.com, 5-26-04

A crowd of fans usually follows Dale Earnhardt Jr. at the track.

Races

NASCAR races are now huge events. In the early days, drivers showed up at the track, raced, and left. Today's race events last several days. With practice and qualifying, the Busch Series and the Nextel Cup races take an entire weekend.

NASCAR has expanded to tracks in the west, such as California.

NASCAR added truck racing in 1995.

NASCAR added the Craftsman Truck Series in 1995. Drivers race pickup trucks in these races. Some weekends, fans can see races from each of the three series at the same racetrack.

NASCAR started in the southeastern United States. NASCAR races are now held all over the country. The Nextel Cup Series now has races in Texas, Illinois, Arizona, Nevada, and California. NASCAR has even traveled to Japan for a race.

Cars

Today's stock cars are not really stock cars at all. They are specially made high-performance vehicles. Each race team builds race cars from scratch. They are designed to be safe, fast, and strong.

A NASCAR race team needs millions of dollars to be successful. The team must build cars, pay mechanics, and travel across the country. Some of that money is won back at races.

A large amount of money for race teams comes from sponsorships. A business gives money to a race team. In exchange, the business advertises itself on the driver's uniform and car. In the early days, stock cars looked like regular cars with numbers painted on the sides. Today, decals and paint jobs cover the cars. People identify drivers with their cars.

Sponsors help race teams pay for the expense of cars and equipment.

CHAPTER 4

Famous Drivers

During NASCAR's history, many famous drivers have helped define the sport. Some drivers have won so many races that they have become legends.

Richard Petty

Richard Petty started his NASCAR career in 1958 when he was 21. His father, Lee Petty, was one of the great drivers in NASCAR's early years. Lee won 54 races in 13 years. Richard picked up where his dad left off.

Richard Petty holds almost every important NASCAR record. He has won more races, led more races, and driven more miles than any other driver in NASCAR history. In 1967, Petty won 27 races. Only about 20 drivers have won more than 27 races in their entire careers. Petty did it in one season.

Petty became known for wearing a cowboy hat and sunglasses.

Learn about:

→ **The King**
→ **The Intimidator**
→ **The Kid**

23

Between 1960 and 1984, Petty won seven championships and finished in the top-ten in all years but one. Petty retired in 1992 with 200 wins. Only one other driver has even half that many wins. People call Petty "the King." Many people say that the sport could not have been as successful as it is without Richard Petty.

Earnhardt was one of the most popular drivers in NASCAR history.

Dale Earnhardt

Like Richard Petty, Dale Earnhardt came from a racing family. His father, Ralph Earnhardt, was a good driver in the first years of NASCAR. Dale joined NASCAR's top series full time in 1979. That year, he won the Rookie of the Year award. The next year, he won the championship. Earnhardt went on to win six more championships, tying Petty's record. He won 76 Cup races.

Even though Earnhardt won many races and championships, he always seemed to have bad luck at the Daytona 500. He badly wanted to win NASCAR's most popular and important race. He finished in second place four times. After 19 years, he finally won the race in 1998. Every driver and crew member formed a line on pit road to congratulate him after the race.

> **"I care about winning races, not if they like me."**
> —Dale Earnhardt, *Sports Illustrated*, 9-7-87

Earnhardt was an aggressive driver. Fans loved him for this. They called him "the Intimidator." In 2001, Earnhardt died in a wreck on the last lap of the Daytona 500.

Jeff Gordon

Jeff Gordon is one of the biggest stars currently driving in the Nextel Cup Series. When Gordon was 18, the ESPN TV network sponsored Gordon at a stock car racing school. They paid his expenses, and he agreed to be filmed. Fans thought he was a good driver for his age.

When Gordon first started driving and winning, people called him "the Kid" because he was so young. Since then, Gordon has won 69 races. He has also won four championships. He has finished in the top-ten in the standings every year since 1994.

These stars and many others made NASCAR popular. Today's best young drivers include Dale Earnhardt Jr., Matt Kenseth, Jimmie Johnson, and Ryan Newman. These drivers are ready to become the stars of tomorrow and draw more fans to the sport.

Gordon always contends for the championship.

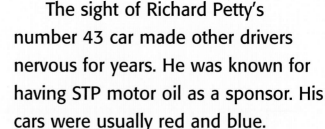

Famous cars are usually famous because of their drivers. Lead cars are the ones that people notice.

The sight of Richard Petty's number 43 car made other drivers nervous for years. He was known for having STP motor oil as a sponsor. His cars were usually red and blue.

Race fans knew Dale Earnhardt simply by the number on his car. For years, people called him "Three." For much of Earnhardt's career, his car was painted black. Other racers hated seeing his black car in their rearview mirrors.

Jeff Gordon's number 24 car is so noticeable that it gave him a nickname. His car had many colors on the sides and hood. It looked like a rainbow. People nicknamed him "the Rainbow Warrior."

Time Line

1947   NASCAR forms in Daytona Beach, Florida.

1948   The first NASCAR races are held for modified cars and roadsters.

1949   NASCAR holds its first big stock car race in Charlotte, North Carolina.

1959   Daytona International Speedway opens. The first Daytona 500 takes place.

1967   Richard Petty dominates by winning 27 races.

1979   The Daytona 500 is the first complete NASCAR race to be shown live on TV.

1980   Dale Earnhardt wins his first of seven NASCAR championships.

1992   Richard Petty retires, holding nearly every NASCAR record.

1994   Jeff Gordon wins the first stock car race to be run at Indianapolis Motor Speedway, the Brickyard 400.

2001   Dale Earnhardt dies in a crash on the last lap of the Daytona 500.

2004   The Winston Cup Series becomes known as the Nextel Cup Series.

Glossary

aggressive (uh-GRESS-iv)—strong and forceful

broadcast (BRAWD-kast)—to send out a program on TV

manufacturer (man-yuh-FAK-chur-ur)—a person or company that makes something

promoter (pruh-MOH-tur)—a person or company that hosts a racing event

qualifying (KWAHL-uh-fye-ing)—the timed laps drivers run before a race to earn a starting spot in the race

sponsor (SPON-sur)—a person or company that gives money or other support to someone in order to gain publicity

Read More

Brock, Ted. *Fast Families: Racing Together through Life.* The World of NASCAR. Excelsior, Minn.: Tradition Books, 2003.

McGuire, Ann. *The History of NASCAR.* Race Car Legends. Philadelphia: Chelsea House, 2000.

Woods, Bob. *Dirt Track Daredevils: The History of NASCAR.* The World of NASCAR. Excelsior, Minn.: Tradition Books, 2003.

Internet Sites

FactHound offers a safe, fun way to find Internet sites related to this book. All of the sites on FactHound have been researched by our staff.

Here's how:

1. Visit *www.facthound.com*

2. Type in this special code **0736837744** for age-appropriate sites. Or enter a search word related to this book for a more general search.

3. Click on the **Fetch It** button.

FactHound will fetch the best sites for you!

Index

He looked up at me from under bushy eyebrows. "You a relative of the deceased?" he asked, an edge of challenge in his tone.

"My name is Compton," I said. "I do investigations for the Spiders."

"What kind of investigations?"

"Investigations they need me to do," I said. "Was he poisoned, or wasn't he?"

Witherspoon looked at the server still standing silently across the room, then back at me, then over at the other side of the room, where Kennrick and the other two Shorshians were consulting in low voices with the Filly doctor. "He was definitely poisoned," he said, lowering his own voice. "The problem is that Shorshians are highly susceptible to poisons, and there are a thousand different ones that can create symptoms like this. Without an autopsy, there's no way to know which one killed him."

I nodded and turned to Bayta. "Where can we set up for an autopsy?" I asked her.

"Wait a minute," Witherspoon protested before Bayta could answer. "Even if I was practiced at non-Human autopsies, we don't have the kind of equipment aboard to handle something like that."

"How about just a biochem autopsy?" I asked.

"That takes almost as much equipment as the regular version," he said. "Not to mention a truckload of specialized chemicals and reagents."

"A spectroscopic test, then?" I persisted.

"Mr. Compton, just how well equipped do you think Quadrail trains are?" he asked, his patience starting to crack at the edges.

"Obviously, not very," I conceded. "Luckily for us, I happen to have a spectroscopic analyzer in my compartment."

"Right," Witherspoon said with a sniff. He took another look at my face, his derision level slipping a notch. "You *are* joking, aren't you?"

The conversation between Kennrick, the Filly, and the two Shorshians had faded away into silence. "Not at all," I assured the whole group. "I trust you at least know which tissue samples would be the most useful?"

"Yes, I think so," Witherspoon said, still staring at me. "You have a *spectroscopic analyzer*? In your *compartment*?"

"I use it in my work," I explained. "Do you have the necessary equipment for taking the tissue samples, or will the Spiders need to scrounge something up?"

"The Spiders have sampling kits," Bayta put in.

"I also have a couple in my bag," Witherspoon said, gesturing to the cabinet where a traditional doctor's bag was sitting on one of the shelves. "May I ask what kind of investigations you do that you require a spectroscopic analyzer?"

"Show me the medical relevance of that information and I may share it with you," I said. "Otherwise, let's get on with it."

Witherspoon's lip twitched. "Of course." He looked over at the Shorshians. "But I'll need permission for the autopsy."

Kennrick, who'd been staring at me in much the same way Witherspoon had been, belatedly picked up on the cue. "Master Bofiv?" he asked, turning to the taller of the two Shorshians. "Can you advise me on Shorshic law and custom on such things?"

[It is not proper that such be done by strangers,] Master Bofiv said, his Shishish sounding harsher than usual here in the dead of night. Or maybe it was the presence of the recently deceased that was adding all the extra corners to the words.

"I understand your reluctance," Kennrick said, giving a respectful little duck of his head. "But in a case of such importance, surely an exception can be made."

"And indeed *must* be made," I put in.

[We cannot grant this permission,] Bofiv said. [We are not kin, nor of similar path.]

"What about *di*–Master Strinni?" Kennrick asked. "I believe he and Master Colix were of similar paths."

The two Shorshians looked at each other. [That may perhaps be proper,] Bofiv said, a little reluctantly. [But the approach is not mine to make.]

[Nor mine,] the other Shorshian added.

"I understand, Master Tririn," Kennrick said, nodding to him. He looked over at me. "It was Mr. Compton's idea. Mr. Compton can ask *di*-Master Strinni."

[That is acceptable,] Bofiv said before I could protest.

I grimaced. But there was no way out of it. Not if we wanted to find out what had killed the late Master Colix. "Where's *di*-Master Strinni now?" I asked.

"He has a seat in first class," Kennrick said. "I'll take you there."

"Thank you," I said. "Bayta, you might as well wait here."

"I could—" she began, then broke off. "All right," she said instead.

I gestured to Kennrick. "After you."

We left the dispensary and headed down the darkened, quiet corridor toward the front of the train. "Thanks so very much for this," I murmured to him as we walked.

"My pleasure," he said calmly. "I still have a business relationship with these people. If they end up being mortally offended at someone, I'd rather it be you than me."

"Can't fault the logic," I had to admit. "What exactly is this *similar path* thing Bofiv mentioned, and how come he and a *di*-Master are at the same place on it."

"It's a religious thing," Kennrick said. "The Path of

something unpronounceable and untranslatable. Very big among the professional classes at the moment."

"Really," I said, frowning. Major changes in alien religious alignments were one of the things Human intelligence agencies worked very hard to keep tabs on. "I don't remember any briefings on that."

"It really only took off in the past couple of years," Kennrick said. "A lot of Shorshians call it a cult and look down their bulbous snouts at it."

"What's *your* take?" I asked.

He shrugged. "I'm just a lowly Human. What do I know?"

Di-Master Strinni's seat was near the center of the rear first-class car. Unlike the seats in second and third, those in first could be folded completely flat for sleeping, with extendable canopies instead of the far less roomy cylindrical roll-over privacy shields that were standard in the lower classes. Strinni himself hadn't bothered with the canopy tonight, but was merely lying asleep with his inner eyelids closed against the soft glow of the car's night-lights and the scattered handful of reading lamps still operating.

I'd never had cause to try waking a Shorshian from a sound sleep, and it turned out to be harder than I'd expected. But with Kennrick's encouragement I persisted, and eventually the inner eyelids rolled back up and Strinni came fully conscious.

He wasn't at all happy at being woken up out of his sleep. But his annoyance disappeared as soon as he heard the grim news. [You believe this not merely a random tragedy?] he asked after I'd explained the situation.

"We're not sure," I said. "That's why we need to test some tissue samples."

[Might there be a Guidesman of the Path aboard?]

"No idea, *di*-Master Strinni," Kennrick said.

"I could ask one of the conductors," I offered.

The inner eyelids dipped down. I was just wondering if he'd gone back to sleep when they rolled up again. [No need,] he said. [If there was one, that truth would have been made known to me.]

Kennrick and I looked at each other. "So is that a yes?" I suggested.

[No,] he said flatly. [You may not cut into Master Colix's flesh.]

I braced myself. "*Di*-Master Strinni—"

[The subject is closed,] he cut me off. He settled back in his seat, and once again the inner eyelids came down.

This time, they stayed there. "What now?" Kennrick asked.

I frowned at the sleeping Shorshian. Without some idea of what had knocked Colix off his unpronounceable Path, our options were going to be severely limited. "Let's go talk to his traveling companions," I said. "Maybe they'll have some idea of who might have wanted him dead."

The crowd in the second/third dispensary had shrunk considerably by the time Kennrick and I returned. Only Bayta, Witherspoon, and Master Tririn were still there. And Colix's body, of course. "Where'd everyone go?" I asked as Kennrick and I joined them.

"Dr. Aronobal—she's the Filiaelian doctor—went off to work up her report on the death," Bayta said. "Master Bofiv wasn't feeling well and returned to his seat."

"Well?" Witherspoon asked. During our absence, he'd laid out a small sampling kit, complete with scalpel, hypo, and six sample vials.

"Sorry," I said. "*Di*-Master Strinni wouldn't give his permission."

[Did you explain the situation?] Tririn asked.

"In detail, Master Tririn," Kennrick assured him.

"Unless there's a Guidesman of the Path around to supervise, we aren't allowed to cut into Master Colix's body," I added.

"Are we sure there *isn't* someone like that aboard?" Witherspoon asked.

"We'd have to ask the Spiders," I said, looking at Bayta.

She gave me a microscopic shrug. "I suppose we could make inquiries," she said.

Translation: she'd already asked. Either there wasn't a Guidesman aboard or else it wasn't something the Spiders routinely kept track of.

"Speaking of Spiders," Kennrick said, "where's the one that was here earlier?"

"He's gone about other duties," Bayta said. "Did you want him for something?"

"As a matter of fact, I did." Kennrick pointed to the drug cabinet. "I notice that none of those bottles are labeled."

"Actually, they are," Bayta said. "The dot patterns along the sides are Spider notation."

"If a passenger needs something, the Spider prints out a label in his or her native language," Witherspoon explained. "Saves having to try to squeeze a lot of different notations onto something that small."

"I'm sure it does," Kennrick said. "But that also means none of the rest of us has any idea what's actually in any of them."

Bayta frowned. "What do you mean by that?"

"I mean we don't actually *know* that the drugs Dr.

Witherspoon and Dr. Aronobal injected into Master Colix were actually helpful," Kennrick said. "It could easily have been just the opposite."

"Are you accusing the Spiders of deliberately causing him harm?" Bayta asked, a not-so-subtle challenge in her tone.

"Maybe," Kennrick said. "Or else someone might have sneaked in here while the Spider was absent or distracted and changed some of the labels."

I stepped around the body on the table and went over to the drug cabinet. I'd noted earlier that the doors were glassed in; up close, I could see now that it wasn't glass, but some kind of grained polymer. Experimentally, I gave it a rap with my knuckles, then tried the latch.

The door didn't budge. "That would have to be one hell of a distracted Spider," I said, turning back to Kennrick. "Besides, wasn't Master Colix showing symptoms of poisoning before they even brought him in here?"

"Symptoms can be counterfeited," Kennrick said. He looked at the body on the table. "*Or* faked."

"You mean Master Colix might have faked his own poisoning so as to get brought in here so he could get pumped full of something lethal from the Spiders' private drugstore?" I asked.

"Well, yes, if you put it that way I suppose it sounds a little far-fetched," Kennrick admitted. "Still, we need to cover all possibilities."

I turned to Tririn. "Did Master Colix have any addictions or strange tastes?"

[I don't truly know,] Tririn said, a bit hesitantly. [I wasn't well acquainted with him.]

"You *were* business colleagues, correct?"

[True,] Tririn said. [But he had only recently joined our contract team.] He ducked his head to Kennrick. [I would say that Master Kennrick probably knew him as well as I did.]

"And I only met him a couple of months ago," Kennrick put in.

Mentally, I shook my head in disgust. Between *di*-Master Strinni, Kennrick, and Tririn, this was about as unhelpful a bunch as I'd run into for some time. "How about Master Bofiv, then?" I asked. "Did *he* know Master Colix?"

[I don't know,] Tririn said. [I believe *di*-Master Strinni knew him best.]

I looked at my watch. I'd already had to awaken Strinni once tonight, and I wasn't interested in trying it again. "We'll start with Master Bofiv," I decided. "Where is he?"

"Four cars back," Kennrick said. "I'll take you."

"Just tell me which seat," I said, taking Bayta's arm and steering her toward the door. "You should stay with Master Tririn."

"I'm going with you," Kennrick said firmly. "These people are my business colleagues. Whatever happened to Master Colix, we need to resolve it before it poisons relations between us." He winced. "Sorry. Poor choice of words."

"I'll stay here with Master Tririn," Witherspoon volunteered. "There may be a couple of tests I can do that don't involve cutting."

"I'll stay, too, then," Bayta said. "I'd like to watch."

I eyed her. Her face was its usual neutral mask, but there was something beneath the surface I couldn't quite read. Probably she didn't like the idea of the body being left alone with a couple of strangers with no Spider present. "Fine," I said. "Come on, Kennrick."

THREE :

Second-class seats weren't as mobile as those in first class, but they were movable enough to allow families and friends to arrange themselves into little conversation and game circles. Those circles usually remained into and through the nighttime hours, which gave a cozy sort of sleeping-bags-around-the-campfire look to those cars when everyone set up their privacy shields.

Not so in third. In third, where the seats were fixed in neat rows of three each on either side of the central aisle, the rows of cylindrical privacy shields always looked to me like the neatly arranged coffins from some horrible disaster.

"He's down there," Kennrick murmured, pointing.

I craned my neck. Master Bofiv was in one of the middle seats to my right, his seat reclined as far as it would go, his privacy shield open. "I see him," I confirmed. "Quietly, now."

We headed back, making as little noise as possible. Third-class seats weren't equipped with sonic neutralizers like those in first and second, leaving it up to the individual passenger to spring for his or her own earplugs or portable neutralizers or else to hope for quiet neighbors.

Bofiv was lying quietly when we reached his row. One of the passengers three rows up from him had his reading light on, which had the effect of throwing the Shorshian into even deeper shadow than he would have been in without it.

Still, I could see him well enough to tell that his inner eyelids were closed. "I woke up *di*-Master Strinni," I whispered to Kennrick. "It's your turn."

"But you're so good at it," Kennrick said, gesturing. "Please; go ahead."

"You're too kind," I said, frowning. On Bofiv's left, against the car's side wall, was an empty seat, presumably that of his compatriot Master Tririn.

But on Bofiv's right, where I would have expected to find the empty seat of the late Master Colix, was the smooth half-cylinder of a closed privacy shield. "Who's that?" I asked, pointing at it.

"A Nemut," Kennrick said. "He's not part of our group."

"Why isn't that Colix's seat?" I asked. "Didn't he want to sit with his buddies?"

"I don't know," Kennrick said, frowning. "Huh. I hadn't really thought about that. You think maybe the others didn't like him?"

"Or vice versa," I said, making a mental note to ask Bofiv and Tririn which of the party had come up with the seating arrangements. "So where *was* Colix sitting?"

"There," Kennrick said, pointing to an empty middle seat across the aisle and two rows forward of the sleeping Bofiv.

I backtracked for a closer look. The late Master Colix's seat was flanked by a pair of privacy shields. Irreverently, I wondered if one of the shields concealed an attractive female Shorshian. Maybe that was why he'd chosen to ditch his colleagues.

And then, as if on cue, the aisle shield retracted to reveal a young Human female.

A *really* young female, in fact. She couldn't be more than seventeen, and even that was pushing it. Her face was thin and drawn, with the look of someone who'd just gone two rounds with food that didn't agree with her.

Make that three rounds. Even before the privacy shield had retracted completely into the armrest and leg-rest storage lip she was on the move, heading toward the front of the car at the quick-walk of the digestively desperate.

I eyed the remaining privacy shield in that particular three-seat block. Maybe *that* was the knockout Shorshic female.

"Well?" Kennrick prompted.

"Well, what?" I countered, turning around to watch the girl. She reached the front of the car and disappeared into one of the restrooms.

"Are we going to ask Master Bofiv about Master Colix's habits and appetites?" Kennrick elaborated.

"In a minute," I said, a sudden unpleasant tingling on the back of my neck as I stared at the closed restroom door. Colix had gotten sick and died . . . and now one of his seatmates had suddenly made a mad dash for the facilities?

Kennrick caught the sudden change in my tone. "What is it?" he asked.

"I don't know," I said. "Maybe nothing."

"Or?"

"Or maybe something," I said, glancing at my watch. Five minutes, I decided. If the girl wasn't back in five minutes I would grab a Spider and send him in to find her.

It was something of an anticlimax when, three minutes

later, the door opened and the girl reappeared. She started a little unsteadily back down the aisle toward her seat, looking even more drawn than she had before.

"Or nothing, I take it?" Kennrick murmured.

"So it would seem," I agreed. The girl's eyes were fixed on me as she came toward us, a wary and rather baleful expression on her pale face. I waited until she was about five steps from us and then tried my best concerned smile on her. "You all right, miss?" I asked softly.

"I'm fine," she said, clipping out each word like she was trimming a thorn hedge. If my concerned smile was having any effect, I sure couldn't detect it. "You mind?"

I wasn't even close to blocking her way, but I gave her a little more room anyway. "I just wondered if you were unwell."

"I'm fine," she said again, brushing past me and flopping down into her seat. She adjusted herself a bit and reached for the privacy shield control.

"Because your seatmate had a bad attack of something," I went on, kneeling down beside her. No point including any more eavesdroppers in this conversation than absolutely necessary. "You might have noticed when his friends took him to the dispensary?"

She slid the control forward, and the shield started to rotate into its closed position. "The dispensary, where he died?" I finished.

The shield closed. I counted off three seconds; and then, the shield opened again. "What did you just say?" the girl asked, her face suddenly tight.

"I said Master Colix is dead," I repeated.

For a long moment she just stared at me. Her eyes flicked up to Kennrick, then back to me. "How?" she whispered.

"He was poisoned," I said. "What's your name?"

She hesitated. "Terese," she said. "Terese German."

"Frank Compton," I introduced myself in return. "How well did you know Master Colix?"

"Hardly at all," Terese said, looking at Kennrick again.

"You didn't talk to him?" Kennrick asked.

Terese hunched her shoulders. "Mostly I read or listened to music."

"But you must have at least occasionally talked to him," Kennrick persisted. "You've been sitting together for the past two weeks, after all."

"He's the one who did all the talking," Terese growled. "Mostly about his job. Oh, and he showed me a few holos of his family, too."

"He was married?" I asked.

A shadow of something crossed her face. "No, they were pictures of his parents and brothers," she said.

"Are *you* married?" Kennrick asked.

"Is that any of your business?" she countered stiffly, giving him an icy look.

"I was just wondering if you were traveling alone," he said in a tone of slightly wounded innocence.

"Then *ask* that," the girl bit out.

"Our apologies," I said hastily. "*Are* you traveling alone?"

"Yes," she said.

"Do you remember Master Colix mentioning feeling ill prior to tonight?" I asked.

"Not to me," she said. She let her glare linger on Kennrick another couple of seconds, apparently making sure he got the message, then looked back at me. "As far as I could tell, he felt fine. At least, up to a couple of hours ago."

"What did he say?" I asked.

"Nothing," she said. "But he was shifting in his seat a lot and making these funny noises."

"What kind of noises? What did they sound like?"

"Mostly uncomfortable-sounding grunts," she said. "Like his stomach was bothering him."

I gestured toward her abdomen. "Like the way your stomach was bothering you a minute ago?"

"It's not the same thing," she said tartly.

"How do you know?" I countered.

"I've got some stomach trouble, that's all," she insisted. "Nothing I'm going to die from."

"Okay," I said, wondering if Colix had been thinking the same thing up to the point where the doctors started poking hypos into him. "What happened then?"

"I was just wondering if I should give up and go to the bar for a while to get away from the noise when he got out of his seat and headed back to his friends," she said.

"How long ago was this?" Kennrick asked.

"Like I said, a couple of hours," she told him.

"Any chance you can pin it down a little more closely?" he asked.

"No, I can't," she said. "I was trying to sleep. I wasn't exactly looking at my watch."

"That's all right," I assured her. "Did anything in particular happen just prior to that time? Had he just returned from the dining car, or had a snack?"

"Or had he been talking to anyone other than you and his other seatmate?" Kennrick asked.

"He hadn't been anywhere or done anything that I saw." Terese nodded at Kennrick. "And the only visitor I saw was you."

I frowned at Kennrick. "You were back here this evening?"

"Early afternoon," he corrected. "I was working on the plans for a traditional Shorshic halfway-celebration meal for next week and wanted Master Colix's advice on menu and procedure."

"How long was this before the uncomfortable grunts started?" I asked Terese.

"Oh, hours," she said. "He had dinner afterwards. And if he had any snacks, I didn't see them."

Dead end. "Did Master Colix go anywhere else this evening? Maybe back to talk with his colleagues a couple of rows back?"

"No." Terese hesitated. "Actually, I had the feeling he didn't get along too well with them."

"How so?"

"For one thing, he didn't want to sit with them," she said. "The Nemut in the aisle seat offered to trade with him right after we left Homshil, but he turned him down."

I looked at Kennrick. "And you didn't notice any of this undercurrent during your meetings on Earth?"

"No, but that doesn't necessarily mean anything," he said. "Shorshians are very good at social compartmentalization. They can all behave in a perfectly friendly way in a business setting even if they personally can't stand each other."

"Not even now that they're on their way home?" I asked. "Wouldn't one of them have at least mentioned it?"

"They wouldn't have mentioned it to me," Kennrick said. "I work for Pellorian Medical, so wherever I am is by definition a business setting. Ditto whenever the Shorshians are with any of the four Filiaelians in our group."

"Are any of the Filiaelians in this car?" I asked, glancing around.

"No, they're all up in first," he said. "And I doubt any of them has made the trek back here since the trip started." He cocked an eyebrow. "But the fact the Shorshians won't talk about their problems to *me* doesn't mean they won't open up to *you*."

I made a face. "In other words, it's time for me to nudge, shake, or otherwise drag Master Bofiv back to the land of the living?"

"Just be persistent," Kennrick advised. "As you saw, they *do* wake up eventually."

He headed back toward Bofiv's seat. "Nice guy," Terese muttered.

"He's all that," I agreed, getting back to my feet. "Thanks for your time."

I joined Kennrick at Bofiv's row. The Shorshian was still lying on his back, his inner eyelids closed. As far as I could tell, he hadn't moved at all since our arrival. "Master Bofiv?" I called softly, giving his arm a cautious shake.

There was no response. "Master Bofiv?" I called again, wiggling the arm a little harder.

Still nothing. I glanced toward the front of the car, wondering if there might be a Spider nearby who I could commandeer for this duty. There wasn't, but I did note that Terese was leaning around her seat watching us.

I turned back to Bofiv. "Master Bofiv, I need to talk to you," I said. I shook his arm again, still without effect, then reached up to try patting the side of his neck.

It was cold. Not cold in the way a sleeping person's skin might get if he forgot to tuck his blanket all the way up to his chin. Bofiv's skin was much colder.

I pulled out my flashlight and flicked it on. The deep shadows had hidden his skin earlier, but I could see now that it had the same mottling that Colix's skin had shown there at the end.

I gazed down at his empty face, a hard knot forming in my stomach. No one was going to be nudging, shaking, or otherwise dragging Bofiv back to the land of the living. Not anymore.

I looked back at Terese. She was still peering around the side of her seat, her curiosity starting to drift over into uncertainty. "What's the matter?" she stage-whispered.

"Do me a favor," I told her. "Go find a conductor and tell him that I need him and another Spider back here right away. And have them get Dr. Witherspoon out of the second/third dispensary and bring him along."

Terese got out of her seat, her eyes on Bofiv's still form. "Is he sick?" she asked.

"No," I told her. "He's dead."

"Without tests I can't be certain," Dr. Witherspoon said as he straightened up. "But in my opinion, he died from the same poison that killed Master Colix."

I looked down at the dispensary's treatment table, where the late Master Bofiv now lay side by side with the late Master Colix. It was a cozy fit. "Great," I said. "We've got a pattern going."

"God help us all," Kennrick muttered. "What are we talking about, Doc, some kind of plague?" He looked pointedly over at the server Spider again standing unobtrusive vigil on the other side of the dispensary. "Something new the Spiders' fancy sensor net let slip through?"

"If it is, it would have to be something both new and very

slippery," Witherspoon said. "I've seen lists of what those sensors catch. Nothing harmful gets through, I assure you."

"Then it has to be something they ate," Kennrick concluded. "If it's not airborne, that's all that's left."

I looked at Tririn, who was standing against the wall beside the Filly doctor. His skin wasn't mottled like the late Master Bofiv's, but it definitely looked paler than it had earlier.

Small wonder. Two of his companions had now bitten the dust, companions who had probably been eating the same food and had definitely been breathing the same air he had over the past two weeks. In his place, I'd have been pretty nervous, too.

"There was nothing dangerous in the food," the server said in his flat Spider voice.

Every head in the room turned at that one. Servers were usually quiet, unassuming little Spiders, with a normal conversational range that was limited to asking a dining car patron what he wanted for lunch or telling a barfly that, sadly, the train was completely out of Jack Daniel's. To have one of them volunteer information, especially information like this, was unheard of.

Kennrick recovered his voice first. "So *you* say," he countered. "I'd want some actual proof of that."

"What about something one of the group brought aboard?" I asked. "Some foodstuff that maybe wasn't packaged properly and went bad?"

"I suppose that's possible," Witherspoon said. "Bacteria-generated toxins can certainly be nasty enough. But it's hard to imagine Master Colix or Master Bofiv eating something that was obviously tainted."

"Which makes it all the more urgent that we get an analysis

of the victims' blood and tissue," I said. "Until we know which poison was responsible, there's no way to backtrack it and figure out where it came from."

"And how do you intend to do that?" Kennrick demanded. "*Di*-Master Strinni has already said no autopsies."

"No, *di*-Master Strinni said no autopsy on Master Colix," I corrected. "He hasn't said anything about Master Bofiv."

"And why would he—?" Kennrick broke off. "You're right," he said, sudden interest in his voice. "Master Bofiv wasn't on the same Path *di*-Master Strinni is."

"Which means he might be willing to let us work on Master Bofiv," I said.

"It's worth a try," Kennrick agreed. "Go ahead. We'll wait here."

"You're the one who knows him," I reminded him.

"You're the one who knows how to wake him up," he countered.

"I've already had to do this twice," I said.

"Once," Kennrick corrected. "You didn't actually wake up Master Bofiv."

"What is the *matter* with you two?" Witherspoon snapped "There are people lying *dead* here."

"And I don't want to be the one to break that news to a business associate," Kennrick said coolly. "It was Compton's idea. He can do it."

Witherspoon rumbled something under his breath. "Oh, for—never mind. *I'll* do it."

He stripped off his examination gloves, tossing them onto the dispensary counter. With a final glare at me, he strode toward the doorway.

He'd made it halfway there when the obvious problem

belatedly caught up with him. "Only I can't, can I?" he growled with frustration and embarrassment. "*Di*-Master Strinni is in first class."

"I think that in this case the conductors will be willing to pass you through," I said.

"You will be permitted," the server confirmed. "A conductor will meet you in the rearmost first-class car and accompany you to *di*-Master Strinni's seat."

"Thank you," Witherspoon said. He got two more steps, then once again hesitated. "Perhaps, Master Tririn, you would accompany me?" he asked, turning to the remaining Shorshian.

Tririn looked at Kennrick, then back at Witherspoon. [Very well,] he said. He murmured something to Aronobal that I couldn't catch; then he and Witherspoon left the room and headed forward.

That left Kennrick, Aronobal, Bayta, and me. Plus the Spider, of course. "Well, that went well," I commented.

"He'll learn," Kennrick said cynically, his gaze lingering on the empty doorway. "Dr. Witherspoon, I mean. Everyone thinks dealing with Shorshians is a walk down the escalator. But he'll learn."

He looked at Aronobal. "But I don't have to tell *you* that, do I?" he went on. "The Filiaelian Assembly has been dealing with them for at least six hundred years now."

"I have never had trouble with the Shorshic people," Aronobal said diplomatically.

"Then you're the exception," Kennrick said. "Half my job seems to consist of smoothing those waters." He turned back to me. "So what now? We wait until they get back?"

"Unless you want to risk Strinni's wrath by starting before the opening bell," I said.

He grimaced. "No, thanks." He started to say something

else, but instead gave a wide yawn. "Hell with this. I'll be in my compartment if you need me."

"On your way, you might consider briefing the Filiaelians in your party about the situation," I suggested as he headed for the door.

"Forget it," he said. "You think waking up Shorshians with this kind of news is a bad idea, you should try it with Filiaelians." His lip twitched and he looked back at Aronobal. "At least with *santra*-rank Filiaelians," he amended.

Aronobal inclined her head but said nothing. Kennrick held his pose for a moment, probably trying to think of some other way to apologize further without looking like either a boor or an idiot, then gave up and looked back at me instead. "Call me if you learn anything."

With that, he escaped into the corridor. I drifted to the doorway, arriving just in time to see the vestibule door leading into the next car close behind him.

"He is not very diplomatic," Aronobal said darkly. "I am surprised that someone chose him to manage dealings with more civilized beings."

The insult had clearly been directed at Kennrick, but I found myself wincing a little anyway. Things that smudged one Human had a tendency to smudge all of us. "He may be better when he's not woken up in the middle of the night to deal with multiple deaths," I suggested.

Aronobal gazed down her long face at me, her nose blaze darkening a little. "A well-trained manager should know how to deal with even the unexpected."

"Maybe he's not as well-trained as we all might like," I said, turning to Bayta. "The server said there wasn't anything in the Shorshians' food. How sure is he of that?"

"Very sure," Bayta said firmly. "The packaging was intact,

and there's nothing in the ingredients of any of the Shorshic-style foods aboard that could be a problem."

"Unless there was some unexpected contamination during the cooking or packaging process," I said. "Maybe we should check that out. If the Spiders don't mind, that is."

From the expression on Bayta's face, it was clear that the Spiders did, in fact, mind. But she knew better than to have this discussion in front of a stranger. "We can certainly ask," she said instead. "The third-class dining car is four cars back."

I nodded and looked at Aronobal. "Keep an eye on Masters Colix and Bofiv, will you?"

"I will," she said. "You will let me know if you find anything?"

"You'll be the first," I promised.

We headed out, turning in the direction of the third-class dining room. I glanced at Bayta's profile as we walked, noting the stiffness in her expression. "If it helps," I said quietly, "I don't actually think this was caused by any negligence on the Spiders' part."

"Neither do I," Bayta said, her voice as stiff as her face.

"But we still have to check it out," I continued. "If for no other reason than to clear them of any responsibility."

"That's not the point," Bayta said. "The Spiders don't want passengers getting into their sections of the train." She sent me a furtive glance. "Not even you."

"I guess you'll just have to go to bat for me on this one," I said.

She gave a soft snort. "I *do* go to bat for you, Frank," she said. "More often than you know."

I studied her profile again, noting the smooth line of her nose, the curve of her cheekbones, and the softness of her skin. That was all most people saw when they looked at her, and while it made for a pleasant enough treat for the eyes, it also effectively hid all the solid stuff below the surface, the character strengths the casual tourist never saw. Intelligence, determination, loyalty, courage—they were all in there, ready to come boiling out whenever they were needed.

And she was right. She'd put her butt on the line for me time and time again. And those were only the times I knew about. "You're right," I acknowledged. "Let's do it this way. I'll wait outside while you go in and look at the facility. I can tell you what to look for, and walk you through anything that needs follow-up."

I could tell she was tempted. It would make life simpler, and give her one fewer telepathic battles to fight. "What would I have to do?" she asked.

I shrugged. "No way to know for sure until we get there. But probably nothing complicated."

She hesitated, then shook her head. "I don't think we can risk it," she said with a sigh. "You're the expert. You really need to look for yourself."

"You sure?" I asked. "I wouldn't want to be stuck on a Quadrail for four more weeks with a whole trainful of Spiders mad at us."

She gave me a wry look, and as she did so some of the tension in her face went away. "Since when do you care what other people think?"

"Oh, I don't care about *me*," I said. "I was worried about *you*."

"Well, don't," she said. "I can take care of myself." She nodded ahead. "Come on—the server's expecting us."

FOUR :

The third-class dining room was deserted when Bayta and I arrived, with only a single server Spider standing a lonely vigil behind the counter along the room's back wall. The counter, in turn, was separated from the area behind him by a slat curtain.

"The door's over here," Bayta said, leading the way toward the side of the serving counter. As we approached, a concealed panel popped open in front of us. I nodded my thanks to the Spider, got the usual lack of reaction in return, and followed Bayta through the doorway.

One of the perennial topics of conversation aboard Quadrails was exactly how the Spiders managed to prepare so many meals for so many travelers. Now, standing in the food preparation room, I finally had an answer to that question.

It was a definite letdown. The prep room was lined with shelves loaded to the gills with flat white boxes covered with Spider dot codes. "Prepackaged meals," I identified them.

"Of course," Bayta said, her tone making me feel a little

ridiculous. "You didn't really think we had full gourmet kitchens on each train, did you?"

"There were rumors," I said, looking around. Along with the food storage shelves, there were other racks containing bottles of water and other liquid refreshments, plus a dozen cook stations that included microwaves, flash-heaters, and rehydrators. Tucked away in one of the back corners was a closed trapdoor with what looked like a wide conveyor belt set vertically against the wall. "For bringing in fresh stock from the storage car?" I asked, pointing at it.

"Yes," Bayta said. "It connects to a conveyor system that runs beneath the cars. We only have those on cross-galactic trains, of course."

I looked back at the food shelves. "I guess we might as well start with the obvious. Which ones are the Shorshic meals?"

"There," Bayta said, pointing to the third stack from the left. "Do you want a list of the meals Master Colix had in the past day? Dr. Aronobal got it from Master Bofiv and Master Tririn earlier while you were speaking with *di*-Master Strinni."

"Did Colix eat the same thing every day?" I asked.

"I don't think so," Bayta said.

"Then I can get the menu later." Stepping over to the Shorshic rack, I picked up the top box.

It was heavier than I'd expected, which probably meant it contained a complete meal instead of appetizers or desserts or something lighter. The box itself was made of a thin but sturdy plastic, sealed with a quick-release strip. Experimentally, I pulled the strip open a couple of centimeters and then tried to reseal it.

It didn't reseal. I tried it again, just to be sure, then tried lifting the corner of the lid, hoping to get a look at the food inside.

But there was a wide flap in the way, and pulling on the

corner merely gained me another couple of centimeters of open strip. "I presume the Spiders would have noticed if one of the meals had shown up unsealed?"

"Of course," Bayta said. "Aren't you going to open it?"

"No need," I said, looking closely at the box in search of punctures or small tears. "What happens to the boxes once the food's been served? Do they get flattened and stored somewhere for reuse?"

"No, they go directly into the recycling system," she said. "The fibers are designed to serve as a catalyst for some of the waste breakdown."

"When you say directly, you mean . . . ?"

"I mean directly," she said, frowning. "Yesterday's packages are already gone. What do you mean, *no need*? I thought you wanted to check the food for contamination."

"I do," I confirmed. "Or rather, I did. But it's clear now that if the food was tampered with, it didn't happen at the kitchen where these things were cooked and packaged. It happened right here aboard the train." I grimaced. "And it happened on purpose."

Her eyes went wide. "Are you saying they were *murdered*?"

"I don't see any way around it," I said. "One death might be an accident. But not two. Not like this."

"But Dr. Witherspoon said Shorshians are especially susceptible to poisoning."

"Exactly my point," I said. "Even small amounts of poisons typically generate obvious symptoms in that species. If Colix and Bofiv had ingested the stuff gradually, over the past few days, the symptoms would have shown up long ago. The only conclusion is that they were both nailed with large, lethal doses, all at once. That kind of dosage doesn't usually happen by accident."

For another few seconds Bayta remained silent. But I could see the shock fading from her face as she realized I was making sense. "All right," she said slowly. "But why would anyone want to kill them?"

"I haven't the faintest," I conceded. "Actually, it's worse than that. We don't even know yet that they were specifically targeted."

Her eyes did the widening thing again. "You mean the killings might have been random?"

"Or the killer was aiming at someone else and missed," I said. "But one thing at a time. The easiest method for delivering poison is by food or drink, since everybody eats and nine out of ten people don't pay that much attention to their food while they're eating it."

"Yes," Bayta said thoughtfully. "Shorshic meals usually include a common dipping dish, don't they?"

"That's what the cultural profiles say," I confirmed. "Which would certainly make surreptitious tampering easier. The downside is that the poisoner pretty much has to be in the same group as the victim—a stranger leaning in so he can sprinkle fairy dust into a dipping dish in the middle of the table would be a little obvious."

"But if the poisoner was also a Shorshian, wouldn't he run the risk of being poisoned himself?" Bayta asked.

"Absolutely," I said. "Which is one of several intriguing questions about this whole thing. Namely, were both Colix and Bofiv murdered by a third party? Or could Bofiv have murdered Colix and then gotten caught in his own backfire?"

"Or vice versa?" Bayta suggested. "Master Colix murdering Master Bofiv?"

"Possibly," I agreed. "Colix would have to be a particularly incompetent killer for that scenario to work, but I've known my share of inept criminals. Still, it's more likely that the killer was someone else at their table."

Bayta's eyes went distant for a moment as she communed silently with the Spiders. "The servers don't have that information."

"That's all right," I said. "We'll corner Tririn later and ask him for yesterday's guest list."

Bayta was silent a moment. "Do you think the Modhri might be involved in all this?"

"That's definitely my default reflex these days," I said. "But we need some kind of motive before we start trying to pin this on the Modhri or anyone else." I cocked an eyebrow. "Why? Is your spider-sense tingling?"

She frowned. "My what?"

"Skip it," I said, making a mental note to add those dit rec adventures to the list of cultural classics I'd been showing her. "Can you think of some reason why he might want to kill a couple of Shorshians?"

"Not really," she said. "But I've been thinking a lot about him lately. Trying to get into his mind, to understand what he wants."

"I thought he wanted to take over the galaxy."

"Yes, but to what end?" she asked. "The Shonkla-raa certainly had a purpose—they wanted him to infiltrate the rebel forces and destroy them from within. But he doesn't have that purpose anymore. He doesn't have *any* real purpose."

"I don't know," I said doubtfully. "To me, taking over the galaxy sounds like a pretty solid reason for living."

"You know what I mean," Bayta said. "The Modhri isn't conquering so that he can institute political or economic changes, or even just so he can loot his victims."

"Okay, so he's unfocused," I said. "So what?"

Bayta shook her head. "I keep thinking that he's like a weapon that's been left on a shelf," she said pensively. "A sword, maybe. He can fall off, and he can do a lot of damage on his way down, but he's still just flailing about without serving a genuine purpose. That has to be frustrating and frightening both."

"So you're thinking he might throw up his hands and quit in disgust?" I suggested dryly.

"I'm wondering if he might go insane."

Something with a lot of cold feet skittered down my spine. "Oh, now *there's* a cheerful thought," I muttered.

"I'm sorry," Bayta apologized. "I probably shouldn't even have brought it up. I just . . . it's been bothering me lately."

"No need to apologize," I assured her. Privately, I thought the whole idea a bit far-fetched—from what I'd seen of the Modhri, he didn't strike me as the neurotic type. But I also knew better than to dismiss anything Bayta said without at least considering it. "It's definitely worth thinking about. Only not right now. Any word from *di*-Master Strinni?"

Bayta's eyes went distant. "He's just given Dr. Witherspoon permission to take blood and tissue samples from Master Bofiv."

"Good," I said, setting the meal box back on its stack. "Let's go make sure he does it right."

"All right." Bayta hesitated. "*Di*-Master Strinni has also insisted that Master Colix's body be removed for storage."

"Removed for storage where?"

"He asked that it be put in one of the baggage cars," Bayta said. "The Spiders are taking it back there now."

"Where are they going to put it?" I asked. "They can't just leave it lying around the aisles. More importantly, how are they going to seal it away from the rest of the train? It's still four weeks to Venidra Carvo, and things are going to get pretty ripe back there if they don't do something."

"They're constructing an isolation tank where they can store the body," she said. "They're also looking into whether they can use the same preservation techniques they use for food."

I tried to visualize the Spiders freeze-drying Colix's body, but I'd had enough disturbing images for one night. "Did Strinni say why he wanted Colix's body moved?"

"Only that he wanted the body to be as much at rest as possible."

More likely he didn't want Witherspoon's scalpel slipping during Bofiv's autopsy and cutting into his fellow Pathmate by accident. "Whatever," I said. "Come on, let's go."

We left the dining car and headed forward. On the way we passed a pair of conductors carrying the late Master Colix, his body wrapped in one of the dispensary's thermal blankets. Briefly, I wondered how many people in third class might be awake, and how many of those might recognize the bundle for what it was. But there was nothing I could do about it, so I put the thought out of my mind.

We reached the dispensary to find Dr. Aronobal and the server Spider still standing their quiet vigil over the remaining body. "The Spiders came in a few minutes ago and removed Master Colix's body," Aronobal said.

"Yes, we passed them on the way," I said, peering at Bofiv's body. It didn't seem to have been touched in the time Bayta and I had been gone.

"You and your companion speak to the Spiders," Aronobal said.

It had been phrased as a statement, not a question. "Of course we do," I said. "Everyone does. We ask them for directions to the dining car, where we can stow our valuables—"

"Not everyone talks to them as you do," she cut me off, her eyes peering unblinkingly at me down her long nose. "You have a special relationship with them."

"We just travel a lot," I assured him. "We've gotten to know the Spiders pretty well."

"Many people travel a lot," Aronobal countered. "Moreover, Humans have only begun to ride the Quadrails, whereas we of the Filiaelian Assembly have traveled among the stars for centuries. How is it that—?"

She broke off abruptly, and in the fresh silence, I could hear the sound of approaching footsteps. "We will continue this later," Aronobal said quietly.

A moment later, Witherspoon and Tririn appeared. "*Di*-Master Strinni has given us permission to take samples from Master Bofiv's body," Witherspoon announced. He stopped short. "Where's Master Colix?"

"The Spiders have already taken care of him," I told him.

"But we only just agreed on that a few minutes ago," Witherspoon protested. He stepped up to the table, looking around as if expecting Colix's body to leap out of hiding and say boo.

"The Spiders are extremely efficient," I said.

"Obviously so." Witherspoon seemed to brace himself. "Very well. Dr. Aronobal, you undoubtedly have more experience with Shorshic physiology than I do. If you would take the samples, I would be honored to assist you."

"Your deference is noted," Aronobal said, inclining her head approvingly. Apparently, this was the sort of servile diplomacy she'd been expecting earlier from Kennrick. Maybe

Witherspoon's humility would redeem the entire Human race a little in her eyes. "In actual fact, I do not have any specialized knowledge in this matter. How often have you performed this type of examination?"

"Thirty or forty times, I suppose," Witherspoon said. "But I've only done it on Humans."

"Your expertise nevertheless surpasses mine," Aronobal said. "You may proceed. I will assist."

Witherspoon glanced at me, took a deep breath, and pulled a pair of gloves from a dispenser beneath the table. "All right," he said. "Let's do it."

I'd seen plenty of dead bodies in the course of my career. Some of them had been spectacularly mangled, and nearly all of them had been pretty bloody. But I'd done my level best to avoid autopsies whenever possible. There was something about the casual, clinical slicing up of a body that bothered me in a way that even the aftermath of thudwumper rounds didn't.

Fortunately, this one wasn't as bad as I'd feared it would be. Witherspoon did the job quickly and efficiently, mostly just nicking off small skin samples or using a hypo to draw blood and other fluids. Only twice did he dig deeper than skin level, and in those instances I was able to keep my focus on the samples as he slid them into the small vials Aronobal held open for him.

Five minutes later, it was over. "That's it," Witherspoon said as he set the last sealed vial into the sample case and handed the Spider the hypos and scalpels he'd been using. "Do you want to bring your spectroscopic analyzer here, or would it be easier if Dr. Aronobal and I accompany you to your compartment?"

"Neither, actually," I told him as I took the sample case. "Bayta and I can handle it."

Witherspoon threw a frown at Aronobal. "That's not proper procedure," he warned.

"Aboard a Quadrail, proper procedure is whatever the Spiders say it is," I reminded him.

[And how will we know if you speak the truth?] Tririn demanded.

"You'll know because I will speak it, and because I have no reason to lie," I told him. "I'm not involved with your group, Pellorian Medical Systems, or any branch of the Human, Filiaelian, or Shorshian governments. I have no ax to grind, no agenda to push, no itches to scratch. More importantly, I'm the one with the necessary equipment and the knowledge and training to use it."

Tririn looked at Dr. Witherspoon, who looked at Dr. Aronobal, who looked back at me. It didn't take a genius to see that none of them was very happy with my executive decision.

It also didn't take a genius to know they didn't have much choice in the matter. [How soon will you have the results?] Tririn asked.

"By midmorning at the latest," I said, taking Bayta's arm. "You might as well all go back to bed. You'll want to get some sleep before the rest of the train wakes up."

We left the dispensary and headed forward. Second class was still pretty quiet, but a few of the passengers were beginning to stir as the early risers mixed with the insomniacs and those hoping to get a head start on the bathroom and shower facilities. First class, in contrast, was still almost uniformly quiet. *Di*-Master Strinni was again sleeping without his canopy, his lidded eyes pointed sightlessly toward the ceiling.

Bayta didn't speak until we were back in my compartment with the door locked behind us. "The analysis won't really take that long, will it?" she asked as I dug out my lighter and multi-tool.

"Not at all," I assured her, flipping the lighter's thumb guard around and positioning it over the flame jet. "But one of the cardinal rules is that you never let people know how long things actually take."

"Why not?" she asked, watching in fascination as I selected the smallest of my multitool's blades and dipped the tip into the vial containing Bofiv's blood sample.

"Because you never know when you might have to do that same something a lot faster than they expect," I told her. Touching the blade to the thumb guard, I deposited a droplet directly above the flame jet. "Here—hold this a second. Keep it vertical."

Gingerly, she took the lighter, holding it at arm's length while I pulled out my reader and data chip collection. The chip labeled *Encyclopaedia Britannica* was one of the oversized ones, as befitted its status as the repository of all Human knowledge.

Or so a casual observer would assume. In actual fact, that particular chip plus my specially designed, one-of-a-kind reader added up to a very powerful sensor/analyzer, one of the finest gadgets the Terran Confederation had to offer. I activated the sensor, took the lighter back from Bayta, and set the reader and lighter at the proper positions relative to each other. "Here we go," I said, and ignited the lighter.

A blue-white flame hissed out, and there was a small puff of smoke as the blood droplet flash-burned to vapor. I shut off the lighter and handed it back to Bayta, then keyed the reader for analysis. "And that's it," I told her. "A few seconds, and we'll have a complete list of what was in Master Bofiv's blood when he died."

"Amazing," Bayta murmured, eyeing the reader. "And Mr. Hardin just let you *keep* it?"

"He was a little preoccupied with other matters at the time," I said, thinking back to my somewhat awkward final confrontation with Larry Cecil Hardin, multitrillionaire industrialist and erstwhile boss. "The trillion dollars I'd just extorted from him was probably weighing a bit on his mind."

"I hope someday he'll learn what his money did for the galaxy," Bayta murmured.

"Actually, I'm not sure he'd really care," I said. "Maybe if you gave him a medal at a big public ceremony."

"After all this time, you still dislike the man that much?"

"I don't dislike him," I told her. "I just see him as he is, not as some idealized person he might someday become if you showed him where the profit was in being noble. Until then, he'll con, finagle, bargain, or outright steal every last dollar he can."

Bayta eyed me thoughtfully. "You practice that speech often?"

"Couple of times a week," I told her. "Still needs a little work."

"Mm," she said noncommittally. "Still, you can't deny that some good did come out of Mr. Hardin's ambitions."

"The trillion dollars," I said. "I believe I mentioned that."

"I was thinking of something even more valuable than that." Bayta gave a little nod toward me. "You."

I felt a lump form in my throat. "Worth more even than a trillion dollars, huh?" I asked, trying to keep my tone light. "I'm honored. Remind me to ask you to speak on my behalf the next time the Chahwyn try quibbling with me over the job we're doing for them."

"I've already done that," she said simply. "One of the other times I went to bat for you."

"Oh," I said, a bit lamely. "Yes, I guess you have."

"You *do* miss a lot not being telepathic," she commented.

I peered at her, wondering if she was being serious or trying to be funny. But her face was its usual neutral, her eyes on the reader in my hand. "I know," I told her. "I've been meaning to work on that."

Her eyes flicked up, the hint of a frown touching her face. Probably wondering if *I* was trying to be funny. "What happens now?" she asked, looking back at the reader. "We test the rest of the samples and look for a common element?"

"Exactly." The sensor beeped, and I watched as the analysis scrolled across the display.

And felt my stomach tighten. "Or not."

"What do you mean?"

"I mean we probably don't really need to test any of the other samples." I turned the reader around to face her. "Second line just above the bottom of the display."

She peered at the line. "Cadmium?"

"A heavy metal," I told her. "Westali's standard course on Shorshians was rather cursory, but heavy-metal poisoning was definitely one of the topics that was covered, mainly because it was considered one of the better ways of quietly dispatching members of that particular species. For the record, it's pretty good against Humans, too."

Bayta's lips compressed briefly. "What exactly does that number mean?" she asked.

"That there's enough in his system to kill a good-sized moose," I said grimly. "Whoever wanted Master Bofiv dead wasn't taking any chances."

Bayta shivered. "Or whoever wanted whoever dead," she said. "You said that he might have missed his real target."

"If he did, that was one hell of a miss."

"Yes," she murmured. "What do we do now?"

"I suppose we might as well run the rest of the samples, just to make sure there aren't any surprises," I said. "After that, we'd better get to bed. Tomorrow's likely to be a busy day."

"Shouldn't we let Dr. Witherspoon and the others know the results?"

I shook my head. "They've all gone back to bed. Not much point in waking them up just to give them bad news. Besides, I want some time to think about this before we spring it on them."

"I thought you said you were going to sleep."

"I said I was going to bed." I looked at the cadmium listing on the analysis. "I never said I was going to get much sleep."

FIVE :

Sure enough, I'd been lying in bed for no more than five hours, and had been asleep for maybe three of those, when I was awakened by someone leaning on my door chime.

Sometimes I hated being right. Stumbling to the door, darkly promising to cripple someone if this wasn't damned important, I keyed it open.

Kennrick was standing there, looking way too fresh and alert for a man who'd been up almost as late as I had. "Compton," he greeted me shortly, taking a step forward as if expecting to be invited in.

"Kennrick," I greeted him in turn, not budging from the doorway and forcing him to stop short to keep from running into me. "Any news?"

"That was *my* question," he said, trying to peer past my shoulder into the compartment. "Dr. Witherspoon told me he and Dr. Aronobal gave you the samples from Master Bofiv's body for analysis."

"And I told *him* that I would let all of you know when I had the results," I said.

"That was over five hours ago," Kennrick countered. "What are you doing, framing the samples for an art-house display?"

"I've been working," I told him stiffly. "These things take time."

"Not *that* much time." He ran a critical eye over me. "And if you don't mind my saying so, you don't exactly look like you just hopped up from your portable lab bench, either."

Silently, I stepped aside. He strode in, his eyes flicking around the room and coming to rest on the reader I'd left on the curve couch. "So what did you find?" he asked as I closed the door again.

"More or less what we expected," I said, brushing past him and picking up the reader. I turned it on, called up the analysis file, and handed it to him.

He frowned, tapping the control to scroll the numbers up and down the display. "How do I read this?" he asked.

I lifted an eyebrow. "I thought you worked for a medical company."

"As an organizer and meeting facilitator," he said patiently. "Not as a doctor. Come on—tell me what this says."

"It says cadmium poisoning," I told him. "Lots of it."

He ran the scrolling again and found the cadmium line. "Terrific," he muttered. "Any chance it could have happened by accident?"

"In theory, pretty much any death could have happened by accident," I said. "But when the string of required coincidences gets long enough, I think you can safely call it murder."

He flinched at the word. "That's insane," he insisted. "Who would have wanted Master Bofiv dead?"

"Wrong question," I told him. "The right question is, who would have wanted Master Bofiv *and* Master Colix dead?"

Kennrick stared at me. "Are you telling me they were *both* murdered? By the same person?"

"Unless you plan to string a few more coincidences together," I said.

He looked back at the reader. "No," he said firmly. "No, this just can't be. It *has* to have been an accident."

"You mean like someone accidentally uncapped a bottle of cadmium powder over their dinner plates last night?" I suggested.

"Or they ingested it some other way," he said. "Cadmium is used in batteries, alloys—all sorts of things. Maybe it flaked off a bad battery in Master Colix's luggage, got on his fingers, and from there into one of their shared meals. Or it could even have come off someone else's stuff and gotten into the air system."

"And then carefully proceeded to target Colix and Bofiv, but not Tririn or any of the other Shorshians in the car?"

"People react differently to infections and toxins all the time," Kennrick said doggedly. "There are cases on record where a group of Humans have eaten the same salmonella-infested food. Some got sick, some died, some hardly even noticed. Why should Shorshic metabolism be any different?"

I could almost feel sorry for the man, straining this desperately to find an explanation that didn't include the word *murder*. But facts were facts, and the sooner we popped all the irrelevant soap bubbles, the sooner we could get down to the unpleasant business at hand. "Because this isn't some random bug running up against a whole range of different immune systems," I said. "For Bofiv to have swallowed that much cadmium, the stuff would have had to be raining down like volcanic ash. I guarantee *someone* at the table would have noticed that."

"You're right, you're right," he said heavily. "What do we do?"

"We let me get on with my investigation," I said. "You said last night that you only met him a couple of months ago?"

"Yes, when he and the contract team arrived on Earth," he said, taking a final look at my reader and then handing it back to me. "Pellorian had invited them in to discuss a proposed joint venture in genetic manipulation."

"Were you the one who organized the conference?"

"I handled the details once the plan was up and running," he said. "But only after the initial contacts had been made and the invitations sent out and accepted. I didn't choose any of the contract team, if that's what you're asking."

"Who did?"

"The corporation's CEO, Dr. Earl Messerly," he said. "I imagine the board probably had some input, too."

"You have their names?"

He eyed me as if I'd just turned a deep and fashionable purple. "Are you suggesting upstanding medical professionals would go to the trouble of bringing a couple of Shorshians all the way across the galaxy just to kill them?"

"You know for certain that none of your upstanding medical professionals is harboring a grudge against the Shorshians?" I countered.

He snorted. "You must be kidding," he said. "I've been to full board meetings maybe three times in the seven years I've been with the company. I barely know their names."

"In other words, you can't vouch for any of them." I keyed my reader for input. "So. Their names?"

Glaring at me, he ran through the list. There were twelve of them, plus CEO Messerly. I keyed in the names as he went, knowing full well that Kennrick was probably right about this being a waste of time.

Still, I had a few Who's Who lists among my data chips, both the straightforward cultural ones and a rather more private set that had been assembled by the Confederation's various law enforcement agencies. Running a check of Pellorian's people against the latter might prove interesting.

But regardless of what the comparison turned up, Pellorian's board was back on Earth, and we were here. "Thank you," I said when Kennrick had finished. "Next question: did either Colix or Bofiv bring aboard any of their own food? Special treats or secret indulgences?"

"You'll have to ask Master Tririn about that," Kennrick said. "He was the one sitting with them."

"He was the one sitting with *one* of them, anyway," I said. "I trust he's well this morning?"

"I actually haven't checked," Kennrick said. "You want me to go ask him if Master Bofiv had a private food supply?"

"Not until we can both be there," I said. "Can you go off and amuse yourself while I shower and get dressed?"

He made a face. "It doesn't qualify as amusement, but I do need to give *Usantra* Givvrac an update. He's the head of the contract team."

"At least you shouldn't have any trouble waking him up at this hour," I said. "Unless he's been dipping into Bofiv's secret stash, of course."

Kennrick's throat tightened. "You think this is funny, Compton?" he growled.

"Not at all," I assured him. "Which is *Usantra* Givvrac's compartment?"

"He hasn't got one," Kennrick said. "He's in the first coach car behind the compartment cars."

I frowned, thinking back to our embarkation at Homshil Station. "And yet you escorted them aboard into a compartment car?" I asked. "Even though they had coach car seats?"

"Into *my* compartment car, yes," Kennrick said. "*Usantra* Givvrac and a couple of the others had some documents they wanted stored in my compartment, and they wanted to drop them off on the way to their seats."

Which wasn't proper procedure, since passengers were supposed to enter a Quadrail only through the door of their assigned car. Apparently, Kennrick and his Fillies didn't have a problem with skirting the rules everyone else had to follow. "Whatever," I said. "I'll pick you up on my way back to talk to Tririn."

Silently, Kennrick left the compartment. As I closed the door behind him, I felt the movement of air that meant the connecting wall was opening. "You heard?" I asked, turning around.

"Most of it," Bayta said. She was dressed in her nightshirt and a thin robe, her dark hair tousled and unwashed. But her eyes were clear and awake. "He sounded upset."

"He looked upset, too," I agreed. I let my eyes drop once to the figure semi-hidden beneath her robe, then forced my gaze back above her neckline where it belonged. Bayta was my colleague and ally in this war, nothing more, and I had damn well better not forget that. "What did you think of his suggestion that the cadmium might have been airborne?"

She frowned. "Didn't you already tell him that was ridiculous?"

"In the way he was thinking about it, absolutely," I agreed. "But he was trying to make it a careless accident. I'm wondering about it as a somewhat more careful murder."

"That still leaves the problem of why only Master Colix and Master Bofiv were affected," she pointed out.

"True, unless someone managed to uncork a bottle of eau de cadmium under the victims' snouts," I said. "Or maybe it was in the form of some cadmium compound that only Shorshians can absorb."

"I don't know," she said doubtfully. "There are toxins that target specific species, but those also get absorbed by everyone else. And most cadmium compounds are as toxic as the element itself, and to nearly all species to one level or another."

I raised my eyebrows. "Impressive."

She shrugged slightly. "I couldn't sleep last night after I went to bed, so I did a little reading," she explained. "The other problem is that since cadmium compounds are inherently poisonous, anything in a liquid or gaseous form should have been screened out by the station sensors."

"Maybe the killer brought the stuff aboard in component form," I suggested. "The cadmium in, say, a battery or alloy, and the delivery chemical as something else."

"The sensors are supposed to watch for that sort of thing."

"*Supposed to* being the key phrase," I said. "Assuming something like that was done, could traces of it have gotten sucked into the car's air filters?"

"Certainly," she said. "All the air in a car eventually travels through those filters."

I nodded. "It's a long shot, but I think it's worth checking out. What would it take to get into one of the air filters in that car?"

"It's not that simple," Bayta said, her eyes unfocusing as she conferred with the Spiders. "There's a whole mechanism that will have to be disassembled. I've sent four mites to start the job, but it'll take a few hours."

"That's okay," I said. "Have them contact you when they're almost done."

"All right," she said. "Are we going to go talk to Master Tririn now?"

"Or we could stop and have some breakfast first," I said. "Your call."

She hesitated, and I had the odd impression that she was searching my face looking for the right answer. "I'm not that hungry," she said.

That was the answer, all right. "Me, neither," I agreed. "Go get ready. We head out in fifteen minutes."

Eighteen minutes later, we passed through the rear vestibule of the third compartment car and entered the first of the first-class coach cars.

I'd rather expected that Kennrick would still be deep in conversation with *Usantra* Givvrac, and I was right. The Human was sitting on the edge of a seat near the right-hand wall, talking earnestly with one of the four Fillies I'd seen him boarding with at Homshil Station.

And now that I was focusing on the Filly himself, I could see that he had the graying body hair of someone well advanced in years.

That alone was mildly surprising. Fillies of that age and rank usually stayed close to home and sent out their younger colleagues and subordinates on fact-finding and contract-making missions. I wondered what kind of lure Pellorian Medical had lobbed into the water to bring out someone of Givvrac's standing.

Kennrick was sitting where he could watch the vestibule door, and as Bayta and I entered the car he spoke a few last words to the Filly and stood up. The alien himself looked at me and nodded a silent acknowledgment as Kennrick maneuvered his way through the little clusters of seats the rest of the passengers had constructed. "That was fast," he commented as he reached us. His eyes flicked to Bayta, but he didn't comment on the fact that I'd brought a guest along.

"Bayta and I can do this alone if you weren't finished with your conversation," I offered.

"No, that's all right," he said. "*Usantra* Givvrac wants me present when you question Master Tririn. He wants to get to the bottom of this even more than you do."

"I'm sure he does," I said, returning Givvrac's acknowledging nod with one of my own. "After you."

The three of us headed aft, walking through the rest of the first- and second-class cars and on into third. As we passed the second/third dispensary I glanced inside, but there was no one there except the server Spider on duty. There were no dead bodies, either, Bofiv having apparently been taken back to the baggage car while Bayta and I slept.

We found Tririn hunched over in his seat, his eyes staring fixedly at the seat back in front of him as he ignored both the exotic alien travelscape playing on the display window to his left and Master Bofiv's empty seat to his right. In the aisle seat of his row was the Nemut Kennrick had mentioned, his rainbow-slashed eyes focused on a reader, his truncated-cone-shaped mouth making little motions like a pre-K child trying to sound out the words.

Two rows ahead of them, Terese German was sitting with her eyes closed, a set of headphones locked snugly around her ears, a silent but clear warning to all and sundry that she wanted to be left alone. Two seats to her right, next to the train's outer side, a young Juri with the unpolished scales of a commoner was gazing intently at the dit rec drama playing on the display window to his right.

We passed their row and came to a halt beside the Nemut. "Master Tririn?" Kennrick called softly. "Master Tririn?"

The Shorshian didn't answer, or even turn to face us. "I don't think he wants to talk," Kennrick concluded. "Maybe we should try again later."

"Or maybe we should try a little harder right now," I said, looking at the Nemut in the aisle seat. "Excuse me?"

"Yes?" the other asked, his deep voice sounding a little slurred. Small wonder; now that I was standing over him I could see that he had an open bag full of small, colorful snack cubes resting in his lap. Apparently, the mouth movements I'd noticed earlier had had nothing to do with the sounding out of words.

"I'd like to get past, if I may," I told him, gesturing toward the empty seat between him and Tririn. I actually didn't need him to move—even third-class Quadrail seats allowed the average passenger plenty of legroom—but it was always polite to ask.

"Certainly," the Nemut said. Getting a grip on his goodie bag, he drew in his knees.

"Thank you." I sidled past him and sat down beside Tririn. "Good day, Master Tririn," I said. "Frank Compton. You may remember me from last night."

[I remember you, Mr. Compton,] Tririn said, the normal harshness of the Shishish tempered by the listlessness in his voice. [And the day is not good. No days from now on will be good.]

"I understand," I said, glancing back at Kennrick. He was still standing in the aisle, glowering at my brazenness at barging in on Tririn's solitude this way. Bayta, for her part, was standing a little apart from him, up near Terese's row, where she wouldn't crowd us but would still be close enough to listen in on the conversation. "Were Master Colix and Master Bofiv close friends of yours?" I asked, turning back to Tririn.

[They were business associates,] he said.

"I understand," I said again, wondering briefly if he was correcting me or agreeing with me. "Tell me, did all three of you eat together yesterday?"

[We ate sundown together,] he said. [Sunrise and midday were eaten individually.]

According to my encyclopedia, that was indeed the standard practice for non-family Shorshians traveling together. Unfortunately, it didn't tell me whether or not the three had been friends or something more distant. "Do you remember what you all ate at sundown?" I asked.

[The common dish was *po krem*,] he said. [It's a shred, a mixture of meat and fruits.]

"Yes, I've heard of it," I said. "What reaches did all of you use?"

For the first time since I'd sat down he turned his face toward me. [My apologies, Mr. Compton,] he said, eyeing me curiously. [I took you to be as other Humans, ignorant of Shorshic custom and honor nodes. For that unspoken slight, I ask your forgiveness.]

"Freely and openly granted," I assured him, giving silent thanks that I'd had the sense to sacrifice an hour of sleep last night in favor of a crash course in Shorshic social customs and terminology.

[Thank you,] he said. [My reach was *galla* bread. Master Colix and Master Bofiv used baked *prinn* scoops.]

So the two dead Shorshians had eaten from the common bowl with the same type of edible scoops, while the Shorshian alive and breathing had used something else. I made a mental note to check with the server Spiders to see if those choices were standard for the three of them, or whether they'd been unique to the fatal evening. "And your individuals?"

[All different,] he said. [*Birrsh* for Master Colix, *valarrki* for Master Bofiv, *sorvidae* for me.] His eyes flicked briefly past my shoulder. [Yet the Spiders said the death was not in the food. Do you believe otherwise?]

"I don't believe there was any death in the food when it was served to you," I told him. "But possibly something happened after that. Do you remember anyone approaching your table while you ate? Perhaps to ask a question, or to engage one of you in conversation?"

Tririn cocked his head in thought. I watched him closely, wondering if he was searching his memory or just trying to think up a good lie. [I don't believe so,] he said at last. [There were servers, of course, but no one else approached.]

"Did you happen to notice who was sitting at the nearby tables?" I asked.

Tririn's brow wrinkled. [We sat at a corner table,] he said. [There was only one table near us. Unfortunately, my back was to the occupants.]

I grimaced. "I see," I said. "Well, then—"

"I saw them," the Nemut on my other side volunteered.

I turned to him in surprise. "*You* saw them?"

"They were Humans," he told me. "One female, one male."

One female . . . "Was it by any chance that female up there?" I asked, pointing two rows ahead toward Terese.

Or rather, toward Terese's empty seat. Terese herself had vanished.

So had Bayta.

"Kennrick?" I demanded, standing up for a better look. Neither of the women was anywhere to be seen.

"Take it easy—they're in the restroom," Kennrick said, nodding toward the front of the car. "The German girl headed off—kind of fast, actually—and your friend followed."

"Ah," I said, frowning as I sat back down. That was at least twice now that Terese had suddenly been taken ill. "Let me rephrase the question," I said to the Nemut. "Was the woman you saw the same one who usually sits there?"

"I believe so," he said. "Though Humans are difficult to distinguish between."

"I understand," I said. "Can you remember anything about the male Human?"

The Nemut's angled shoulder muscles quivered briefly in one of their equivalents of a shrug. "His hair was white," he said. "That is all I remember."

"That's fine—you've been very helpful," I assured him. "Thank you." I turned back to Tririn. "My apologies," I said. "For the interruption in our talk, I ask your forgiveness."

[Freely and openly granted,] he assured me. [Do you believe the death was in these Humans?]

"I don't know yet," I said. "Two further questions, if I may. First, do you know whether either Master Colix or Master Bofiv had a private food supply? Something they brought aboard, as opposed to something supplied by the servers aboard the train?"

[Master Bofiv had no such supply,] Tririn said. [I would surely have seen if he had.]

"And Master Colix?"

[I don't know,] Tririn said. [You would need to inquire of one of his seatmates.]

"I'll do that," I promised. "Final question, then. Whose

idea was it for Master Colix to sit away from you and Master Bofiv?"

[It was Master Colix's choice,] Tririn said. [He asked specifically for that seat.]

Which was more or less what Terese had implied earlier. "Was there some trouble between the three of you?" I asked.

[Not at all,] Tririn said. [Master Colix prided himself on his knowledge of alien languages. He hoped that seated between a Human and Juri he would have the opportunity to practice and improve his skill at both languages.]

"Really," I said. "I was under the impression that Shorshic vocal apparatus couldn't handle either of them."

Tririn seemed to draw back, as if suddenly realizing he had strayed onto forbidden territory. [There are ways,] he said, his tone guarded.

"Ah," I said, keeping my expression neutral. According to my reader's data files, that was an outright lie. Shorshians were completely incapable of speaking anything but Shishish and a smattering of Fili unless they'd had what was rather sarcastically referred to as the Gibber Operation.

Had Colix gone under the knife? I couldn't tell—Tririn's phrasing had left that ambiguous, possibly deliberately so. It *was* clear, though, that he didn't want to discuss it further.

But there were other ways to get the answer to that one. If Master Colix had been able to speak English or Juric, one of his seatmates would surely know it. "I thank you for your time and patience, Master Tririn," I said. "Especially on this day of sadness. I hope you'll be equally gracious should I need to discuss the matter with you further."

[I will be most pleased to do so, Mr. Compton,] he said. His eyes flicked to Kennrick. [*You* are welcome to approach at any time.]

"Thank you," I said. "Good day, Master Tririn."

I sidled past the Nemut with a nod of thanks, brushed by Kennrick, and headed up the aisle toward the front of the car. I was passing Terese's empty seat when Kennrick caught up with me. "Wait a minute," he said in a low voice. "Damn it, Compton—*wait*."

"Problem?" I asked, not breaking stride.

"Yes, *problem*," he gritted out. "You may be the hotshot detective, but even I know that basic investigative technique includes double-checking everyone's story."

"That's exactly what I'm doing," I told him. "Or had you forgotten that Ms. German is up here in the restroom?"

"I was thinking about the Juri in the other seat," he growled, jerking a thumb back at Terese's row. "The one Master Tririn claims Master Colix was speaking Juric to."

"And you think I should question the Juri about that?" I asked mildly.

"Absolutely," Kennrick said. "You were right—Shorshic vocal apparatus—"

"You think I should question the Juri about it while Master Tririn is within earshot of the conversation?"

"It wouldn't be—" He broke off. "Oh. Right. That wouldn't be very politic, would it?"

"Hardly politic at all," I agreed. "But if you want to try it, be my guest."

Kennrick grimaced. "I guess you've noticed that Master Tririn and I don't get along very well."

"It's a little hard to miss," I agreed. "What's the problem?"

"I just can't connect with him," he said. "I really don't know why."

"Did you have the same problem when you were on Earth?"

"If we did, I didn't notice it," he said. "It was only after we came aboard the Quadrail at Terra Station that things started to go downhill." He shrugged. "Of course, it could just be that he was on his best behavior during the discussions at Pellorian. Maybe even back then he didn't really like me. *Or* the others."

"He didn't get along with the others?"

"I had that impression," Kennrick said. "But it's just an impression. Like I said, if there was trouble between them they probably wouldn't confide in me. But it makes sense that if he had trouble with me, he might have had trouble with the others, too."

"Perhaps," I said. Though privately I could easily see how someone could love his fellow man and still not like Kennrick. "I'll try to sound him out about that later."

The outer restroom door was still closed when we reached it. I considered going inside and seeing if I could figure out which stall Terese was in, decided she would probably take violent offense if I tried, and found a place by the door where I could lean against the wall and cultivate patience. Taking his cue from me, Kennrick found a spot of his own a little farther up the car and did likewise.

Patience is always rewarded. A couple of minutes later the door opened and Terese stepped out. She looked a little pale, which meant that when she reddened with anger at seeing me standing there her color came out just about right. "Good morning, Ms. German," I said, stepping into her path.

I expected her to try to push her way around me. Instead, she fired a withering glare in my direction, spun a hundred eighty degrees, and headed forward at the fastest walk she could manage without actually breaking into a jog. By the time I recovered from my surprise at her sudden about-face, she was into the vestibule and out of sight.

"Well, *that's* inconvenient," Kennrick growled.

"Relax," I soothed him. "Where's she going to go on a Quadrail?" I looked back at the restroom door as Bayta emerged. "What's the verdict?" I asked her.

"She was throwing up," Bayta said. "I don't know how bad it was—she wouldn't let me help her."

Kennrick swore under his breath. "So she's definitely sick," he said. "Compton, this has gone way beyond serious."

"Relax," I advised him, eyeing the vestibule door and thinking back to that last view I'd had of Terese's face. In my experience, people with serious illnesses usually didn't have the mental and emotional strength to spare for that level of annoyance. At least not against relative strangers.

"Because if you were wrong about the cadmium, and the Shorshians had something contagious—"

"I said *relax*," I repeated, more firmly this time. "Let's not start a panic until it's absolutely necessary, all right?"

He made a face, but nodded. "So what do we do?"

"We go after her," I said. "Either she's on her way to the shower/laundry car, which is unlikely since she hasn't got a change of clothing with her, or else she's headed for the dining car for something to settle her stomach."

"Fine," Kennrick asked in a tone of overstrained patience. "So can we go?"

In answer, I took Bayta's arm and headed for the vestibule. Assuming Terese kept up the same pace that she'd left here with, by the time she reached the archway into the third-class dining car she would have quick-walked for most of three long Quadrail cars. All that exercise, plus her stomach trouble, should take some of the starch out of her and make her a little easier to question.

We walked through the shower/laundry car, then the storage car, and finally through the vestibule into the third-class dining car. As with all such cars, the aisle here veered all the way to the right side of the car so as to avoid cutting the dining area in half. There were large, slightly tinted windows in the wall that separated the dining room from the corridor, allowing the patrons to watch those passing by and vice versa. "Any sign of her?" I asked, slowing down as I peered in through the windows.

"Not yet," Kennrick said. "Maybe she went past and has gone to ground somewhere forward."

"There," Bayta said, pointing.

I followed her finger. Terese was standing at the bar at the forward end of the car, talking earnestly to a tall Filly I didn't recognize. "Anyone seen that Filly before?" I asked.

"No," Bayta said.

"Me, neither," Kennrick said. "Does he look a little drunk to you?"

"Not really," I said. "You two stay out here. Be ready to corral her if she makes another break for it." Squaring my shoulders, I walked through the archway into the dining area.

I was halfway through the maze of tables and chairs when the Filly detached himself from Terese and headed toward me. "May you be well," I said in greeting as he got within earshot.

"You will not bother the Human female," he said, his tone flat and unfriendly.

"I'm not bothering her," I assured him, coming to a halt. "I just want to ask her a few questions."

"You will not bother the Human female," he repeated, his hands bunching into fists as he continued toward me.

I sighed. Apparently, Terese hadn't come here for something to settle her stomach. She'd come here looking for a white knight to protect her.

And she had apparently found one.

SIX :

"Easy, now," I cautioned, holding my hands out toward the Filly as I reversed direction, backing toward the archway and the corridor beyond. The last thing I wanted was to get involved in a brawl with one of the other passengers. The *very* last thing I wanted was for that brawl to take place in a dining room.

But the Filly kept coming, the thought of broken tables, crockery, and bones apparently not bothering him in the least. I continued giving way, still making useless soothing noises. The carefully designed privacy acoustics of Quadrail dining cars meant that none of the other patrons could really make out what either of us was saying, but pretty much everyone facing our direction had spotted the gathering storm and had clued in their dining partners. If I'd ever wanted to get beaten to a pulp in front of an audience, I reflected sourly, this was my big chance.

Apparently, Bayta was thinking along the same lines. The *kwi* snugged away in my pocket tingled as she telepathically activated the weapon.

I could certainly see her point. The Filly probably outweighed me by ten kilos, and while his species wasn't known for their prowess at unarmed combat, they weren't complete slouches at it, either. The chance to drop him where he stood was a very tempting proposition.

Unfortunately, the presence of an audience put that option off the table. Using a weapon, even a nonlethal one, on a supposedly weapons-free Quadrail would draw way too much unwelcome attention.

Fortunately, the *kwi* wouldn't be necessary. I'd backed up nearly to the archway now, and had finally reached my goal: a small section of empty floor space.

Time to make my move.

"All right, this has gone far enough," I said firmly, coming to an abrupt halt with my hands still held out in front of me, my palms toward the Filly. "I'm going to question Ms. German, and that's all there is to it."

He took the bait. "You will not bother the Human female," he said, continuing forward and reaching for my left wrist. As he stretched out his arm, I smoothly withdrew mine, bringing it inward toward my chest. He picked up his pace, reaching even more insistently toward me.

And with his complete attention now focused on the wrist that was somehow managing to remain just out of his grasp, I reached across with my right hand, grabbed his hand and bent the wrist in on itself, then snaked my left hand behind his elbow.

An instant later he found himself pinned upright in place, his arm locked vertically at his side, his weight coming up on his toes as I pulled the bent wrist upward and inward. "Now," I said softly to the long face and startled eyes fifteen centimeters from my own. "I'm going to ask Ms. German a few questions, and then she can go about her business. Is that all right with you?"

For a couple of heartbeats he remained silent. "A few questions only," he replied at last.

"Thank you," I said.

Releasing his arm, I took a step backward. I was taking something of a risk, I knew—he was uninjured, he still had those ten kilos on me, and he was perfectly capable of backing out of his verbal agreement if he chose to do so.

But he didn't. Apparently, he was smart enough to realize that someone who had just showed my brand of restraint in round one was likely to have more painful options available for round two. Stepping to the side, he gestured me back into the dining area.

Terese was still standing by the bar, her mouth hanging slightly open. Apparently, she hadn't expected her white knight to be vanquished quite so easily.

Which meant she'd had some expectations to begin with, either about me or about the Filly. I tucked away that little bit of data for future consideration. "Hello, Ms. German," I said, nodding politely as I came up to her. "Remember me?"

She clamped her mouth closed. "What do you want?"

"The answers to a few questions," I said. "A *very* few questions." I gestured her to one of the bar stools. "Have a seat?"

Reluctantly, she plopped down on the stool. I took the next one and sat down facing her. Out of the corner of my eye I saw that Bayta and Kennrick had now come into the dining area and were watching us from across the room. "I heard a rumor that Master Colix might have brought along some private snacks," I said. "Did you notice him with anything like that?"

Terese shrugged. "He might have had something."

"Were they in a bag?" I asked. "A nice box? A tube dispenser?"

"It was a dark brown bag," she said. "Small, like a meal from a quick-food spot. But I don't know where it came from." She gave a flip of her fingertips that somehow managed to take in the entire room. "He could even have gotten it from here, for all I know."

"We can check on that," I said. "Did you notice anything specific about the bag or its contents, anything about how either looked? Or were there any strange aromas that might have caught your attention?"

She shook her head. "Like I said, I didn't really pay much attention to him."

"So who *should* I be talking to about this?"

"The Juri on his other side," she said. "The two of them were jabbering all the time." She wrinkled her nose. "It was like bad Chinese or something."

That was actually a pretty fair description of how Juric sounded. "You said he showed you holos of his family?"

"Once," she said. "Mostly, he just talked about his job."

I nodded. "How was Master Colix's English, by the way? I'm told he was trying to brush up on his language skills."

She wrinkled her nose again. "He still had a long way to go."

"But you *could* understand him?"

"As much as I wanted to. Look, can I go now?"

"Sure," I said, gesturing her toward the exit. "You know, you really ought to see a doctor about that stomach of yours."

That got me another glare as she slid off her stool. "I'm fine," she insisted. "It's not contagious, if that's what you're worried about."

"Not really," I said as she turned away and took a step toward the archway. "I'm sure Dr. Witherspoon would have said something to the Spiders if you were."

Even with her back to me, I could see her reaction to Witherspoon's name. "Who?" she asked, stopping but not turning around.

"Dr. Witherspoon," I repeated. "The man you had dinner with last night."

"I didn't have dinner with him," she said, still keeping her face away from me. "I was eating by myself and he came over and sat down."

"And you immediately told him to take a hike, right?"

She hesitated, and I could see the tension in her shoulders as she tried to guess how much I knew, and therefore how much bending of the truth she could get away with. "He might have stayed for a few minutes," she conceded. "He said he'd noticed my stomach problem and wanted to ask me about it."

"What did you tell him?"

She gave me an oblique look over her shoulder. "Can I leave now?"

"I already said you could," I said. "Thanks for your cooperation."

She might have expelled a sarcastic snort as she strode off, but with the dining car's acoustics I couldn't tell for sure. She glared at the Filly who she'd sent to stop me, strode past Bayta and Kennrick without a glance at either of them, and headed back down the corridor toward her car.

"Well, that was interesting," Kennrick commented as he and Bayta joined me at the bar. "What exactly did you say to her there at the end?"

"I take it there was a reaction?" I asked.

"Oh, a beaut," Kennrick assured me. "What did you say?"

For a moment I considered not telling him. But he'd already heard the Nemut mention that Terese had met a white-haired

Human over dinner, and it wouldn't take much of a deductive leap on his part to tag Witherspoon for the part. "I asked about her dinner with Dr. Witherspoon," I said.

"Really," Kennrick said. "And?"

"She denied it was an actual dinner," I said. "According to her, he just dropped by to see how she was feeling."

Kennrick grunted. "Did you get anything about her sickness?"

"Not a whisper," I said. "I wonder if you could do me a favor."

He cocked an eyebrow, possibly noting the irony of a former Westali agent asking a former fugitive for help. But if he was tempted to make a comment to that effect, he managed to resist it. "Shoot," he invited.

"I want you to track down Dr. Witherspoon," I said. "Find out what the symptoms are of heavy-metal poisoning in Humans."

Kennrick looked at the archway where Terese had just exited. "You think *she's* the one who poisoned them?"

"No idea," I said. "But she seems to be the only one who was in the victims' immediate vicinity who's also noticeably ill."

"Yes, but *her*?" Kennrick persisted. "She doesn't exactly have that icy killer look about her."

"Not very many icy killers do," I said. "Maybe her stomach trouble has nothing to do with this. But if it does, I'd like to find it out before someone else joins the choir invisible."

"Point," Kennrick said heavily. "Any idea where Witherspoon might be?"

I looked at Bayta. "His seat is two cars back from Ms. German's," she said. "I don't know if he's there, though."

"But there are only fifteen third-class cars," I added helpfully. "He has to be there somewhere."

"Thanks," Kennrick growled. "If and when I find him, where will you be?"

"In my bed," I said, yawning widely. "I'm still way too short on sleep."

"I know the feeling," Kennrick said. "Talk to you later." With a nod at Bayta, he left the dining area and headed toward the rear of the train.

"Do you want me to see if the Spiders can locate Dr. Witherspoon?" Bayta asked.

"Even if they could, I'd just as soon have Kennrick wander around on his own for awhile," I said. "I know he's worried about his precious contract team, but I don't especially like having him underfoot. How's the disassembly of the air filter system going?"

"Slowly," Bayta said. "I don't think one of these has ever been taken apart while the train was in motion, and the mites are having to figure it out as they go. Do you think Ms. German is the killer?"

"My first impression is no," I said. "But I'm not ready to write anyone off the suspect list quite yet. She's certainly had enough access to the victims over the past two weeks. *And* she's definitely hiding something."

Bayta looked at the archway. "Do you suppose she could be running away from home?"

"Jumping a Quadrail is a pretty pricey way of escaping Mom and Dad," I reminded her. "On the other hand, without access to the Spiders' station-based records, there's no way to know the circumstances of her coming aboard."

"No, there's not," Bayta murmured thoughtfully. "Do you suppose that's why the killer chose a cross-galactic express? So that we wouldn't be able to get anyone's records?"

"Could be," I said. "Or so we wouldn't be able to call for

help, get quick and complete autopsies, or get out of his line of fire. Pick one."

Bayta shivered. "You think he's planning more killings, then?"

"I would hope that two dead bodies would be enough for anyone," I said soberly. "But I wouldn't bet the rent money on it."

"No." She took a deep breath, and for just a moment her mask dropped away to reveal something tired and anxious. It was a side of her that I didn't see very often, and there was something about it that made me want to take her hand and tell her, don't worry, it'll be all right.

But I didn't. I didn't dare. Among his other tricks, the Modhri employed something called thought viruses, suggestions that could be sent telepathically from a walker to an uninfected person. In one of the lowest ironies of this whole miserable business, thought viruses traveled best along the lines of trust between friends, close colleagues, or lovers.

Which meant that once the Modhri had established a colony in one person, the walker's entire circle of friends was usually soon to follow, lemming-like, in the act of touching some Modhran coral and starting their own Modhran polyp colonies. The Modhri had used that technique to infiltrate business centers, industrial directorates, counterintelligence squads, and even whole governments.

Bayta and I were close. We had to be, working and fighting alongside each other the way we were. But at the same time, we had to struggle to maintain as much emotional distance between us as we possibly could. Otherwise, if the Modhri ever got to one of us, he would inevitably get the other one, too.

Bayta knew that as well as I did. The moment of vulnerability passed, her mask came back up, and I once again forced my protective male instincts into the background. "So what's our next move?" she asked.

"Exactly what I told Kennrick." I yawned again. "I'm going to get some sleep. You coming?"

"I think I'll wander around a little longer," she said. "Maybe go watch the air system disassembly. I don't think I could sleep just now."

I eyed her, that brief flicker of vulnerability coming back to mind. But her professional self was back in charge, cool and confident and competent.

And it wasn't like she would be alone out here. Not with hundreds of people milling around and other hundreds of Spiders watching her every move. "Okay," I said, pushing myself off the bar stool. "Just be careful. And let me know if anything happens."

"What if what happens isn't especially interesting?" she asked.

"This is a murder investigation," I reminded her grimly. "*Everything* is interesting."

This time I got nearly four hours of sleep before I was awakened by a growling stomach, the realization that I hadn't eaten since last night, and the delectable aroma of onion rings.

"I thought you might be hungry," Bayta said as she carefully balanced the onion rings and a cup of iced tea on the edge of my computer desk's swivel table.

"Very," I confirmed, sniffing at the plate with mild surprise. Offhand, I couldn't think of any other time when Bayta had brought me something to eat purely on her own initiative. Either she was finally getting the hang of this girl-Friday stuff, or else I was looking even more old and decrepit and pitiable than usual lately. "Thanks. Have a bite?"

"No, thank you," she said, her cheek twitching. "My stomach's been bothering me a little today."

"You're probably just hungry," I suggested as I sat down and took a sip of the tea. It was strong and sweet, just the way I liked it.

"No, I had a vegetable roll a couple of hours ago," she said. "I'm just feeling a little odd today, that's all."

I frowned at her as I bit into one of the onion rings. "Odd enough to have you checked over by one of the doctors?"

"Oh, no, it's nothing like that," she assured me. "Like I said, my stomach's just a little sensitive."

"Okay," I said, making a mental note to keep tabs on her digestive rumblings. With two confirmed poisonings, and Terese German apparently heaving her guts on a regular basis, I wasn't ready yet to chalk up Bayta's oddness to normal travel indigestion. "Any news on the air filter?"

"It's almost ready," she said. "Another hour, maybe."

"Good," I said, biting a third out of the next onion ring in line and washing it down with a swig of tea. "You didn't happen to bump into either Kennrick or Dr. Witherspoon while you were wandering around, did you?"

"I didn't spot either of them," Bayta said. "But I wasn't really looking. I was mostly talking to *Tas* Krodo."

"Who?"

"Master Colix's other seatmate," she said. "The one Ms. German said he mostly talked to."

I frowned at her. "You talked to him? Alone?"

"Not alone, no," she said evenly. "There were other passengers in the car."

"That's not what I meant," I said, setting down a half-eaten onion ring. Was that what the unexpected tea service had been all about? Some kind of preemptive peace offering? "Interrogation is an art, Bayta."

"It wasn't an interrogation," she said, her voice stiff. "We were just two people having a conversation."

I took a careful breath, the old phrase *poisoning the well* flashing to mind. Putting potential witnesses on their guard—or worse, accidentally planting suggestions as to what you wanted to hear—could wreck an entire session. Especially when aliens and alien cultures were involved. "Bayta—"

"I'm not a child, Frank," she snapped. "Don't talk to me as if I were. I've watched you enough times to know the kinds of questions to ask."

"All right," I said as calmly as I could. A fight right now wouldn't help either of us, or the situation, in the slightest. "What kinds of questions did you ask?"

"I first confirmed that he did talk a great deal with Master Colix," she said. Her tone was a near-perfect copy of a junior Westali agent reporting to a superior. "I also confirmed that Master Colix was able to speak both English and Juric. Apparently, Master Colix spent a lot of time talking to *Tas* Krodo about the Path of Onagnalhni."

"The—? Oh, right." I nodded. "Kennrick's Path of the Unpronounceable and Untranslatable. Not entirely unpronounceable, I see."

"Pretty close, though," Bayta said, relaxing slightly. For all her stubbornly defiant talk about doing her own bit of investigating, she really *had* been worried about how mad I would be at her. "He also said that Master Colix had a dark brown bag of what he thought were some kind of fruit snacks."

"He tasted one?"

"No, Master Colix never offered to share," Bayta said. "But they had a fruity scent."

"Sounds harmless enough," I said.

"Yes, it does," Bayta said. "But when I went to look for them in the overhead and underseat storage compartments, I couldn't find them."

I frowned. "The *locked* overhead and underseat compartments?"

"Those compartments, yes," she said grimly. "Only by the time I got to them they weren't locked anymore."

"Well, now, that's very interesting," I murmured, picking up another onion ring and chewing thoughtfully at it. "Did you notice anything unusual about the locks? Any damage to the catches or scratch marks anywhere?"

"I didn't see anything." Bayta's lips compressed briefly. "But I probably don't know what to look for, do I?"

"You'd have noticed if the locks had been forced," I assured her. "That's usually pretty obvious. But the differences between key and keypick aren't nearly so blatant."

"Keypicks don't work on Quadrail locks," Bayta said.

"If something can be coded to be unlocked, somebody will eventually find a way to fake that code," I said, picking up the last two onion rings and cramming them into my mouth. "That, or they'll get hold of a copy of the actual key."

"The passenger's ticket is the only key."

"So I've heard," I said. "So unless the thief forced the locks, we arrive at the conclusion that he also absconded with Colix's key."

"Before he died?"

"Or afterward," I said. "Dead people are much less argumentative when you're going through their pockets."

Bayta shivered. "Sounds awful," she murmured.

"It isn't high on anyone's pleasant-activities list," I conceded as I stepped into the half-bath to wash the onion ring breading off my hands. "But there's still a chance that someone simply broke in. We'll need to go take a look to be sure."

"All right," Bayta said slowly. "But why would anyone want to steal Master Colix's fruit snacks? You can get things like that in the dining car."

"Maybe you can't get his specific brand," I said. "Or maybe there's some other reason entirely." I scratched my head as a sudden ferocious itch ran through my scalp. "But one question at a time. Let's figure out first how the compartments were opened. Then we can tackle the who and why of it."

My plan was to first check out the late Master Colix's storage compartments and then hunt down Kennrick to see what, if anything, he'd learned from Witherspoon about heavy-metal poisoning symptoms in Humans.

Like most of my plans these days, this one didn't survive very long.

We were passing through the last first-class coach when we spotted both Kennrick and Witherspoon. They had pulled up a pair of chairs to face *di*-Master Strinni. Witherspoon was examining the Shorshian, who was gesturing oddly as he talked in a low voice.

And from Witherspoon's expression, I could tell something was wrong.

The doctor glanced up as we approached. "Mr. Compton," he greeted me absently, his mind clearly elsewhere.

"Dr. Witherspoon," I nodded back. "We having a conference?"

"Not exactly," Witherspoon said as he peered closely into Strinni's eyes.

"*Di*-Master Strinni is feeling strangely stressed and nervous," Kennrick explained. "He asked the conductor to allow Dr. Witherspoon into first to administer a sedative."

I eyed Strinni. His muscles were trembling beneath his skin, his breath was coming in short bursts, and his eyes were darting back and forth between the four of us. He certainly looked stressed. "How long before it takes effect?" I asked.

"I haven't given it to him yet," Witherspoon said. "This is something more than simple stress."

I felt my throat tighten. "You mean like—?"

"No," Witherspoon interrupted, throwing me a warning look under his eyebrows. "The symptoms aren't right for that."

"What *are* they right for?" I countered. "No—never mind. Let's just get him to the dispensary and see if—"

[No,] Strinni cut me off. His voice was harsh and dark and as shaky as his musculature. [I will not be poisoned by Spider medicine. The Spiders seek to destroy us all. I will not be placed within their metal claws.]

I frowned. Granted that I hadn't spent more than a few minutes with him before now, such a rabidly anti-Spider attitude was still a surprise. "I'm just suggesting a visit to the diagnostic table," I said. "They're Fibibib design, actually—nothing Spider about them."

[On such a table is where my comrades expired,] Strinni countered. [I do not wish to join them in the silence of death.]

"I'm sure their deaths had nothing to do with the table," I said, deciding to skip over the fact that Master Bofiv, at least, had died long before he reached the table.

"And we won't take you there against your wishes," Kennrick added, his eyes on Witherspoon. "Doctor?"

"I don't know," Witherspoon murmured, touching the edge of Strinni's armpit where the most prominent Shorshic pulse was located. "His pulse is thready, his skin conductivity is bouncing around, and he's so weak he can barely walk. But what that all adds up to, I don't know."

"Seems to me that it's time for a full-press consultation," I said. "Let's get Dr. Aronobal up here and see if she's got any ideas."

[No!] Strinni spat before Witherspoon could answer. [I will not be treated by a Filiaelian!]

"I've already suggested that Dr. Aronobal be brought in," Witherspoon told me grimly. "But *di*-Master Strinni absolutely refuses to see anyone but me."

[I will not be debased so,] Strinni insisted, his arm flailings widening their range.

"No one will force that on you, *di*-Master Strinni," Witherspoon said, holding out his hands. "Please, try to stay calm."

"We're just trying to help you," I added, catching Kennrick's eye and giving him a questioning frown. Wordlessly, he gave me a helpless shrug. Apparently, Strinni's freshly exposed bigotry and paranoia was a new one on him, too.

But my attempt at soothing noises had come too late. [You're with them!] Strinni snarled abruptly, leveling two fingers at my chest. [You serve and obey them!]

And without warning he heaved himself to his feet, knocked Witherspoon sideways out of his chair with a sweep of his right arm, and lunged straight at me.

I did my best to get out of his way. But I was caught flat-footed, my attention still on Kennrick, and standing between Bayta and the next chair over with zero maneuvering room.

My only chance was to back up as fast as I could and hope I could get to a better position before he reached me.

But Strinni was already in motion, and my combat reflexes were sadly out of shape. I'd barely gotten a single step when he slammed into me like a Minneapolis snowplow, his momentum shoving the two of us backward toward whatever bone-wrenching obstacles might be lurking in our path. His big arms wrapped around my back and neck, squeezing my torso and crushing my face against his shoulder. I caught a whiff of something sickly sweet—

Abruptly the bear hug was lifted, and I found myself tottering backward alone. I blinked my eyes to clear them, and found that Strinni had gained two new attachments: Bayta and Kennrick, one of them hanging on to each of his arms like terriers on a bull.

A single sweep of Strinni's arm had sent Witherspoon to the floor. Assuming Strinni was thinking at all, he was undoubtedly thinking he could shake off his new attackers with similar ease. With a bellow, he bent at the waist, half turning and swinging his arms horizontally like massive windmill blades.

Kennrick managed to hang on for about a quarter turn before he lost his grip and flew two meters across the floor to pile himself against the back of one of the other chairs, eliciting a startled bark from the Fibibib seated there. With one of his arms freed, Strinni now shifted his attention to freeing the other one.

But Bayta was stronger than she looked. She held on stubbornly as Strinni swung his arm and torso ponderously back and forth. I got my balance back, grabbed a quick lungful of air, and headed back toward the melee.

Only to be brought up short as a Filly forearm appeared out of nowhere to bar my way. "That is no way to behave toward one who is ill," the alien chided as he glared down a distinctive rose-colored blaze at me. His skin was flushed, his pupils wide with too much alcohol or excitement or both. "He must be treated with respect and care."

"You want to try respect and care, be my guest," I bit out, trying to push his arm out of the way.

But Rose Nose was as determined as I was, and I still didn't have all my wind back. For a couple of seconds we struggled, him still spouting platitudes, me trying very hard not to simply haul off and slug him.

It was just as well that I didn't. The Filly's delay meant that Kennrick recovered his balance and got back to Strinni before I did.

Which meant that it was Kennrick, not me, who caught a swinging Shorshic forearm squarely across the left side of his rib cage.

There was too much noise for me to hear the crack of breaking ribs, if there actually was such a crack. But even over Strinni's paranoid gaspings and Rose Nose's admonitions I had no trouble hearing Kennrick's strangled grunt as the arm sent him flying across the room again. He slammed hard into the floor, and this time he didn't get up.

But his sacrifice hadn't been for nothing. The rest of the car's passengers had finally broken out of their stunned disbelief at Strinni's bizarre attack, and even as I continued to struggle with my self-appointed Filly protector a Juri and a Tra'ho moved in from opposite sides and tackled the berserk Shorshian.

Even then Strinni didn't give up. Still ranting, he continued to stomp around the floor, trying to throw off his attackers the way he'd disposed of Kennrick. But Bayta was still hanging on, and neither the Juri or Tra'ho was giving way, either, and Strinni began to stagger as he burned through his adrenaline-fueled energy reserves.

And then Witherspoon was on his feet again behind the clump of people, reaching past Bayta's head to jab a hypo into the back of Strinni's neck.

For another few seconds Strinni didn't react, but kept up his bizarre unchoreographed four-person waltz. I finally got past my guardian Filly and headed in, balling my hands into fists as I aimed for a couple of pressure points in the Shorshian's thighs that ought to drop him once and for all.

But even as I cocked my fists for a one-two punch, Witherspoon's concoction finally reached Strinni's motor control center. His legs wobbled and then collapsed beneath him, and he and the others fell into a tangled heap.

I looked at Witherspoon. "If this is so weak he can barely walk," I said, still panting, "I'd hate to see what frisky looks like."

"We need to get him to the dispensary," Witherspoon said grimly. He was breathing a little heavily himself. "Can I get some help in lifting?"

"No need," Bayta said, pushing herself out of the pile and getting carefully to her feet.

I looked toward the rear of the car. A pair of conductor Spiders had emerged from the vestibule and were hurriedly tapping their way toward us. "Everyone off and out of the way," I ordered. "The Spiders can carry him."

"He doesn't like Spiders," Rose Nose reminded me. With the excitement over, his eyes were starting to calm down.

"He's unconscious," I reminded him. "I won't tell if you don't."

From across the room came a rumbling groan. I looked in that direction to see Kennrick pulling himself carefully up from the floor, one hand on the nearest chair armrest, the other pressed against his side where Strinni's arm had slammed into him. "You okay?" I asked, stepping over to offer him a hand.

"Oh, sure—I do this every day," he gritted out. "What the hell was *that* all about?"

"You tell me," I said, looking back as the two Spiders picked up the unconscious Strinni, each of them using three of their seven legs to form a sort of wraparound hammock. "This sort of thing happen often?"

"If it does, it's been the galaxy's best-kept secret." He winced as I helped him the rest of the way to his feet. "I've never heard *di*-Master Strinni even raise his voice in an argument."

"Except maybe with Spiders or Filiaelians," I said, easing Kennrick to the side as the Spiders maneuvered their burden past us toward the forward vestibule and the dispensary four cars ahead.

"Well, that was just plain crazy," Kennrick said firmly. "We have four Filiaelians right here on his contract team. *Ow!*"

"Sorry," I apologized. "How bad is it?"

"Like I've been kicked by a cow." He smiled wanly. "And I worked summers on a dairy farm, so I know exactly what that feels like."

"You need help getting to the dispensary?" I asked. Bayta was disappearing through the vestibule door, and I could see Witherspoon's shock of white hair just in front of her. "I can get a Spider if you want."

"No, I can make it," he said. "Just give me a hand."

"Sure," I said, getting an arm around his shoulders. "Easy, now."

"You see?" Rose Nose said sagely as we passed him. "I said that was no way to behave toward one who is ill."

"Thanks," I said. "I'll try to remember that."

SEVEN :

Three of Kennrick's ribs had been slightly cracked in the fight, fortunately not badly enough to require a cast or even a wrap. His side apparently hurt like hell, though. Witherspoon gave him a bottle of QuixHeals and another bottle of painkillers and ordered a regimen of rest and sleep. Kennrick allowed that he could probably manage that and toddled off toward his compartment.

Strinni's case, unfortunately, wasn't nearly so easy to fix.

"I've run the blood scan twice," Witherspoon said as he gazed down at the Shorshian now securely strapped to the diagnostic table. "We've got not one, but *two* different poisons that have invaded his system. The first is a relative of printimpolivrebioxene, which the analyzer lists as a sort of combination hallucinogen and paranoic."

"That certainly fits his performance just now," I agreed. "Is that the sickly-sweet odor I caught when he was trying to crush in my ribs?"

"Probably." Witherspoon's throat tightened. "The other

poison appears to be a heavy metal. Probably the same cadmium that killed his two colleagues."

"How surprising," I murmured. "Are we in time to do something about this one?"

"I don't know," Witherspoon said. "I've got him on a double dose of Castan's Binder, which should be able to bond to the metal still in his bloodstream. But if too much has already gotten into his deep tissues—" He shook his head.

I looked at Bayta. She was gazing down at Strinni's closed eyes, absently massaging her right wrist. "Bayta, is there anything the Spiders can do?" I asked.

"Nothing that Dr. Witherspoon isn't already doing," she said. "I was just wondering if we should wake him up. Maybe he knows who did this to him."

"That would definitely explain why they slipped him a Mickey," I agreed.

"A Mickey?" Witherspoon asked, frowning.

"A Mickey Finn," I explained. "Knockout drops, usually."

"Yes, I'm familiar with the term," Witherspoon growled. "But *I'm* the one who gave him the sedative."

"I was referring to the hallucinogen," I said. "Maybe the poisoner was afraid *di*-Master Strinni knew something important, so he made him go berserk in the hope that we'd go ahead and knock him out ourselves, thereby saving himself the trouble."

"I suppose that's possible," Witherspoon said. "One problem: I believe printimpolivre-bioxene is on the Spiders' prohibited list."

I looked at Bayta. "Is it?"

"All hallucinogenic chemicals are supposed to be there," she confirmed. "Unless it was already in *di*-Master Strinni's system, it shouldn't have gotten past the sensor screening."

"It definitely wasn't in his system," Witherspoon said. "Like the heavy-metal poisoning, printimpolivre-bioxene's effects would have shown up very quickly. Within hours, most likely. Certainly long before the two weeks we've been traveling."

"This is starting to sound like a locked-door murder mystery," I said. "So what about Bayta's suggestion that we wake him up?"

"I don't know," Witherspoon said, rubbing his shoulder where Strinni's first attack had landed. "I'd prefer to let him just sleep off the sedative instead of adding another chemical to the mix that his system's already dealing with. Besides, until his kidney-primes are able to oxidize the printimpolivre-bioxene and flush it from his system, he'd most likely just wake up into the same frenzied state he was in before."

Which would make anything we *did* get out of him fairly useless. "How long before that happens?"

Witherspoon shrugged. "Three hours. Maybe four."

"We'll come back then," I said, taking Bayta's arm. "If his condition changes, or you need anything, just tell the Spider."

"And the word will somehow magically get back to you," Witherspoon commented, glancing at the server standing silently by the drug cabinet. "Yes, Dr. Aronobal told me you two seem to have an interesting relationship with them."

"We travel a lot," I said, steering Bayta toward the dispensary door.

"I don't believe that any more than Aronobal does," Witherspoon said, peering closely at us. "But it's not really any of my business, I suppose."

"You suppose correctly," I agreed. "See you later."

We headed out into the corridor. "Where are we going?" Bayta asked as I turned us toward the front of the train. "I thought you wanted to look at Master Colix's storage compartments."

"I do," I said. "But first we both need to get something in our stomachs."

She looked sideways at me. "Yours bothering you, too?"

"Yes, but that could just be the onion rings," I said. "I gather you're still running at half speed?"

"It's not that bad," she assured me. "Besides, I already told you that I had something to eat."

"A whole vegetable roll," I said, nodding. "And that after having missed breakfast *and* lunch."

"The vegetable roll *was* lunch."

"I've had Quadrail vegetable rolls," I reminded her. "Those are appetizers, not meals. If you really don't want to eat anything, fine. But at least come keep me company."

"All right," she said reluctantly. Maybe she was wondering about the propriety of stuffing our faces while Strinni was in the dispensary dying of cadmium poisoning.

But my gut was rumbling something fierce, and I needed to get something down there to keep it busy. Whether she thought so or not, Bayta probably needed something, too.

The main section of the dining car was mostly empty when we arrived. That wasn't particularly surprising, since we were between the normal lunch and dinner hours and most of the passengers were elsewhere reading, chatting, playing games, or watching dit rec dramas and comedies.

The bar end of the car, in contrast, was packed with passengers, some having pre-dinner drinks, others possibly not yet finished with their lunchtime libations. I glanced in through the smoked plastic dividers as we entered the dining section, just as glad we weren't going to try to get a table in there.

With my digestive sensitivity in mind, I'd already decided

to steer clear of anything exotic or heavy on spices. Accordingly, I ordered a simple steak and vegetable combo, passing on the half-dozen optional sauces offered by the menu.

Bayta, ignoring my raised eyebrows, just ordered another vegetable roll and a glass of lemonade.

"People *do* get indigestion on trips, you know," I reminded her as the Spider headed away from the table. "Especially long trips like this one."

"Maybe," she said. Her eyes were on the center of our table, her attention clearly on her rumbling intestinal tract. "But I've never had indigestion. Not like this. Never."

Abruptly, she looked up at me. "Did you ever find out from Mr. Kennrick or Dr. Witherspoon what the Human symptoms of heavy-metal poisoning were?"

"You were there the whole time," I pointed out. "That part of the conversation got short-circuited by Strinni's one-and-a-half-gainer into the deep end."

"I just thought you might have asked Mr. Kennrick about it while you were helping him to the dispensary."

"Never even occurred to me to bring up the subject," I admitted. "We were a little preoccupied with his ribs at the time."

"So we don't know if"—she glanced down at her abdomen—"if this is a symptom or not."

"Not specifically, no," I said as soothingly as I could. "But we know that the train's food supply isn't contaminated, and no one's been leaning over our dinner plates sprinkling cadmium garnish on our salads."

"What if it's airborne?" Bayta asked. "We still don't know about that."

"We will as soon as we finish dinner," I said. "You said they'll have the filter disassembled in, what, another half hour?"

Her eyes unfocused briefly. "About that."

"So we'll eat and then head back and take some samples," I said. "Five minutes after that we'll know whether the stuff was in the air or not."

"Compton?" Kennrick's voice came from behind me.

I turned, wincing as the movement strained freshly tenderized joints. Kennrick was standing a couple of feet back, his expression that of a man who's just eaten a bad grape. "I thought you were heading back to your compartment," I said.

"I was," he said. "Other matters intervened. *Usantra* Givvrac would very much like a word with you."

"I'd be delighted to give him one," I said. "Just as soon as we finish our meal."

Kennrick's eyes flicked pointedly to the empty table in front of us. "Or possibly beforehand?" he suggested. "*Usantra* Givvrac is right here, over in the bar section." His lip twitched. "We were discussing the situation when he spotted you coming in."

"You're as well informed about this mess as anyone," I reminded him. "What does he think I can add to the discussion?"

Kennrick glanced at Bayta. "He feels you may have a better handle on what's happening than I do."

"And you resent the implications?"

"What I resent or don't resent is irrelevant," he said evenly. "I'm Pellorian Medical's representative to these people, and the head of the contract team has made a request of me. The rule is, if you can satisfy such requests, you do."

"True enough," I agreed, feeling a twinge of sympathy. In my early days in Westali, when most of my missions boiled down to VIP-babysitting duty, I'd often found myself in the same unenviable position. "Well, we can't have you ignoring your mandate, can we? Tell *Usantra* Givvrac I'd be honored to give him a few minutes of my time."

"Thanks," he said, and headed back toward the bar section. I waited until he was out of earshot, then turned to Bayta. "Anything you want me to ask him?" I asked her. "Upper-rank Fillies are notorious for speaking only to the senior person present."

"No, I don't think so," Bayta said. "We can always ask him later if I think of something."

"Careful," I warned. "In classic dit rec dramas, putting off a conversation usually means that person is the next one to die."

Bayta shivered. "I wish this *was* a dit rec drama," she murmured. "At least then there would be some sense to it."

"Oh, there's sense to it," I promised her grimly. "We just don't know what it is yet. But we will."

"I hope so." She looked up again, her eyes focusing somewhere over my shoulder. "Here he comes."

Earlier, when I'd seen Kennrick and Givvrac conferring in the latter's coach car, I'd noted that the Filly looked fairly elderly. Now, as I watched him crossing the dining car toward us, I was struck by not only how old he was, but also how fragile. He walked carefully, as if balance was a conscious decision instead of something his body automatically did on its own. His eyes continually scanned the tables and chairs alongside his path, with the air of someone who fears a casual bump might break delicate bones. Kennrick walked close beside him the whole way, his eyes alert, his hand poised for an instant assist should the other need it.

I stood up as they approached, swiveling my chair partway toward them. "I greet you, *Usantra* Givvrac," I said, gesturing to the seat. "Please take my chair."

"I thank you, Mr. Compton," Givvrac said, sinking gratefully onto his knees on it in the standard Filly sitting position. He waited for the chair to reconfigure for his body, and then gestured to the chair across the table beside Bayta. "Please—sit. You as well, Mr. Kennrick."

"Thank you," I said, stepping around the corner of the table and sitting down in the indicated chair as Kennrick took the other empty seat beside Givvrac. "If I may be so bold, *Usantra* Givvrac, I'm surprised to see someone of your age so far from home."

"With age comes experience, Mr. Compton," Givvrac replied. "With experience comes wisdom and perspective. Or so one hopes."

"Your people thought such wisdom and perspective would be necessary in this contract discussion?" I suggested.

"They did," Givvrac confirmed. "And so it was. But I came here to question you, not to be questioned by you."

"My apologies," I said, inclining my head. "Please state your questions."

"I'm told by Mr. Kennrick that you are an investigator," Givvrac said. "Let us begin with a list of your credentials."

"I'm a former agent of Earth's Western Alliance Intelligence service," I said. "During those years, I traveled over fairly large stretches of our end of the galaxy, and gained experience dealing with members of several of the Twelve Empires."

"And now?"

"Now I travel the galaxy with my associate Bayta," I said, nodding toward her. "We do odd jobs and assist with investigations for the Spiders."

"I see," Givvrac said, and I could see him wondering, just as Witherspoon had, what sort of investigations the Spiders might possibly need assistance with. Unlike the good doctor, though, Givvrac was too polite to ask. "Any other credentials?"

For a moment I was tempted to tell him about my brief employment with Larry Hardin, who had hired me to find a way to steal, bribe, or extort control of the Quadrail away from the Spiders. Givvrac's reaction to such a revelation might have been interesting. "Various odd jobs when I was in school," I said instead. "Nothing remarkable."

Givvrac nodded, a rather awkward looking motion for that head and neck combination. Clearly, it was a gesture he'd picked up solely to use with Humans and a couple of other species. "Tell me what you've learned of the present situation."

"Unfortunately, at this point I probably don't know much more than you do," I said. "Yesterday evening Master Colix came down with cadmium poisoning, source unknown, and quickly succumbed to it. Shortly thereafter, Master Bofiv died from the same cause. It appears now that *di*-Master Strinni has also been poisoned, plus he's been dosed with a drug called printimpolivre-bioxene."

Givvrac looked at Kennrick. "Are you familiar with this drug?"

"Dr. Witherspoon says it's a hallucinogen," Kennrick said. "It was apparently the reason for *di*-Master Strinni's violent behavior earlier in his car."

"I've not heard of this drug before," Givvrac said, looking back at me. "Is it common?"

"It's common enough," I said grimly. "In the illegal drug trade, its street name is *necrovri*."

Givvrac sat up a bit straighter. "Necrovri," he murmured. "Yes, I've heard of it. A blight among the Shorshic and Pirkarli lower classes." His nose blaze darkened. "But how could such a thing have drawn in one of *di*-Master ranking?"

"The upper ranks of any species aren't immune to the lure of the forbidden," I reminded him. "However, in this case, I don't think *di*-Master Strinni took the drug on his own. I believe it was given to him without his knowledge, possibly to prevent us from learning something from him about the other two murders."

"Murders," Givvrac murmured, his blaze darkening a little more. "Mr. Kennrick said he believed the deaths were not accidental. Now you add your same opinion to his?"

"Yes, I do," I said, diplomatically passing over the fact that Kennrick wouldn't have had any such insight if I hadn't taken the time to beat it into him. "Dr. Witherspoon is trying to reverse *di*-Master Strinni's cadmium poisoning. If he succeeds, we should be able to question *di*-Master Strinni and see what he knows. If anything."

"Do you know how this poisoning was accomplished?" Givvrac asked.

"Not yet," I said. "Part of the problem is that we don't have a motive for the attacks. Typically, motives for murder fall into one of three categories: passion, profit, or revenge. Passion is out—clearly, these killings were carefully planned and executed. That leaves us profit and revenge." I raised my eyebrows in silent question.

"Clever, Mr. Compton," Givvrac said, a touch of amusement in his voice. "So in order for you to answer my questions, I must first answer yours?"

"All investigations require questions and answers," I pointed out. "Can you think of how anyone would profit from the deaths of Masters Colix and Bofiv?"

"No," Givvrac said, his tone leaving no room for doubt.

"Leaving us with revenge," I said. "Can you think—?"

"Just a minute," Kennrick interrupted. "Your pardon, *Usantra* Givvrac, but there *are* reasons of profit that could explain these deaths."

"No, there are not," Givvrac repeated, giving Kennrick a warning glare. "Your next question, Mr. Compton?"

"Let me first rephrase my previous one," I said, eyeing Givvrac closely as I thought back to his answer. I'd seen this before, usually with suspects trying to beat a polyline test by finding loopholes in the interrogator's questions. Teenagers, I recalled from years gone by, were also adept at the technique, especially during parental cross-examinations. "Can you think of how anyone would profit from Master Colix's death?"

Givvrac hissed out a quiet sigh. "Perhaps," he said reluctantly. "There was some disagreement among us as to whether we would grant Pellorian Medical Systems the genetic-manipulation knowledge and equipment they seek."

"Let me guess," I said, watching Kennrick out of the corner of my eye. "Master Colix was against the deal?"

Kennrick's expression didn't even twitch. "In actual fact, Mr. Compton," Givvrac said, "Master Colix was one of the strongest proponents *for* the contract."

"Interesting," I said. "I gather, then, that Master Bofiv was *against* the contract."

"He was," Givvrac confirmed, frowning. "Did he tell you that before he died?"

"Unfortunately, he didn't speak to me at all," I said. "I deduced that from your earlier statement that no one would profit by *both* Master Colix's and Master Bofiv's deaths. Ergo, they must have been on opposite sides of the disagreement, with both deaths together thus returning the contract team to its original status quo."

"Hardly the exact status quo," Kennrick said. "There were no more than two or possibly three of the eight in opposition to our proposal. With the unfortunate deaths of Masters Colix and Bofiv, the percentage of members favorable to Pellorian has actually increased."

"Not precisely true, Mr. Kennrick," Givvrac said. "In actual fact, before these deaths the contract team was evenly split on the matter: four for, and four against."

Kennrick stared at him. "You never said—" He broke off, glancing sideways at me. "I was unaware the contract team's feelings were running so closely."

"It's not a matter of your company's expertise and learning," Givvrac assured him. "You've proved that beyond doubt. The question is solely whether or not your species in general has the wisdom to use these methods properly."

"I see," Kennrick said, and I could sense his reflexive desire to argue the point in Pellorian's and humanity's defense. But this wasn't the time or place to reopen the negotiations. "Forgive my intrusion. Please continue."

"Thank you," I said. "So what you're saying, *Usantra* Givvrac, is that the original four-to-four deadlock has been reduced to a three-to-three deadlock?"

"Deadlock implies the matter may end without resolution," Givvrac corrected me sternly. "That will not happen. The decision *will* be made before Mr. Kennrick leaves the Assembly for his return home."

"Understood," I said. "May I ask which members of your group are currently on which side?"

Givvrac hesitated. "That's privileged information," he said. "I'm not sure even the current situation justifies my telling you."

Kennrick, to his credit, picked up on the cue. "Excuse me a moment, *Usantra* Givvrac," he said, getting to his feet. "It just occurred to me that we never told the server that we would be over here instead of back in the bar. I'll go get our refreshments."

He headed across the dining car toward the bar. "Speaking of refreshments, *Usantra* Givvrac, I must again extend my apologies," I said. "I neglected to ask if you would care to join us in a meal."

"No, thank you," Givvrac said. "Food does not interest me at the moment."

I frowned. Fillies liked their food as well as anyone else in the galaxy. "Is something you ate bothering you?"

"Most likely," he said. "I have been feeling somewhat delicate over the past few hours."

"There seems to be a lot of that going around," I commented, my own gut rumbling in sympathy. "While Mr. Kennrick is gone, perhaps you'd be willing to tell me which members of your team are for this deal with Pellorian?"

"You will agree not to share my words with Mr. Kennrick?"

"Of course," I said. "I'll sign a contract to that effect if you wish."

Givvrac visibly relaxed. Written contracts were very important to Fillies. Even if he and I never actually signed anything, my willingness to do so would go a long way toward putting me in the trustworthy category. "No need," he said. "*Di*-Master Strinni was the next strongest proponent of the Pellorian contract."

"Really," I said. So that was two aye votes either dead or on the critical list. "What about Master Tririn?"

"He stands against the contract," Givvrac said. "Oddly enough, the four Shorshians were evenly split."

"And of course, all of them knew where all the others stood?"

"Indeed," Givvrac said. "The eight of us had several meetings together during the torchliner voyage from Earth to the Terran Tube Station."

"Without Mr. Kennrick present, I presume?"

"You presume correctly," Givvrac said. "Only in his absence

can we speak freely on the subject." He cocked his head in a Filly posture of consideration. "Though such opportunities were uncommon. He often joined one or another group of us for our meals."

"Taking care to talk up the benefits of dealing with Pellorian Medical, no doubt?"

"Correct," Givvrac agreed. "He is a tireless representative of his company."

"I'm sure he is," I said diplomatically. He'd probably been a tireless representative of Shotoko Associates, too, right up until the day Westali had swooped down and broken up DuNoeva's spy ring. "So Master Colix and *di*-Master Strinni were for the contract. Who else?"

"*Asantra* Muzzfor is also on their side of the discussion," Givvrac said. "He is one of my colleagues."

"Yes," I said, catching the subtle vowel difference. Colleagues they might be, but an *asantra* like Muzzfor was lower in rank than an *usantra* like Givvrac. "And the fourth?"

"I also lean in that direction," Givvrac said. "I therefore count myself among them, though I have not entirely made up my mind."

I nodded. "And the other opponents would then be the other two Filiaelians?"

"*Esantra* Worrbin and *Asantra* Dallilo are also against the contract," he confirmed.

"Where do they and *Asantra* Muzzfor sit aboard the train?"

"All three have seats in the second of the first-class coaches, the one directly back of the exercise/dispensary car."

"Do they sit together for the most part?"

"Yes," Givvrac said. "To anticipate your next question, the four of us have frequently discussed the contract during this trip. *Di*-Master Strinni often joined us, as he too has a seat in first class."

"And the other three Shorshians?"

"I presume they also held such conversations, though I cannot say for certain." A shadow seemed to pass across his face. "Or rather, I presume they did when there were still three of them."

"You haven't spoken to them about the matter?" I asked.

"We travel in first class," Givvrac said. "They travel in third."

"Yes, of course," I said. "I just thought that since Mr. Kennrick had gone back there on occasion to talk to them you might have done similarly."

"I have not, nor have my colleagues," Givvrac repeated firmly. "Those of first class do not mingle with those of third while aboard the train."

Bayta nudged me, and I looked over Givvrac's shoulder to see that Kennrick had reappeared on our side of the car, a pair of drinks in hand. "Thank you for your openness and honesty," I said to the Filly, inclining my head. "Perhaps we can speak now of the other possible motive for these horrific crimes, namely that of revenge. Can you think of any reason why someone would be carrying anger or hatred toward either Master Colix or Master Bofiv?"

"Here we go," Kennrick said as he came up to the table. He set the drinks down and then resumed his seat beside Givvrac. "My apologies for the delay."

"No apologies required," Givvrac said. "As to your question, Mr. Compton, I believe it would be inappropriate for me to speak of another's life after his voice is silenced."

"I understand," I said, suppressing a grimace. Was it inappropriate to gossip about the deceased at all, or was it only inappropriate because Kennrick was now back in the conversation? "In that case, I think that's all I need for the moment. I thank you deeply for your time and wisdom, *Usantra* Givvrac."

"You are welcome," Givvrac said. "Feel free to approach me with further questions if you have the need. Will you also wish to speak with *Esantra* Worrbin, *Asantra* Muzzfor, or *Asantra* Dallilo?"

"Perhaps later," I said. "If I do, I'll be sure to obtain your permission first."

"No need," he said. "I hereby grant you open access to all Filiaelians under my authority aboard this train."

"I appreciate that," I said, inclining my head again. Fillies weren't the obsessive sticklers for protocol that Juriani were, but they had definite ideas of rank and chain of command. Violating those rules would burn whatever goodwill I might have started with, and could conceivably get the whole crowd of them to clam up on me completely. With Givvrac's carte blanche in hand, at least I didn't have to worry about that.

"Then we take our leave," Givvrac said, placing both hands on the table and carefully getting to his feet. "Perhaps, Mr. Kennrick, you'll assist me back to the bar area?"

"Certainly," Kennrick said, scrambling quickly to his feet and holding out a hand where the Filly could grab it if necessary. "Compton, could you give me a hand with the drinks? I can't handle both of them and offer *Usantra* Givvrac assistance at the same time."

"Certainly," I said, standing up.

"No need," Givvrac said, waving me down again. "My drink has lost its taste, and Mr. Kennrick can easily handle his own."

"Are you sure?" I asked. "It's no trouble, I assure you."

"I'm sure," Givvrac said. "Thank you for your time, Mr. Compton. Mr. Kennrick?"

"Ready," Kennrick said, picking up his own drink. As I sat down again, they turned away and started across the dining room.

And then, two steps away, Givvrac paused and retraced his steps back to our table. "One other thing, Mr. Compton," he said. "If I may be so bold as to offer you advice in your area of expertise."

"In my area of expertise there's always more to learn," I assured him, gesturing to the chair he'd just vacated. "Please speak on."

"Thank you," he said, making no move to sit down. "You stated that the motives for murder were passion, profit, and revenge. In your place, I would consider two additional possibilities."

"Those being?" I asked.

"The first is honor," he said. "With Filiaelians and Shorshians alike, damage or endangerment to one's honor can be reason to eliminate the one who presents that threat. I don't know if Humans feel similar motivations."

"We do, though perhaps to a different degree," I told him.

"And to varying degrees within our species," Kennrick added. "Certainly there are Earth cultures that hold honor very important."

"True," I said. "And the second motive, *Usantra* Givvrac?"

His eyes burned into me. "Insanity."

For a moment the word hung in the air like a bubble of black in a dark gray silence. Then, Givvrac gave me a final nod. "Thank you for your time, Mr. Compton. Good day."

"Good day, *Usantra* Givvrac," I replied. "Good health to you."

"Perhaps," he said. "We shall see."

He headed back across the dining area, Kennrick at his side. "What do you think?" I asked Bayta.

"I was just wondering if Mr. Kennrick has figured out who was on which side of the contract discussion," she said, her voice thoughtful.

"If Mr. Kennrick is worth anywhere near his salt, one would certainly hope so," I said.

"Could he want the contract enough to kill to make sure it went through?"

"Possibly," I said. "The problem with that theory is that, at the moment, two-thirds of the poisoning victims were already on his side."

"Unless he misread their intentions."

"True," I said. "But if we're going down the profit side of the street, it would make more sense if the killer was on the other side of the deadlock."

"Master Tririn?"

"He certainly shows promise," I said. "He's opposed to the contract, and he had easy access to two of the victims."

"But not to the third," Bayta pointed out. "*Di*-Master Strinni was in first class, where Master Tririn wouldn't have been able to get to him."

"Unless Strinni liked to go back and visit the others like Kennrick did," I said. "Givvrac implied that he didn't, but Givvrac may not know for sure. Or Tririn might have come up here if someone in first asked for him."

Bayta frowned into space. "No one asked Master Tririn to come forward," she said.

I shrugged. "It was a long shot. It's not like Master Tririn's been in high demand around the train the way Dr. Aronobal and Dr. Witherspoon have."

"True," Bayta agreed. "It also occurs to me that we only have *Usantra* Givvrac's word that Master Tririn was actually opposed to the Pellorian contract."

"Very good," I said approvingly. "As I told Givvrac, investigations require questions and answers. But you don't necessarily believe those answers. Any other thoughts?"

"Just this." She pointed at Givvrac's abandoned drink. "Do you know what this is?"

I picked it up and gave the contents a sniff. The concoction had a tangy, exotic aroma, but with no scent of alcohol that I could detect. "Not a clue," I said.

"It's *miccrano*," she said. "A traditional Filiaelian remedy for serious stomach and digestive trouble."

"Is it, now," I said, eyeing the drink with new interest. "Sounds like he may be feeling more than just a bit delicate. Has he had a chat with either of our two doctors?"

Bayta's eyes defocused as she again consulted with the Spiders. As she did so, the server appeared from the rear of the dining area with the meals we'd ordered before Kennrick first came to our table. I'd actually expected the food to show up during our conversation, which could have been a little awkward since Givvrac would certainly have insisted on a polite departure. Knowing Bayta, she'd probably telepathically instructed the Spider to hold the meals until we'd finished and our visitors had left.

Bayta's eyes came back. "He had a conductor bring Dr. Aronobal up from third class about an hour ago," she reported. "Dr. Aronobal is the one who recommended the *miccrano* to him."

"Which also probably explains why Kennrick was here instead of in his compartment," I said as the Spider set our plates in front of us. "Givvrac would have been in the bar, working through his tummy-soothers, when Kennrick passed by on his way to lie down. Do we know how many of them he had?"

"This was his third," Bayta said, nodding at the glass.

"Which he never touched," I commented, rubbing my chin. "I wonder why he decided to abandon it."

"Maybe he was feeling better," Bayta suggested.

"Or decided that the first two hadn't done him any good anyway," I said, something prickly running up my back as I eyed the glass. If someone had poisoned the drink . . .

I snorted under my breath. No—that one *was* pure paranoia. Even if Kennrick was the killer, he'd have to be crazy to poison Givvrac at a time when we knew they were having a drink together.

Still, it couldn't do any harm to check. "Bayta, can you have the server in the dispensary bring me one of those little vials from the sampling kit?" I asked.

"Yes, of course," she said, her voice suddenly uncertain. "You think there's something in *Usantra* Givvrac's drink?"

"No, but we might as well be thorough about this." I picked up my fork. "Meanwhile, this isn't getting any warmer. Let's eat."

The meal was up to the usual Quadrail standards. Unfortunately, it was impossible for me to properly enjoy it with my gut rumbling the way it was. Halfway through, I gave up and pushed the plate away.

Bayta was either feeling better than I was or else was stubbornly committed to not wasting any of the food her Spider friends had hauled across the galaxy for our benefit. She made it all the way through her vegetable roll, chewing silently but determinedly.

She was just finishing off her lemonade when a server Spider appeared and set a sampling vial and a small hypo on the table beside my plate.

"Thank you," I said. Taking the hypo, I extracted a couple

of milliliters of Givvrac's drink and injected it into the vial. "I said thank you," I repeated, looking at the Spider.

"He's waiting for you to give back the hypo," Bayta explained.

"Ah," I said, reversing the instrument and holding it up. The Spider extended a leg and took it, then folded the leg up beneath his globe and tapped his way back out of the dining area. "Any news on the air filter?" I asked Bayta.

"It's nearly done," she said. "It should be ready by the time we get back there."

"Good," I said, standing up and slipping the sample vial into my pocket. "Let's go."

EIGHT :

It was getting toward train's evening, and the third-class passengers were starting to drift back to their seats after a busy day in the entertainment car, the exercise area, or the bar.

Which meant there was a large and curious audience already in place when Bayta and I moved toward the rear of the car and the disassembled air filter system waiting there for us.

I'd never asked Bayta what exactly the disassembly procedure entailed. Now, as we joined a group of knee-high mite Spiders and a pair of the larger conductors, I could see why the job had taken this long. A section of ceiling nearly a meter square had been taken down, probably with the help of the two conductors, and was currently hanging by thin support wires attached to its four corners at about throat level over the back row of seats. The occupants of those seats, not surprisingly, had found somewhere else to be for the moment.

"We couldn't bring in a couple of cameras so the whole train could watch?" I grumbled as we passed our third knot of rubberneckers.

"I thought you'd want to take the sample yourself," Bayta countered, a slight edge to her voice. Clearly, she didn't like having the Quadrail's innards exposed to the paying customers this way any more than I did, and she didn't appreciate me getting on her case about it. "There's no way you could have reached the filter while it was still in place."

And given the tight tolerances of Quadrail floor space, there was probably nowhere more private where they could have lugged the filter assembly for the procedure. "I suppose," I conceded.

We reached the hanging plate, and I took a moment to study its upper side. The filter assembly consisted of about a dozen boxes of various sizes and shapes scattered across the plate, all of them marked with incomprehensible dot codes. They were connected to each other by a bewildering and colorful spaghetti of tubes, ducts, cables, and wires. Other tubes and conduits, carefully sealed off, ran to the edges of the plate, where presumably they connected to equipment tucked away above the rest of the ceiling. The plate itself had sixteen connectors, four per side, for fastening it to the rest of the ceiling. The connectors, I noted, were accessible only from above. It was pretty clear that no one was going to tamper with the system without Spider help. "Which one do I want?" I asked Bayta.

"That one," she said, pointing to the largest of the boxes. "The Spiders will take off the cover for you."

"Thanks," I said, looking down at the mites grouped around us like shiny seven-legged lap dogs. "Do they need a boost?"

"No," Bayta said, and I quickly stepped back as a pair of fist-sized twitters appeared from inside the ceiling and deftly slid down the corner lines onto the exposed machinery. Picking their way across the miniature landscape, they reached the box Bayta had indicated and started removing one of its sides.

"Here," Bayta said, pressing a pair of sample vials into my hand. "Will you need a hypo or scraper?"

"Got one, thanks," I said, pulling out my multitool and selecting one of the blades. The twitters got the filter's side off, and I leaned in for a closer look.

I'd expected to find some sort of thin but tangible layer of fluffiness, the sort of thing you might find in an office building air filter that hadn't been replaced for a few weeks. But the dimpled white material sitting in front of me looked as clean and fresh as if it had come right out of the box.

It looked, in fact, like some industrious Spider had given it a thorough cleaning sometime in the past few hours. And if one of them had, this whole thing was going to be a complete waste of time. "You *did* warn the Spiders not to clean it, didn't you?"

"Of course," Bayta said. "It hasn't been touched since Homshil."

"Looks pretty clean to me," I pointed out.

"It's the third-stage filter," she said. "It always *looks* clean."

I suppressed a grimace. Of course it did. All the larger dust and lint particles would have been captured by a larger-mesh filter somewhere upstream in the system. But it was this filter that would have a shot at trapping impurities the size of cadmium atoms and compounds. "Just making sure," I said, trying to salvage a little dignity.

Experimentally, I gently scraped the multitool blade along one edge of the filter. A small cascade of fine white powder appeared and drifted slowly downward. Moving the blade to a different part of the filter, I held one of the vials in position and scraped more of the white powder into it. I waited until the dust had settled and then handed the vial to Bayta for sealing. I repeated the operation on a third section of the filter, again handing the vial to Bayta when I was done. "That should do it," I told her. Folding the blade back into the multitool, I turned around.

And stopped short. Standing three meters away, right in the center of the ring of gawkers, was the Filly I'd had the brief tussle with earlier that day in the third-class bar. He was staring at me with an intensity I didn't at all care for. "Can I help you?" I asked.

"What do you do here?" the Filly asked, his long nose pointing toward the filter assembly.

"Just a routine maintenance sampling," I said in my best authoritative-but-soothing voice. "Nothing you need to be concerned about."

I'd used that voice to good advantage many times over the years. Unfortunately, this particular Filly wasn't buying it. "Is there danger in the air?" he demanded. "Is there risk to us all?"

"There's no risk to anyone," I said firmly if not entirely truthfully. "As I said, this is just a routine maintenance check."

But it was no use. A low-level murmur was already rippling through the rest of the onlookers, some of whom had probably ridden this line before and knew that there was nothing routine about what we were doing. "If there is risk, we deserve to know the truth," the Filly said firmly, his volume rising to a level that would reach most of the car instead of just the group assembled here at the rear.

"There is no risk," I said again, letting my gaze drift over the crowd as I tried to think up an answer that would satisfy them. "But you're right, you deserve to know the truth. If you'll all be quiet a moment?"

I stopped, waiting for them to pick up on the cue. I could

feel Bayta's eyes on me, and her concern as she wondered what exactly I was doing.

I wondered what I was doing, too. Telling them there was a murderer aboard the train was definitely out—we could wind up with a riot on our hands, with nowhere anyone could escape to. But I'd had enough experience with rumor mills to know that if we didn't give them *something* the situation would only get worse, possibly leading to the same riot I was hoping so hard to avoid.

Ergo, I had to give them some truth. The trick, as always, would be to figure out how much.

Slowly, in bits and pieces, the mutterings faded away. "Thank you," I said. "I presume you're all aware that two of your fellow travelers died yesterday."

The last mutterings abruptly vanished. I had their full attention now, all right. I heard Bayta mutter something under her breath, but it wasn't like the rest of the passengers wouldn't have noticed the two newly empty seats. "What I'm doing here is checking for the presence of what are called *afterelements*," I went on. "Those are bits of nucleic acid residue, antibodies, mucousids—the sorts of things that might have been exhaled by a person in his last battle against a lethal congenital defect."

The Filly's nose blaze darkened a bit. "A congenital defect? In both victims?"

"I can see no other likely conclusion," I said, noting in passing his unusual use of the word *victims*. "No one else in the car has shown any signs of illness, which eliminates the possibility that they died from some contagious disease."

I gestured toward a pair of Shorshians near the rear of the crowd. "It can't even be something specific to Shorshians, since other Shorshians in the car haven't been affected."

"So you say it was a congenital disease," the Filly said, his tone a bit odd.

"As I said, there's no other likely conclusion," I repeated. "Nothing for any of you to be concerned about. So please, return to your seats and try to put these unfortunate events from your minds."

A fresh set of mutterings began to circulate through the onlookers. But the tone was definitely calmer, and at the rear of the group the passengers began obediently heading back toward their seats. Within a minute, the whole crowd had joined the mass migration.

Everyone, that is, except the Filly whose questions had gotten everyone riled up in the first place. He stayed right where he was, his eyes never leaving my face, as the rest of the passengers dispersed. "Was there something else?" I asked.

He took a step closer to me. "You are lying," he said quietly. "If you sought a congenital disease, a proper investigation would begin with samples taken from the bodies of the victims."

"I'd like nothing better," I said. "But there are questions of religious protocol, and the leader of their group has prohibited me from taking direct samples."

The Filly looked at Bayta, his blaze darkening a little more. "Perhaps that prohibition will yet be lifted," he said.

"Perhaps," I said.

He took another step toward me. "But should you discover a different cause of death," he went on, lowering his voice still more, "I would urge you to let me know at once."

"In such an unlikely event, I'm sure the Spiders will let everyone know at the same time," I assured him.

"I would appreciate it very much," he said, putting an emphasis on the last two words. "Even small bits of preliminary knowledge would be worth a great deal to me."

"I'll keep that in mind," I promised. "If I should happen to learn anything, whom shall I ask for?"

He studied me another couple of heartbeats. "I am *Logra* Emikai," he identified himself. "My seat is four coaches forward, in the car just to the front of the dining car."

"Understood," I said. "A pleasant evening to you, *Logra* Emikai."

"And to you." With a brief nod of his head, he turned and headed down the aisle toward the front of the car and his own seat four coaches away.

"Interesting," I murmured, catching Bayta's eye and nodding toward the departing Filly. "You catch all that?"

"You mean the fact that he just tried to bribe us?" Bayta asked, her voice stiff.

"Well, yes, that too," I said, turning back to watch Emikai's progress. He was moving briskly, adroitly dodging around the slower-moving passengers who weren't in nearly so much of a hurry. "I was mostly referring to the fact that he seemed to know we'd already taken samples from Master Bofiv's body."

"How do you know that?" Bayta asked, her moral outrage at the bribery attempt starting to fade into fresh interest.

"From his reaction to my comment that *di*-Master Strinni hadn't let us take samples," I said. "The question is, how did *he* know? Okay—let's see what he does."

"With what?" Bayta asked, craning her neck to see over the crowd.

"Not with *what*," I corrected. "With *whom*. Specifically, with Master Tririn. Or hadn't you noticed that Tririn didn't bother to come back here to see what we were doing?"

"Maybe he's just tired."

"Or he already knows what we will or won't find," I said.

"Or he didn't need to come himself because he already had a friend on the scene."

"*Logra* Emikai?"

"Could be," I said. "You have any idea what sort of rank *logra* is?"

"Not in that form," Bayta said. "It could be a dialectal variant of *lomagra*, one of the middle artisan classes."

"Or else it's something new, something private, or something he made up out of thin air," I said.

"And you think he and Master Tririn are working together?"

"We'll know in a second," I said. "Even if they just know each other, there ought to be some signal or at least recognition as Emikai passes him."

But to my disappointment, the Filly passed by Tririn's seat without so much as a sideways glance in the Shorshian's direction. "Or not," I said. "Well, that tells us something, too," I added, turning away.

"Wait a second," Bayta said, her voice suddenly urgent.

"What?" I asked, turning back.

"*Logra* Emikai's head dipped to his right just there," Bayta said. "Like he was saying something to—"

And right on cue, Terese German stood up and stepped into the aisle.

"To our young friend with the bad stomach?" I suggested.

"Exactly," Bayta said. Terese made a show of stretching as she casually but carefully looked around her, then headed after the departing Filly. *Logra* Emikai reached the vestibule and disappeared inside, heading for the next car. A few steps behind him, Terese did likewise. "Coincidence?" Bayta asked.

"I don't think so," I said. "I've been assuming that when we were in the bar earlier she just grabbed the first likely-looking lug to protect her from me. The whole incident makes a lot more sense if the choice wasn't nearly that spur-of-the-moment."

Bayta pondered that for a moment. "Thought it still could be perfectly innocent," she pointed out. "They've been passengers on the same train for the past two weeks. If they'd already gotten to know each other, she would naturally go to him for help."

"Maybe," I said. "But she's never struck me as the gregarious sort. Come on—time to go."

"Where?" Bayta asked as I took her arm and steered us forward down the aisle. "We're not going to follow them, are we?"

"We just happen to be going the same direction, that's all," I assured her as we wove our way around the other passengers wending their way to and fro down the aisle. "Tell the Spiders they can put the filter equipment back together again. We're done here."

My original plan—actually, at this point we were probably on my second or third original plan—had been to have a look at the late Master Colix's storage compartments while we were checking on the air filter. But again, things weren't working out the way I'd hoped. This time, it was the large number of passengers still watching our every move that persuaded me to put off the compartment exam a little longer. Convincing them that two deaths a few hours apart had been just an unhappy happenstance would be a much harder sell if I was seen rooting through the personal effects of one of the dearly departeds. Hopefully, we could come back later tonight when things had quieted down.

As I'd promised Bayta, we did indeed follow Terese and

Emikai toward the front of the train, but only because we all happened to be going in the same direction. The girl and the Filly only made it as far as the bar end of the dining car, I noted as we passed, whereas Bayta and I were going four cars farther, to the second/third dispensary.

"What are we doing here?" Bayta asked as I ushered her into the small room.

"Finding a place where we can be alone," I said. "Is there a curtain or something we can close over this doorway?"

In response, the server Spider standing his post by the drug cabinet skittered over and slid a cleverly hidden pocket door over the opening. "Thank you," I said, stepping over to the treatment table and laying out my newly filled sample vials. "More importantly, I wanted someplace I could do a quick analysis without a lot of people looking over our shoulders."

"Why don't we just go back to our compartments?" Bayta asked as I pulled out my reader and lighter.

"Because our next real stop is the first-class dispensary to check on Strinni, and I don't want to go all the way forward and then have to backtrack," I told her. "I don't know about you, but I'm getting tired of all this walking."

I started with Givvrac's untouched drink. I hadn't really expected to find anything sinister lurking there, and for once I was right. "As I said, even if Kennrick *is* involved, he wouldn't be stupid enough to lace a drink only he had access to," I reminded Bayta as I set the vial aside. "These others may be more interesting."

They were. But not in the way I'd expected.

"What *is* all that?" Bayta asked, staring in bewilderment as the chemical list scrolled across my reader's display.

And scrolled some more, and then kept on scrolling, for another four pages. Whatever the Spiders' third-stage filter was collecting, it was collecting a lot of it. "Whatever it is, the good news is that the air isn't the source of the poisoning," I said. "You can see—right there—that there's barely a trace of cadmium in the whole mix."

"Not enough to kill them?"

"Not even enough to make them sick," I said. "As to the rest of this soup, be patient. The analyzer has a huge database, and it'll take some time for it to sort through everything."

I watched the reader as the first trace compound ID came up, a type of perfume used by Fibibibi to mask some of the pheromones that appeared in females at potentially awkward times. "We've got a make on Contestant Number Two," I said as the next part of the analysis came up. "Actually, make that Contestants Two through Eight. It's a cluster of digestive exhalation products. Pirkarli, mostly."

Bayta wrinkled her nose. "There *were* two Pirks back there."

"And I'm sure the rest of the car is grateful for the focused ventilation system you have by Pirk seats," I said, looking over at the locked drug cabinet. Neither Witherspoon's nor Aronobal's kits were there. "I thought doctors' kits were supposed to be kept locked up."

"They are," Bayta said. "Both kits are in the first-class dispensary right now."

I frowned. As third-class passengers, neither doctor had normal access to that part of the train. "Are their owners up there with them?"

"Dr. Witherspoon is," Bayta said. "He's monitoring *di*-Master Strinni. Dr. Aronobal left her bag in first so it would be available in case she was called on again to treat *Usantra* Givvrac's stomach trouble."

"Digestion has always been the Fillies' weak spot," I commented, looking down at my reader. "Our next mystery guest has now signed in. Looks like this one's actually a group, too."

"More Pirkarli emissions?"

"Not unless our Pirks are also hypochondriacs," I said. "These are three different antibacterial sprays, the kind people like to waft around themselves to protect against alien germs." I cocked an eyebrow. "I wonder if one of them might belong to our friend *Logra* Emikai. He certainly seemed concerned about the train's overall air quality."

"He's not seated in that car."

"But his friend Terese is," I reminded her. "Maybe he gave her some of his spray. Or maybe they're both hypochondriacs." I gestured to the reader. "One more to go. How's *di*-Master Strinni doing?"

"He's conscious," Bayta said slowly, her eyes unfocusing as she communicated with the server in the first-class dispensary. "He seems to have calmed down, too."

"Good," I said. "As soon as this is done—" I broke off, glaring at the display. "Oh, for—"

"What is it?" Bayta asked, craning her neck to see.

"Contestant Number Whatever turns out to be nothing but fragmented Juriani scale material," I said, pointing to the line. "Apparently fragmented small enough to sneak through the other filters."

"Is that a problem?" Bayta asked, frowning.

"Hardly," I said, shutting down the reader and putting it back into my pocket. "But I doubt Larry Hardin's high-end techs worked this hard to design and build this thing just so I could use it to identify Jurian dandruff."

I took the sample vials and dropped them into my pocket

beside the reader. "Come on—let's see if *di*-Master Strinni is up to answering some questions."

We arrived at the first-class dispensary to find Strinni lying quietly on the diagnostic table, his skin showing the same mottling that Master Colix and Master Bofiv had demonstrated just prior to their deaths. Not a good sign. The Shorshian's breathing was labored, his eyes dull and listless. But at least he no longer looked inclined to throw the furniture around. "Good evening, *di*-Master Strinni," I greeted him, glancing around. Aside from Strinni himself and the server standing by the drug cabinet there was no one else in the room. "How do you feel?"

[Like I'm dying,] he said grimly. [It's good of you to come, Mr. Compton. And you,] he added, giving Bayta a small acknowledging nod. [I very much wanted to apologize for my behavior earlier.]

"No problem," I assured him. "I'm sure that was just the necrovri talking. You use the stuff often?"

A bit of fire came into his eyes. [I do not *use* any such poisons,] he said, the words coming out as crisp and emphatic as individual thudwumper rounds. [I don't know how it came to be in my body. But I assure you it was none of *my* doing.]

"I believe you," I assured him. Actually, I only believed him about eighty percent, but I wasn't going to call him a liar to his face. "Any idea how it could have gotten into your system?"

His brief surge of passion faded away. [Perhaps it was placed within my food without my noticing,] he said.

"Perhaps," I agreed. "Who have you shared a meal or drink with over the past three or four days?

[Only the others of my contract team,] he said. [Those in first class, of course.]

"No one else?" I asked.

[Do you accuse me of lying?]

"Just double-checking," I soothed. "Do you happen to know where Dr. Witherspoon is, by the way?"

[He went for food,] Strinni said.

"For *food*?" I asked, frowning. Bayta and I had just come up from the rear of the train, and we hadn't passed Witherspoon along the way. "When did he leave?"

[A few minutes only before your arrival.]

"He didn't go back to third," Bayta spoke up. "The Spiders are letting him eat in first tonight."

"Ah," I said, nodding. Unlike the third-class dining car, which was half a train back, the first-class dining car was just three cars away toward the front. All the same, I found it damned odd that Witherspoon would just take off and leave a desperately ill patient all alone this way. "He didn't ask Dr. Aronobal to take over while he was gone?" I asked Strinni.

[I didn't *want* Dr. Aronobal to take over,] Strinni said, a flicker of life again peeking through the weariness. [*I* sent Dr. Witherspoon for his food, Mr. Compton. He didn't abandon me, as you so obviously think. He's already done all that he can for my broken body.]

"My apologies," I said, not feeling particularly apologetic. Hungry or not, ordered out or not, Witherspoon still shouldn't have deserted his patient. "If I may suggest, though, in a case like this two sets of eyes and minds are always preferable to one. I'm sure Dr. Aronobal would be happy—"

[I will not be treated by that Filiaelian,] Strinni cut me off. [I will not be so debased.]

He'd said the same thing earlier, during the drug-driven

fracas in his coach car. At the time, I'd assumed it was the necrovri talking. Apparently, it wasn't. "I understand your reluctance," I said. "But still—"

"Frank," Bayta said, touching my arm warningly.

Grimacing, I nodded and shut up. There was a lot of specism in the galaxy, lurking in the dark corners where supposedly civilized people didn't like to look. In general, Shorshians and Fillies got along reasonably well, but there were fringe elements in any group. "Fine," I said to Strinni. "I gather you don't have any such reservations about Dr. Witherspoon?"

[Why would I?] he asked. [Dr. Witherspoon is part of our group.]

I stared down at him. "He's *what?*"

[He's a physician with Pellorian Medical Systems,] Strinni said. [He sat in with the contract team during many of our meetings, and travels now with us to Rentis Tarlay Birim to examine our facilities.]

"I didn't know that," I said, giving Bayta a quick look. Judging by her expression, this was news to her, too. "How come no one ever mentioned this to me?"

[Why was it any of your concern?] Strinni countered. [You're not part of our group. Neither have you any official authority or investigative position—]

He broke off in a fit of loud, wet-sounding coughs. "Are you all right?" I asked as the coughing showed no sign of stopping.

And then, abruptly, the mottling of his skin dissolved into a chaotic flow of black, white, and gray as all semblance of a normal Shorshic color pattern disappeared. "Bayta!" I snapped, grabbing for Strinni's arm as his body began convulsing.

"One of the conductors is getting him," she said tightly. "Shall I have Dr. Aronobal brought up, too?"

"Yes," I said. The hell with Strinni's prejudices—his life was on the line here. "Where is she?"

"In her normal seat," Bayta said. "Eighteen cars back."

I swore under my breath. Eighteen cars was a long ways away. "Yes, get her here," I ordered. Maybe Strinni was in better shape than he looked.

I had barely completed that thought when the Shorshian gave a final convulsion and collapsed into an unmoving heap on the table.

Not breathing at all.

"Get Witherspoon here *now*," I snarled at Bayta as I grabbed the bright orange LifeGuard unit off the wall by the drug cabinet. I punched the selector for Shorshic configuration and hurried back to the table. "Here," I said, pulling the arm cuff free of its holder.

Bayta took the cuff and fastened it around Strinni's arm. "Ready," she said. I made a final check of the breather mask I'd set over Strinni's face and punched the start button.

The LifeGuard chugged to life. I gazed down at Strinni's face, knowing full well that this was almost certainly an exercise in futility. But I had to do *something*.

And then, to my astonishment, Strinni's eyes stirred and opened to slits. [Compton,] he murmured, his voice muffled by the mask.

I frowned at the LifeGuard. The device hadn't finished running its diagnosis, but red lights were already beginning to wink on all across the display. This had to be the most heroic effort at last words on the books. "I'm here," I said, leaning closer to him as I gazed into those half-closed eyes. "What is it?"

[Don't desecrate . . . my . . . body,] he said, his voice fading until it was almost too soft to hear. His eyes closed again, and the lights on the LifeGuard's display went solid red.

I looked at Bayta. "Don't desecrate my body?" I echoed. "What in the world does *that* mean?"

"Probably that he doesn't want an autopsy," she said, her eyes aching as she gazed at this, the third dead body she'd seen in two days. "He's a member of the Path of Onagnalhni, remember?"

"Right," I murmured. "I'd forgotten."

There was the sound of racing footsteps out in the corridor, and I turned as Witherspoon burst panting into the dispensary. "Don't bother," I told him as I stepped aside to let him see the unmoving figure on the table. "He's dead."

NINE :

Witherspoon wasn't willing to take my word for it. Or the LifeGuard's electronic evidence, either. Silently, grimly, he set to work with analyzers and hypos and modern medicine's magic potions.

In the end, he accepted the inevitable.

"I shouldn't have left," he said wearily, stepping over to the side of the room and touching a switch. A seat folded out from the wall, and he sank heavily onto it. "I should have stayed here with him."

"He told us he'd ordered you to go get some food," I reminded him.

"So what?" he countered. "I'm a doctor, not a servant."

"No, but when your patient orders you away, there's not a lot you can do," I said.

"I could have ignored him," Witherspoon said, dropping his gaze to the floor. "Or I could have stayed just outside in the corridor where I would have been available when he needed me." He hissed between his teeth. "Instead, I was out feeding my face."

"For whatever it's worth, I don't think you could have done anything even if you'd been here," I said. "He already had too much cadmium in his tissues. We don't have the facilities aboard to have cleaned it out fast enough."

"I know," Witherspoon said. "I should have been here anyway."

For a minute the room was silent. I gave him another minute to mourn his companion, or to sandpaper his conscience, then got back to business. "*Di*-Master Strinni said you were part of his contract team."

"Yes," Witherspoon acknowledged without hesitation. "Though technically, Mr. Kennrick and I are with Pellorian Medical, not the contract team per se."

"It might have been nice to know this earlier," I commented.

He turned puzzled eyes on me. "Why?"

"Because in case you've forgotten, this is a murder investigation," I said. "High on the list of useful things to know are the relationships between victims and suspects."

A whole series of emotions chased each other across his face, with outrage bringing up the rear. "Are you saying I'm a *suspect*?" he demanded. "How *dare* you!"

"I dare because we now have three unexplained deaths aboard our cozy little Quadrail," I said calmly. "*And* because you were in recent contact with at least two of the three victims."

"That's a gross misstatement of the situation," Witherspoon insisted stiffly. But his expression was rapidly fading from righteous anger to cautious apprehension. He'd surely seen enough dit rec thrillers to know how high the victims' doctor usually ended up on the cops' suspect list. "Besides, all three victims were showing symptoms before I was brought in."

"True," I agreed. "Tell me about Terese German."

He blinked. "Who?"

"The young Human woman you had the consultation with over dinner last night."

A flicker of recognition crossed his face. "Oh," he said. "Her."

"Yes, her," I said. "What did you—?" I broke off as another set of hurrying footsteps sounded out in the corridor and Dr. Aronobal came charging into the dispensary, her chest heaving even more than Witherspoon's had been at his entrance. But then, Aronobal had had farther to jog. "Dr. Aronobal," I greeted her gravely. "My apologies for dragging you all the way up here—"

"How is he?" Aronobal asked, slowing to a fast walk as she headed toward the table.

"—especially as it turns out to have been unnecessary," I finished. "I'm afraid *di*-Master Strinni has passed on."

Aronobal shot me a look as she came to a halt by the body. "My bag," she said tartly, jabbing a finger at the Filiaelian medical kit locked in the drug cabinet.

Obediently, the Spider unlocked the cabinet and handed over the bag. For all the good it would do. "Where were we?" I asked, turning back to Witherspoon. "Oh, yes. Terese German."

Witherspoon's eyes flicked over my shoulder. "What about her?"

"Let's start with what you talked about," I suggested.

Witherspoon hunched his shoulders in a shrug that I was pretty sure was supposed to look casual. "Not much," he said. "I'd noticed that she seemed to be having stomach or digestive trouble—frequent trips to the restroom and all—and I asked if there was anything I could do."

"You noticed that all the way from two cars back?" I asked. "You must have eyes like a hawk."

"Well, no, I—I mean," he stammered. "I mean—"

"Your seat *is* two cars back from hers, right?" I asked.

"Yes, but—" He broke off, his eyes flicking over my shoulder again. "I mean I noticed at the times I was in that car. When I was visiting Master Colix, Master Bofiv, and Master Tririn."

"And was there?"

"Was there what?" he asked, thoroughly lost now.

"Was there anything you could do for her?"

Again, his eyes flicked over my shoulder. "I really can't say anything more. I'm sorry."

I looked over my shoulder, wondering what Witherspoon found so fascinating over there. Aronobal was standing squarely in Witherspoon's line of glance, hunched over the table with her back to us. "You *do* remember that this is a murder investigation, right?" I asked, turning back to Witherspoon.

"It would be hard to forget with you reminding me every two minutes," Witherspoon said acidly. With the brief break, he was on balance again. "I'm sorry, but this is a matter of doctor/patient privilege."

"Dr. Witherspoon?" Aronobal called, not turning around. "A word with you, if you please?"

"What is it?" Witherspoon asked, getting up and crossing to the table.

I crossed to the table, too, circling the foot and coming up on the other side from the two doctors. "Look at this," Aronobal said, pointing to Strinni's hands.

The forefinger of Strinni's right hand was curved around

to touch the tip of his thumb like an okay sign, the other fingers sticking stiffly straight out together. His left hand, in contrast, was curved like he'd been holding on to a thick pipe that had been subsequently removed. "What did you do that for?" I asked.

"I did nothing," Aronobal insisted. "They were like this when I first reached him."

"Were they, Frank?" Bayta murmured as she came to my side.

"I don't know," I had to admit. "I wasn't focusing on his hands at the time."

"Was he holding anything earlier?" Aronobal asked. "In either hand?"

"No," I said. That much I *was* sure of. "There was nothing within reach, either."

"Your arm, perhaps?" Aronobal suggested, reaching over the table and wrapping her hand experimentally around my wrist.

"No," I said again. "I have no idea why his hands would have curled—"

"It's sign language," Witherspoon said suddenly.

I studied Strinni's hands. Now that Witherspoon mentioned it, they *did* look like finger-spelling letters. The letters F and C, in fact.

My initials.

"Can you read them?" Aronobal asked.

"Just a second," Witherspoon said as he started contorting his own hand. "The left hand is the letter C," he said. "The right hand . . . that's an F."

"CF," Aronobal murmured thoughtfully.

"More likely FC," Witherspoon said. "That's the order they're in as you look down at them."

"Or even more likely pure coincidence," I said. Whatever

had happened with Strinni's hands, the last thing I wanted was for Witherspoon or Aronobal to think there was a connection there to me. "Some trick of that last set of convulsions. He had enough breath to warn us not to autopsy his body, after all—if he'd wanted to leave a dying clue, he could have just said something."

Witherspoon looked sharply at me. "FC," he said. "*Frank Compton.*"

I held his gaze, a sinking feeling running through me. Damn. "That's ridiculous," I insisted.

"Is it?" Witherspoon countered. "Of course he couldn't say anything, not with you and your friend the only ones in the room. What other clue could he leave?"

"Okay, fine," I said. "Let's say those really are F and C signs—"

"Oh, please," Witherspoon growled. "There must be a hundred encyclopedias aboard that can confirm *that.*"

"I meant as opposed to random hand configurations," I said patiently. "That still leaves the question of how *di*-Master Strinni learned Human sign language in the first place. Come to think of it, if we're going down that road, we ought to be looking into what those mean in *Shorshic* sign language."

"There is no such thing," Aronobal said. "Deafness is curable or treatable among Shorshians, and hence is essentially unknown. Any signing system would have been lost generations ago."

"Ditto for most other species," Witherspoon agreed. "If *di*-Master Strinni knew any sort of sign language, it would be the Human variety."

"Which still doesn't prove he actually did know it," I said. "Besides, I only met him yesterday. What possible motive would I have for killing him?"

"That *is* the question, isn't it?" Witherspoon said, his tone going all dark and ominous. He would have been great in a dit rec mystery. "Perhaps we should get Mr. Kennrick in here and see if he can shed some light on this."

"Mr. Kennrick isn't an investigator," I said.

"No, but he seems to know something about you," Witherspoon said. "Maybe there are some dark secrets in your past—"

"Just a minute," Bayta spoke up suddenly, her eyes unfocusing. "*Usantra* Givvrac is in great pain. He's asked a conductor to bring him a doctor."

"You sure it's *Usantra* Givvrac, and not one of the other Filiaelians?" Witherspoon asked, a sudden anxiety in his voice.

"I'm sure," Bayta said. "But one of the other Filiaelians in his car is also feeling ill."

"I'd better go," Witherspoon said, gesturing to the Spider to hand him his bag.

"I'll do it," Aronobal said calmly, laying a hand on Witherspoon's shoulder. "I have more experience with Filiaelian medicine than you."

"You both need to go," Bayta said. "A Filiaelian four cars back, *Osantra* Qiddicoj, is also calling for a doctor."

"Four back?" I repeated, mentally doing my own count of the cars. "*Di*-Master Strinni's car?"

"Yes," Bayta confirmed.

Where Strinni had been poisoned with both heavy metal and a hallucinogen. Interesting. "Sounds like we suddenly have plenty of patients to go around," I said, looking back and forth between Witherspoon and Aronobal. "How do you want to sort it out?"

"Dr. Witherspoon can treat *Osantra* Qiddicoj," Aronobal said, already halfway to the door. "I will treat *Usantra* Givvrac and the other in his car."

"And I'll go with Dr. Witherspoon," I volunteered, falling into step behind Witherspoon as he headed toward the door.

"That's not necessary," Witherspoon said.

"I don't mind," I assured him.

Witherspoon stopped dead in his tracks. "Let me make it clearer," he said coldly, "I don't want you along."

"Sorry to hear that," I said. "Let *me* make it clearer: I don't give a damn what you want. You've got a sick patient. We both want to see him. You want me to stay here, you're welcome to try and make me. Otherwise, stop complaining and get moving."

He pressed his lips tightly together. "Fine," he said. "You first."

I rolled my eyes and moved into the doorway in front of him. "Bayta, stay here and watch *di*-Master Strinni's body," I said. "We'll be back in a minute."

We headed out, Aronobal hitting the corridor and branching left, Witherspoon and I branching right. "What is it with all this Filly stomach trouble?" I whispered over my shoulder to Witherspoon as we reached the first coach car and passed through the sea of canopied seats and sleeping passengers. "More heavy-metal poisoning?"

"It's not acting like it," Witherspoon whispered back. "But with gleaner bacteria in their intestines doing the bulk of waste processing and removal, Filiaelians are highly susceptible to digestive trouble."

"Like Terese German?" I asked.

He didn't answer. "I said—"

"I heard you," he interrupted. "And I already told you my dealings with her are confidential. Quiet, now—we don't want to wake anyone."

We passed through the rear vestibule and entered the first-class entertainment car. From the faint reflections of flickering light I could see from the various dit rec cubicles as we passed, it was clear there were still a few night owls up and about. We finished with that car, passed through another coach car full of canopied seats and sleeping travelers, and arrived at last at *Osantra* Qiddicoj's car.

Most of the passengers here had deployed their canopies, though a few seats contained Shorshians who, like *di*-Master Strinni, apparently preferred sleeping in the open air. Near the rear of the car, I spotted the soft glow of a conductor call light on one of the uncanopied seats. The seat itself was turned away from us, hiding its occupant from view, but I doubted that the call light was marking someone who merely wanted to know when the dining car started serving breakfast. "There's our boy," I murmured, heading toward it.

We were halfway back when I heard a soft thud behind me. Frowning, I started to turn—

Something exploded against the side of my neck, and the darkened Quadrail car went completely black.

I woke up slowly, with the nagging but persistent feeling that I wasn't at all comfortable.

I tried to bring my hands up to my eyes to help rub them open. But the hands didn't want to move. In fact, I wasn't even sure where exactly my hands were. I tried turning my head to look for them, but my head wouldn't move either.

Was I paralyzed?

That delightful thought snapped me fully awake. With my heart pounding, I opened my eyes.

In front of me was an unrelieved curtain of dark gray, and for another horrible second I thought I'd gone blind as well as paralyzed. Then my eyes focused, and I realized that what I was staring at was exactly that: a curtain of dark gray. I was sitting in a first-class seat with the sleep canopy deployed around me.

And the reason I'd thought I was paralyzed was that my wrists, ankles, and forehead were taped to that selfsame seat.

I looked downward as far as I could. There were at least four windings of tape around each of my wrists, possibly as many as five or six. I couldn't see my ankles or, obviously, my forehead, but I had no reason to suspect my assailant had been any less generous there than he had with my wrists.

Experimentally, I tried twisting my arms, hoping I could break free. Nothing. I tried the same move with head and feet, with the same lack of results. At this rate, I'd be pinned here like a prize butterfly until lunchtime tomorrow.

My gut gave one of its now all-too-familiar rumbles. The thought of lunchtime, or of food in general, was almost painful. I listened to the fresh growling, trying to figure out if this was the same problem as before or if my assailant had decided to go ahead and poison me while he had the chance. It certainly felt like I was dying from the inside out.

I stiffened, the sudden tightening of my stomach muscles adding a fresh burst to the intestinal turmoil lower down. There it was, damn it—so obvious I should have fallen over it. *Dying from the inside out . . .*

And then, outside my canopy, I heard something. I strained my ears, and the sound resolved itself into a set of quiet footsteps and the equally quiet but very distinctive tap-tap-tap of a Spider.

It was Bayta. It had to be. Clearly, I'd been gone long enough to arouse her misgivings and she'd grabbed a Spider to come looking for me. Feeling a surge of relief, I opened my mouth to call to her.

Only to discover that my friend with the tape had thoughtfully taken the time to gag me, too.

I heaved my shoulders back and forth to the sides, trying to shake the seat enough to catch Bayta's notice. But it was anchored solidly in place, and I doubted I was getting up enough momentum to even disturb the canopy. I tried grunting through the tape over my mouth, but even to my own ears the muffled sound sounded pretty pathetic. Looking in all directions, I searched for inspiration.

And then, my gaze fell on the music controls by my left hand.

It was a long shot, I knew. Quadrail audio systems were heavily focused, precisely to prevent everyone else in the car from being disturbed by someone else's music. I would have to crank it up to eardrum-damaging levels for anyone out there to even hear it.

But it was a risk I had to take. If I didn't get Bayta's attention now, it could be hours before one of the other passengers wondered why this particular traveler was sleeping in so late, and got curious enough to investigate. There were already at least three Fillies out there in serious medical trouble, with possibly more to come. Unless I got out of here, and fast, we were going to have more deaths on our hands.

Cranking the volume all the way up, I set my teeth and touched the switch.

It was like sitting front-row-center at a live concert where each musician had made a bet with all the others that he could get the most sound out of his instrument. I left the music on maybe a quarter of a second before switching it off again, and even with that short an exposure it felt like the my ears were coming off at the lobes.

But I couldn't stop now. I fired it up another quarter second, and then another. Then, bracing myself, I turned it on for a full second.

This time, it felt like the top of my head was joining my ears in their attempt to vacate the premises. I gulped a breath, fired off another full second, and another, and then thankfully returned to three more of the shorter quarter-second bursts of agony.

Bayta had had a sheltered upbringing among the Chahwyn, and had been playing a determined game of intellectual catch-up since then. Still, somewhere along the line, surely even she had learned the significance of a classic SOS.

I was midway through the third repeat, and was wondering if my ears were starting to bleed yet, when the canopy was pulled open, and I saw Bayta's worried face looking down at me.

In the brief time I'd been away, the dispensary had become an emergency room.

Witherspoon was sitting on one of the fold-out seats along the side wall, pressing a cold pack against the back of his head, his posture that of a man who had just gone three rounds with a bulldozer. Two Fillies were twitching in obvious discomfort on fold-out slabs on the other side of the room. One of them turned his head as Bayta and I entered, and I saw it was my friend Rose Nose, the one who'd pulled me out of the scuffle with Strinni earlier in the afternoon, just long enough for Kennrick's ribs to get cracked instead of mine.

Strinni's body, which had been on the diagnostic table when I'd left, was nowhere to be seen. In its place, lying ominously still on the treatment table as Aronobal worked feverishly over him, was *Usantra* Givvrac.

"Whatever you're doing, stop it," I said, wincing as the sound of my words assaulted my sore ears. "It won't work."

"Compton!" Witherspoon exclaimed, looking up at the sound of my voice. "Are you all right? Someone hit me—"

"Save it," I cut him off. "You need to get a load of gleaner bacteria from somewhere and inject it into his intestines."

"What?" Aronobal asked, frowning down her long nose at me.

"Are you deaf?" I bit out. "Their gleaner bacteria's been wiped out. The unneutralized waste is backing up and flooding their systems—that's what's making them sick."

"Impossible," Aronobal insisted. "What could they possibly have eaten that could have done so much damage?"

"They didn't eat it, they inhaled it," I said, disengaging myself from Bayta's supporting arm and making my slightly unsteady way to the table. "I took a sample earlier from one of the train's air filters and found traces of antibacterial sprays."

"You can't kill a Filiaelian's gleaner bacteria that way," Witherspoon said. "Everything they inhale is filtered through the respiratory system—"

"So is everything Humans inhale," I interrupted him. "But Bayta and I are both feeling the effects of something on our own gut flora. Whatever this stuff was our killer was spraying around, it digs deep and packs one hell of a punch."

Witherspoon looked at Aronobal. "Is this reasonable? Or even possible?"

"Do you have any other treatment to suggest?" Aronobal countered. "Very well, Mr. Compton. If your companion will ask the Spiders to find some Filiaelian volunteers, we'll try your suggestion."

"No," a weak Filly voice said.

It took me a second to realize the voice had been Givvrac's. "No what?" I asked, looking down at him.

"No need to find volunteers," he said, his eyes nearly closed, his nose blaze gone so dark now as to be nearly black. "My contract team—*Esantra* Worrbin, *Asantra* Muzzfor, and *Asantra* Dallilo. They will provide what is necessary."

"Works for me," I said, looking over at Bayta. "Can you get the Spiders on it?"

She nodded. "Already done."

"Compton?" Givvrac murmured.

I looked back down at him. "Yes?"

"My final wish," he said softly. "Find this murderer."

"I will," I promised, wondering distantly if Filly law listed any penalties for failing to deliver on a deathbed promise. "But you're a long ways yet from any final wishes," I added. "Half an hour, and you'll be as good as new."

"Find the murderer, Mr. Compton," Givvrac repeated, his voice trailing off into a whisper. "And kill him."

I looked at Bayta, then at Witherspoon, then at Aronobal . . . and there was something in the Filly doctor's eyes that warned there were indeed penalties for reneging on such a promise. "If it's within my power," I said, looking back at Givvrac, "I will."

His eyes closed, and he gave a microscopic nod. "Then will honor and justice be served," he murmured.

Five minutes later, he was dead.

TEN :

"Hold still," Witherspoon ordered as he gently pulled on the back of my right ear and eased the tip of his viewer into the labyrinth within.

"You just watch where you're poking that thing," I warned, wincing as his touch sent my ears' background throbbing onto a new and more exciting rhythm.

"Courage, Compton," Kennrick admonished, glancing around the otherwise deserted first-class bar as he took a sip of his brandy.

Normally this sort of examination would have been held in the dispensary. But the dispensary was more than a little crowded at the moment. Besides, the dispensary didn't serve brandy, which Kennrick apparently liked a lot.

It also didn't serve yogurt, which I didn't like at all, but which my gut badly needed to help replenish its supply of helpful bacteria. "I'm saving my courage for when he pokes something in *your* ear," I told Kennrick, taking a last bite and setting my spoon on the table beside my empty bowl.

"In that case, feel free to yell in agony," Kennrick said agreeably.

"I never scream in front of the help," I said, gesturing toward the server standing a couple of paces behind Witherspoon. The Spider, I knew, was here to keep an eye on Witherspoon's medical bag.

Kennrick, I was pretty sure, was here to keep an eye on me.

Witherspoon let go of my ear. "Other side, please," he instructed.

I swiveled my chair around, putting my back to Kennrick and the table. "We have got to be the saddest lot of travelers in Quadrail history," Kennrick mused as Witherspoon dug his viewer into my other throbbing ear. "Give us a drum and a couple of fifes and we'd be right at home in a Western Alliance historical painting."

"It's worse back in the dispensary," I reminded him.

"They were included in my list," he said, his voice grim. "*Damn* it all. I still can't believe this is happening."

"You mean the fact that your contract team is falling over like dominoes?" I asked.

"*And* the fact that the Spiders haven't lifted a leg to stop it," he growled. "I thought they were supposed to keep weapons off their damn trains."

"What weapons?" I countered. "Like you said earlier, cadmium's found in any number of gadgets used all over the galaxy. And people bring antiseptic sprays onto Quadrails all the time."

"Sprays strong enough to penetrate all the way into Filiaelian intestines?"

"I'll admit that's a new one," I conceded. "The point remains that up to now nothing that's been used has qualified as a standard weapon."

"They're supposed to screen for nonstandard weapons, too," Kennrick growled. "You about done there, Doc?"

"Almost," Witherspoon said. "And I think our energies would be better spent in figuring out how we can prevent this from happening again instead of trying to assign blame."

"Hear, hear," I said. "Actually, that's the main reason I wanted the two of you here while Dr. Witherspoon checked me over. I thought it was about time we all had a nice quiet conversation together."

"*You* wanted me here?" Kennrick asked. "The conductor said it was Dr. Witherspoon who sent for me."

"It was," I agreed. "A quiet conversation is the reason I let him do it. Doc? What's the verdict?"

"No permanent damage that I can see," Witherspoon reported, putting the viewer back into his bag and pulling out a packet of QuixHeals. "But both your eardrums are going to be tender for a while." He grimaced, his fingers digging briefly beneath his shirt collar to gingerly touch the back of his neck. "As will your neck," he added. "A few days on QuixHeals and you should be mostly back to normal."

"So what did you want to talk about?" Kennrick asked.

"Obviously, what's been going on aboard this train," I said. "Dr. Witherspoon has a theory."

The sudden change in conversational direction caught Witherspoon by surprise. "I do?" he asked, sounding bewildered.

"Of course," I said. "You think I did it."

It was Kennrick's turn to be caught flatfooted. "*You?*" he demanded.

"That's right," I said, watching Witherspoon closely. Under our dual gaze, he was starting to look a little squirmy. "*Di-*Master Strinni may have died with his hands making the sign-language symbols for F and C. Dr. Witherspoon thinks they're my initials."

"Ridiculous," Kennrick said. "Sorry, Doc, but it's ridiculous."

"Why?" Witherspoon countered. "We know nothing about Mr. Compton. Who he is, who he's working for, or what he's doing on this train."

"He's annoyed that I pointed out he'd been with two of the victims before they died," I stage-whispered to Kennrick. "Actually, with Givvrac, we're now up to three out of four."

"And who knows how many of them *you* dealt with?" Witherspoon shot back. "You *or* your Spider friends."

"Easy, Doc," Kennrick soothed. "You've got the wrong end of the stick here. Whatever Mr. Compton is now, what he *was* was Western Alliance Intelligence."

Witherspoon drew back a little, his eyes narrowing. "*Westali?*"

"That's right," I confirmed.

"You know this for a fact?" Witherspoon asked.

"I do," Kennrick confirmed.

"How?"

A muscle twitched in Kennrick's cheek. "He was—"

"I was involved in an operation at the law office where he was working a few years ago," I jumped in.

Witherspoon's wary look shifted to Kennrick. "Was Mr. Kennrick the target?" he asked pointedly.

"No," I said. It was mostly true. "And to answer your next question, I left the service voluntarily." That was also mostly true, though I certainly wouldn't have volunteered to resign if I hadn't been pressured to do so. "I can give you references, if you still want to check up on me after we reach Venidra Carvo. Won't do you much good right now, though."

"I'll get the list from you later," Witherspoon said, visibly relaxing a bit. "Did *di*-Master Strinni know about your history? Is that why he left us your initials?"

"We don't even know that they *were* initials, let alone mine," I reminded him. "They could have stood for First Class, Fried Chicken, or even Feeling Crappy. *If* he knew Human sign language at all, which we still haven't established."

"It's not impossible," Kennrick said. "I've seen a number of non-Humans using Human sign language over the years. Business people especially—some companies like to have a way of communicating in private across crowded rooms. I don't know about *di*-Master Strinni specifically, though."

"Maybe Master Tririn will know," I said. "In the meantime, now that my pedigree's been established, I'd like to ask you a few questions."

"I've got one of my own first," Kennrick said. "Are you operating under the authority of the Spiders on this?"

"They've asked me to investigate the deaths, yes," I said.

"Is this a one-time thing, or does your association with them predate this particular trip?" he persisted. "The reason I ask is because Pellorian Medical's policy is to always cooperate with the authorities, even if that cooperation leads to the disclosure of confidential company information. But that only applies to authorities with genuine credentials, not some thrown-together posse of rent-a-cops."

"I could probably order the Spiders to throw you off the train," I offered. "Would that that qualify as adequate authority?"

"I'd say so," Kennrick said. "Sorry, but murders or not, Dr. Witherspoon and I still have to cover our own rear ends here. What do you want to know?"

"Let's start with the obvious," I said. "Do you know of anyone who might have had it in for your contract team?"

"Or Shorshians and Filiaelians in general," Witherspoon put in. "Don't forget, there are two other Filiaelians being treated back there."

I shook my head. "Collateral damage. The members of your team are clearly the targets."

"But that's ridiculous," Witherspoon objected. "We're a *medical* group. Why would anyone want to attack *us*?"

"Because you're a medical group whose decisions will affect the distribution of millions of dollars," I said.

"There's your proof of Westali training," Kennrick commented dryly. "First instinct of every government type is to assume it's about money."

I shrugged. "That's because nine times out of ten it is."

"Maybe this is the once out of ten that it isn't," Kennrick said. "Dr. Witherspoon's right—when you're dealing with Filiaelians and Shorshians, it's just as likely to be about avenged honor." He cocked an eyebrow. "Which, I'll point out, *Usantra* Givvrac also mentioned."

"Fine," I said, giving up. To me, it was obvious this wasn't a revenge killing. That kind of murderer usually wanted everyone to know that honor had been satisfied, which meant killing his victim in a very obvious way. Something else had to be at the root of this, though I still had no idea what.

But Kennrick and Witherspoon were clearly not yet ready to let go of the revenge straw. I might as well humor them and get it over with. "What do you know about the late members of your group?"

"Not much," Kennrick admitted. "Doc?"

"I know that Master Colix and *Asantra* Dallilo have worked together on other projects in the past," Witherspoon said. "So have *Usantra* Givvrac and *di*-Master Strinni. Maybe they managed to offend someone along the way."

"Except that *Asantra* Dallilo is still alive," I pointed out.

Kennrick grunted. "Give it a few hours."

"He could be right," Witherspoon rumbled. "Do you think we ought to put the rest of the contract team under guard?"

"Whose guard would you trust?" I asked. "Yours and Mr. Kennrick's?"

"Or yours," Witherspoon suggested.

"Or the Spiders'?" Kennrick countered.

"I doubt the Spiders have anyone to spare for escort duty," I said, passing over the fact that they wouldn't be much use as guards anyway. "As for me, I don't work for you."

"What if we hire you?" Kennrick asked.

"You couldn't afford me," I assured him. "Next question. I'd like your reading on where each of the recently deceased stood vis-à-vis this deal with Pellorian Medical."

"Didn't *Usantra* Givvrac give you all that earlier?" Kennrick asked, frowning.

"He gave me his take on the lineup," I confirmed. "I want to hear yours."

Kennrick shrugged, wincing as the movement shifted his injured ribs. "I've always assumed that all four Filiaelians were for the deal, along with *di*-Master Strinni and probably Master Colix."

"Leaving Master Tririn and the late Master Bofiv as the only two opposed?" I asked.

"Right." Kennrick grimaced. "But since *Usantra* Givvrac said it was actually four to four, I obviously miscounted some-where."

"So it would seem," I agreed. "Was that the way you saw things, too, Dr. Witherspoon?"

"More or less," he said. "I wasn't so sure *Usantra* Givvrac was on our side, but I was counting on the other three Filiaelians."

"So who else in the group is against us?" Kennrick asked.

"That's unimportant at the moment," I said. "So by your reckoning—"

"Why is it unimportant?" Witherspoon put in.

"Give me a minute and you'll see," I told him. "So by your reckoning, the victims were three for Pellorian and one against?"

"Compton—" Witherspoon began.

"Yes," Kennrick said, holding a quieting hand toward the doctor.

"Just making sure," I said. "Now, the important question: have either of you discussed any part of this with anyone outside Pellorian Medical since the contract team arrived on Earth?"

The light seemed to dawn in Kennrick's eyes. "I get it," he said, nodding. "Unfortunately, no, we haven't. Well, *I* haven't. I assume Dr. Witherspoon hasn't, either."

"What do you mean, unfortunately?" Witherspoon asked. "Why is it unfortunate?"

"Because if we'd told someone about the team, and that someone was relying on our count, it might show up in the pattern of killings," Kennrick told him.

"Exactly," I said. "It's important to get into a murderer's head, but sometimes it can be enough to get into his eyes. If we can figure out how he sees things, we may be able to backtrack him. So, Doctor: did you discuss the contract with anyone outside Pellorian's walls?"

"Absolutely not," Witherspoon said firmly.

"How about on the torchliner from Earth to Terra Station?"

"Again, no," Kennrick said. "Ethics aside, loose talk like that can get you fired on the spot."

"How about discussing the matter with the rest of the contract team when you thought you were in private, but where someone might possibly have been able to eavesdrop?"

"I—" Kennrick broke off, turning a suddenly uncertain look on Witherspoon. "Well, actually, I don't really know," he said slowly. "Torchliner acoustics aren't as well designed as a Quad-rail's. And the four Shorshians and I *did* have several mealtime discussions together."

"Did you ever take straw votes at these discussions?" I asked.

"They never did while I was present," Kennrick said. "But they might have done so after I left. They never talked about things like that in front of me."

"Or me," Witherspoon seconded.

"Understandable," I said. "I'll try asking Master Tririn about it in the morning."

"I'm sorry, but this still doesn't make sense," Witherspoon said. "If it's about whether the contract succeeds or fails, shouldn't the killer be eliminating only the team members who are opposing him?"

"In theory, sure," I said. "In actual practice, focusing exclusively on his opponents would be about as clever as taking out a full-page ad announcing his intentions. He'll need to muddy the water by killing at least one of his own side."

"Which fits the current situation exactly," Kennrick murmured.

"So you think he wants to defeat the contract?" Witherspoon asked.

"Possibly," I said, eyeing Kennrick. He was gazing off into space, a thoughtful look on his face. "But we've got a long way to go before we start jumping at that kind of conclusion. Something else, Kennrick?"

"I don't know," Kennrick said slowly. "I was just wondering if Dr. Witherspoon might be right about this being a revenge thing, only the killer was only after *one* of the victims, not all four of them. Is it possible that he killed the others just to make his real target less apparent?"

Witherspoon hissed between his teeth. "Good *God*."

"It *has* been done before," I agreed. "But again, without knowing anything about the victims' backgrounds, that theory won't get us very far."

"Probably not," Kennrick conceded. "I just thought I should mention it."

"Consider it mentioned," I said. "Let's switch gears a minute. Dr. Witherspoon, can you tell me anything about what happened earlier back in *Osantra* Qiddicoj's coach car?"

"Not really," Witherspoon said, fingering his neck gingerly. "I was following you to his seat when something hit me. The next thing I knew, your friend Bayta and a conductor were standing over me, trying to get me to wake up."

"Did you hear anything before you were hit?" I asked. "The sound of the vestibule door opening behind you, stealthy footsteps, heavy breathing—anything?"

Witherspoon shook his head. "He could have materialized out of thin air for all I know."

"Did you see or hear anything odd after you woke up?"

"Again, no," Witherspoon said. "Bayta and the conductor helped me back to the dispensary—and took *Osantra* Qiddicoj in there, too, of course—then went back to look for you." He grimaced. "And before you ask, I have no idea why anyone would want to attack me."

"Maybe it wasn't you he was after, Doc," Kennrick suggested, eyeing me speculatively. "Maybe he wanted Compton, and you were just in his way."

"That *is* a thought," Witherspoon agreed, giving me a speculative look of his own. "After all, you were the one who figured out what was wrong with the Filiaelians. If he wanted *Usantra* Givvrac dead, you were the one he needed to shut up."

"Except that at the time no one knew I had the answer," I reminded him. "Including me."

"The attacker still might have thought you were getting close," Witherspoon said.

"Or maybe you had something he wanted," Kennrick said suddenly. "You still have those tissue samples from Master Colix and Master Bofiv?"

"I assume they're still in my room," I lied, shifting my elbow slightly against my chest to press reassuringly against the vials in my pocket. The samples from the air filter and Givvrac's drink were indeed an obvious target for the killer to go after, which is why they'd been the first thing I'd checked when Bayta and the Spider got me out of that chair. "Any of your stuff gone, Doc?"

Witherspoon shook his head. "If it is, it's nothing important."

"What do you mean, if it is?" Kennrick asked, frowning. "Haven't you checked your pockets and your bag?"

"Of course I have," Witherspoon said. "My pockets haven't been touched, and he made a mess of my bag when he was looking for tape to tie up Mr. Compton with."

I focused on the medical bag still sitting in the middle of our table. "What kind of mess?" I asked carefully.

"A mess kind of mess," Witherspoon said with a touch of impatience. "Everything got moved or shifted around, with vials and pill cartridges and all dumped in the bottom. That sort of thing."

"He dumped everything in the bottom while he was looking for *tape*?" I asked.

"Yes," Witherspoon said, frowning. "What's your point?"

I looked at Kennrick, saw the light starting to dawn there. "Doc, no one throws a bunch of vials around when they're looking for a roll of tape," I said. "He wanted something else in there."

"Kindly credit me with a *little* intelligence, Mr. Compton," Witherspoon growled. "I've checked on all my painkillers and other potentially dangerous drugs. They're all still there. I doubt anyone would go to this much effort just to steal a packet of QuixHeals."

"So let's find out what *was* worth this much effort." I reached over and opened the bag. "Inventory. Now."

Witherspoon grimaced. "Fine," he said. "But I can tell you right now that we're not going to find anything significant."

"Five bucks says I will," I said nudging the bag a little closer to him.

For possibly the first time that day, I was right.

Bayta was alone in the dispensary, sitting on one of the fold-out seats and gazing wearily at *Usantra* Givvrac's body, when the Spider and I finally returned. "You all right?" I asked, peering at her as the Spider crossed the room and put Witherspoon's bag back under lock and key.

"I was just thinking about this afternoon, in the bar," she said. "When you told me that putting off a conversation usu-ally meant that person will be the next to die."

I winced. "I'm sorry I said that."

"I'm sorry he's dead." Bayta paused. "The killer's not fin-ished yet, is he?"

"Doesn't look like it," I conceded. "You listened in on our inventory of Witherspoon's bag?"

She nodded again. "There's a hypo missing."

"Right," I said. "Inevitable, I suppose, in retrospect. The three basic ways of delivering poisons are inhalation, ingestion, and injection. With the first two mostly off the table, that leaves only the last."

"What do you mean, mostly?" Bayta asked.

"We still haven't totally eliminated the possibility that someone added the cadmium to the Shorshians' food after it was delivered," I said. "Did you check with the servers, by the way, on whether Colix and Bofiv always used the same reaches for the common dish?"

"They didn't," Bayta said. "All three Shorshians switched off between *galla* bread, *prinn* scoops, and *rokbi* sticks, with no particular pattern the servers noticed."

"So no one could have poisoned the reaches, at least not if he was targeting specific victims," I concluded. "That leaves our killer with a choice of poisoning the common dish—or, rather, half the common dish, since Tririn wasn't affected—or two separate individual dishes. *And* all that without anyone at the table noticing. Not impossible, but pretty damn difficult."

"Unless Master Tririn himself is the killer," Bayta said slowly. "According to *Usantra* Givvrac, he was one of the four members of the team opposed to the contract with Pellorian Medical. Three of the four victims were *for* the contract."

"True," I agreed. "But that runs us immediately into another problem. Two problems, actually. If he was trying to stack the vote in his favor, Master Colix's death already accomplishes that. So why keep killing? Especially since the second death, Bofiv's, evens up the vote again?"

"It doesn't make sense, does it?" Bayta admitted.

"Not yet," I conceded. "A bigger problem with Tririn is that you've already proved he hasn't been up to first class since we left Homshil, which means he had no access to Strinni or Givvrac."

Bayta winced. "Actually, that might not be true," she said reluctantly. "It occurred to me—a little late, I'm afraid—to ask the conductors about unlimited first-class passes. They tell me eight passes came aboard the train, but only seven of the holders are actually riding in first class."

I stared at her. "Oh, hell."

"I'm sorry," Bayta apologized. "I should have asked about that sooner."

"Not your fault," I told her. So someone else had the same ability we did to flit back and forth between classes without a single locked door or raised eyebrow. Terrific. "If Spiders were smart enough to volunteer this stuff on their own instead of having to be asked—" I broke off. "Never mind. Water under the bridge. Very interesting water, too."

"Because it shows that the killer had everything planned in advance?"

"*And* because it shows he has some serious financial backing," I said. "I don't suppose there's any way of finding out who has this eighth pass?"

Bayta shook her head. "If it wasn't used to board, the conductors won't have that information."

"Who *would* have it?" I persisted. "The stationmaster back at Homshil?"

"Yes, he would have been the one who informed the conductors about the eight passes in the first place," she said. "But there's no way to get a message back there until we reach Venidra Carvo."

"Why not?" I asked. "There must be a few of your secret little sidings scattered along the way. Can't you shoot the Spiders a telepathic message as we pass, like we did on our last trip back to Earth? They could then load the request onto a message cylinder and send it back to Homshil via one of their tenders."

"It won't be easy," Bayta said doubtfully. "We don't get very close to the Spiders when we pass a siding. That'll make the contact difficult. We're also going much faster then we do when we pass through a station, so we won't be able to send anything very long or detailed."

"Then we'll just have to be clever," I said, trying to kick a few of my comatose brain cells back to life. "What if we give all the conductors aboard the same message and have them line up along the length of the train? Hell, let's give it to the servers, mites, and twitters, too. Maybe between all of them we can get enough of it across to make sense."

For a moment Bayta was silent, either thinking it over or consulting with the Spiders. "It might work," she said at last. "No guarantees, but it might."

"No guarantees expected," I assured her. "When will we pass the next siding?"

"In about six hours," she said. "It'll still take a while for a message cylinder to get from there to Homshil Station, though. And of course the only way to get the information back to us will be though a tender, and depending on where they have to send it from—"

"Yes, yes, I get it," I cut her off. "But even limited information will be better than nothing. Let's figure out the shortest way to phrase the message and then start rehearsing the Spiders."

"All right," she said, running a critical eye over me. "But I can do that. You'd better get to bed."

"I'm on my way," I promised. "One other thing."

I hesitated, wondering if I really wanted to do this. During my last private conversation with a Chahwyn Elder I'd promised that I would hold on to their new secret as long as I could. Not just because he hadn't wanted Bayta to know about it, but also because I agreed with him that the truth would be a troubling shock for her. Besides, at the time I'd made the promise there wasn't any particular reason she needed to know.

But circumstances had changed. We were locked aboard a super-express Quadrail, four weeks from our destination, with a shadowy killer who'd made an art out of sneaking death past the Spiders' sensors. We needed reinforcements, and we needed them now. "Along with the unlimited-pass information," I said, "I want you to put in a request for a couple of the Chahwyn's newest class of Spider."

"There's a new class?" she asked, frowning. "When did you hear about this?"

"When we were delivering Rebekah to her friends," I told her. "There was a Chahwyn aboard the tender, and he and I had a little chat."

Bayta's face had gone very still. "You never told me about that," she said.

"I was asked not to," I said, wincing. The hurt in her eyes was radiating at me like a heat lamp on a bad sunburn. "There was some concern about your possible reaction to the new Spiders."

"But you're telling me about them now," she said slowly. "That means you think I need to know. Because we're in danger, or because the train's in danger. We're alone against a killer—"

She broke off, her face suddenly stricken. "Oh, no," she said. "The *defenders*?"

I blinked. "You know about them?"

She closed her eyes, a wave of pain crossing her face. "The

Chahwyn Elders have talked about the idea for years," she said, her voice tight. "Since long before you were brought in to help us."

"Really," I said, trying very hard not to be annoyed and not succeeding very well. Here I'd been walking around with tape over my mouth for a solid month, worried that I'd let something slip. And now I find out Bayta had known the essentials all along? "Why didn't you tell me about them?"

"Why didn't *you* tell *me*?" she shot back, opening her eyes again to shoot a glare squarely between my eyes. "As far as I knew, the Elders were still just talking about the idea. *You* knew they'd actually created some of them." The glare suddenly evaporated. "I thought you trusted me," she said in a suddenly quiet voice.

"I *do* trust you, Bayta," I said, once again wanting to reach out and take her hand. Once again, I resisted the impulse. *Thought viruses* . . . "I was told to keep it quiet, and I'm sure you were too. It's the Elders' fault, not yours or mine."

"I suppose," she said. But I could still hear the quiet hurt in her voice.

"But I'm glad it's out in the open," I continued, searching for a way to deflect her mind away from thoughts of distrust or betrayal. "I gather you don't think much of the project?"

"Of course not," she said. "It would change the character of the Spiders forever. I don't want that."

"Unless they only make a few of them."

"You really think they'll stop there?" she countered. "With the Modhri threat the way it is? I've read about arms races, Frank. They never stop. Ever."

"Not until one side or the other goes down, anyway," I conceded. "Maybe the Elders don't think they've got any other choice."

"Of course we have a choice," Bayta said, her voice suddenly the color of despair. "We can end it. We can retreat back to Viccai and end everything."

I winced, glancing at the open dispensary door. We really shouldn't be talking about things like this in the middle of a crowded train. But the Spider who'd dropped off Witherspoon's case was standing just outside in the corridor, clearly on guard against eavesdroppers.

As well he should be. The Quadrail was essentially a fraud, the reality of its magic a closely kept secret I'd stumbled across on my first mission for the Spiders. The Tube and trains were nothing more than window dressing for the exotic quantum thread that ran down the center of the Coreline. Traveling close to the Thread was what allowed a vehicle to travel at speeds of a light-year per minute or better, the actual speed depending on how close the closest part of the vehicle was to the Thread. Anything inside the vehicle, connected to it, or even just touching it ran at the same speed, with no tidal or other nasty effects to deal with.

The problem the Chahwyn had faced when hoping to restart interstellar travel after the defeat of the Shonkla-raa was that you didn't need a train for the Thread to do its magic. You could just cozy up to it with a torchliner or torchyacht or even a garbage scow, and you'd be off to the races.

Which would have been fine if the Chahwyn could have trusted everyone in the Twelve Empires to stick with torchliners and garbage scows. Unfortunately, they couldn't. That was how the Shonkla-raa had conquered the galaxy in the first place, sending their warships along the Thread to the galaxy's inhabited systems, destroying or enslaving everything in their path.

And if the Thread's secret became common knowledge,

there was no reason to believe someone else wouldn't take a crack at replicating that achievement. Hence, the Quadrail, with its limited points of entry, its massive station-based sensor arrays, and its strict no-weapons rules.

But if the galaxy ever got a whiff of the truth, it would be all over. "You can't be serious," I said to Bayta, lowering my voice despite the presence of our Spider watchdog. "You destroy the Tube and the Quadrails, and someone's bound to figure out the secret."

"I said we end everything, Frank," she repeated, her voice weary in a way I'd never heard it before. "*Everything.* Including the Thread."

I felt my jaw drop. "You can destroy the *Thread*?"

She nodded. "You already know we can ravel off pieces of it—that's how we create loops and spurs. It's thought that if we ravel the Thread too many times, its mass will drop below a critical level and it will simply evaporate."

I felt a chill run up my back. "And what about the people who would be trapped off their worlds? How would they get home?"

"They wouldn't," Bayta said. "But exile is better than becoming slaves to the Modhri."

Except that most of the worlds where the new exiles would find themselves already had a Modhran presence, and a lot of those worlds also had at least one Modhran coral outpost. The Quadrail would be gone, but the Modhri would go merrily on his way, making slaves of anyone who crossed his path. The only difference would be that he would have to settle for being a whole lot of small, isolated, local despots instead of a single, vast galaxy-wide despot. I couldn't really see what difference that would make for his thousands of small, isolated, local groups of slaves.

Clearly, the Chahwyn who favored this approach hadn't thought it through. Just as clearly, this wasn't the time for a discussion of that shortsightedness. "Fortunately, we're a long way from that kind of irrevocable decision," I said instead. "Let's focus on the here and now. We've got a plan. Let's get it started and see where we go from there."

"All right," Bayta said. Her voice was still tired, but maybe a couple of shades less dark than it had been. "You go ahead. I'll be in later."

"Not too much later," I warned. "You've been up as long as I have, and there's time for at least a few hours of sleep before we pass that siding."

"I won't be long," she promised. "Good night."

"Good night." I headed toward the doorway, stepping past the Spider into the corridor.

And paused. On any normal Quadrail, with a contingent of Spiders wandering around and the station sensors having successfully blocked out all weaponry, I wouldn't have thought twice about leaving Bayta to wander the train alone.

But this was hardly a normal Quadrail. Not anymore.

And she was too important to risk letting our unknown assailant get a crack at her. Too important to our survival aboard this damn train. Too important to our war against the Modhri.

Too important to me.

"On second thought, you can set up your Greek Chorus from inside your compartment," I said, gesturing to her. "Come on—we'll go together."

ELEVEN :

Whoever our murderer was, he'd apparently decided to clock out for the night. I got Bayta to her compartment, made sure both our doors were locked, and just managed to get myself undressed and take one final QuixHeal before collapsing co-matose on my bed.

I slept for ten hours straight, and when I finally dragged myself conscious I found the QuixHeals had done their chem-ical magic and I felt nearly back to full speed again. I took a quick shower, then opened the connecting door between our compartments to check on Bayta.

Only to find that she wasn't there.

Muttering curses under my breath, I left the compartment and headed aft, fervently hoping that she was merely having breakfast and not off doing more solo sleuthing. I reached the dining car and went in.

To my relief, I spotted her sitting at a two-person table be-hind a plate of something Jurian-looking. "Good morning," I said as I sat down across from her.

"Good afternoon," she corrected, her eyes flicking measuringly across my face. "How do you feel?"

"Much better," I said. "How about you?"

"I'm fine," she said. "I got a few hours of sleep before we reached the siding, and was able to sleep a little more afterward."

"That all go okay?" I asked, lowering my voice.

"We think so," she said. "But we can't be completely sure."

"I guess we'll find out," I said. "What's good for breakfast today? Or brunch, or whatever?"

"The *vistren* is good," she said, gesturing toward her plate. "But I understand the servers may run out of livberries before we reach Venidra Carvo."

"Say no more," I said. Livberries were my absolute favorite Jurian fruit. "A Belgian waffle with livberries, if you would, and a glass of sweet iced tea."

Her eyes flattened briefly. No point in dragging a server all the way over to our table to get my order when Bayta had a direct line to the kitchen. "On its way," she said. "I've been thinking about Dr. Aronobal."

"What about her?" I asked.

"Mostly just wondering," she said. "We talked a lot last night about the missing first-class pass. But Dr. Aronobal's been moving fairly freely between third and first ever since Master Colix's death."

"So has Dr. Witherspoon," I reminded her.

"True," she said. "But Dr. Witherspoon wasn't alone with *Usantra* Givvrac for several minutes before she called a conductor to help get him to the dispensary. Dr. Aronobal was."

"You mean just before Givvrac's death?" I shook my head. "No. The damage to his gleaner bacteria was done long before then. The poisons were already backing up into his system when we spoke to him in the bar yesterday afternoon."

"But she could have done something to help the process along," Bayta persisted. "The other two Filiaelians who were affected seem to be recovering just fine."

"Givvrac was a lot older than either of them," I reminded her. "Besides, unless Aronobal's working with a partner, she's off the hook for the attack on Witherspoon and me."

"How do you know?" Bayta asked. "The only conductor in the area was waiting with *Usantra* Givvrac. Couldn't Dr. Aronobal have followed you and Dr. Witherspoon to the rear, attacked you there, and then gone back to *Usantra* Givvrac?"

"For one thing, wouldn't either you or the server in the dispensary have seen her double back?" I asked.

She grimaced. "Actually, probably not," she said. "We were concentrating on *di*-Master Strinni's body, preparing it for transport to the baggage car."

So anyone could have been wandering around without being seen. That was useful to know. "It still couldn't have been Aronobal," I said. "Neither Witherspoon nor I heard the vestibule door open behind us, which means our attacker was already in the car waiting for us."

"Because," Bayta said slowly, "he knew you would come to help *Osantra* Qiddicoj. So could *Osantra* Qiddicoj's poisoning have been a deliberate way of drawing you there so that he could get that hypo?"

"Possibly," I said. "It's not like the killer hadn't already used the same stuff on *Usantra* Givvrac and the others. And of course, with *di*-Master Strinni gone, he even had the perfect hiding place to wait for us."

Bayta's lip twitched. "*Di*-Master Strinni's empty seat."

"Exactly," I confirmed. "And since we saw Dr. Aronobal leave the dispensary heading the opposite direction, there's no way she could have doubled back and gotten to *Osantra* Qiddicoj's car ahead of us."

"All right," Bayta said. "But it still couldn't have been Master Tririn."

Privately, I'd already put Tririn low on my suspect list—poisoning your dinner companions without giving yourself so much as a stomach ache was a little too obvious for someone with our killer's brand of subtlety. But it would be interesting to hear Bayta's reasoning. "Why not?" I asked.

"Because even if he has the missing first-class pass, going up to *di*-Master Strinni and *Usantra* Givvrac would mean approaching people who knew he was supposed to be in third," Bayta said. "Surely someone would have thought to mention that to us."

"Good point," I agreed, leaning back a little as the server appeared at our table and set my breakfast in front of me.

"Besides which, with *di*-Master Strinni's death the team is back to an anti-Pellorian vote count," she continued. "Why then kill *Usantra* Givvrac, too?"

"Let's assume you're right," I said, spreading the berries across the waffle. "Here's what we've got. Opportunity and motive are only so-so for Tririn. Opportunity is good for Aronobal and Witherspoon, but we have no motive for either of them."

"And both doctors also have method, assuming the poison was injected."

"True," I said, taking a bite of my waffle. Now that I knew the meals were prepackaged, damned if they didn't *taste* prepackaged. Sometimes it didn't pay to know how the magician did the trick. "But if either of the doctors is involved, why go to all that effort to clobber Witherspoon and me to steal a hypo? They have plenty of their own. And unlike the rest of the passengers, they have a legitimate reason to carry them around."

"Except that most of the time their hypos are locked up and inaccessible, even to them," Bayta reminded me.

"Unless they're out using them," I said, thinking that one over. "What about people who have to self-medicate? Type Four diabetics, for instance? Do they get to carry their own hypos aboard?"

Bayta shook her head. "The Spiders store them in the drug cabinets along with the doctors' bags. The passenger has to go to his area's dispensary to use them, under a server's watch."

"Any chance someone could smuggle one out of the cabinet?" I asked. "Take one while palming a second, for instance?"

"It wouldn't be easy," Bayta said thoughtfully. "At the very least you'd have to distract the server."

"So he'd probably need an accomplice," I concluded. "You have a list of passengers who have hypos on file?"

"Let me get it." Her eyes unfocused as she consulted with the Spiders. I took advantage of the break to work some more on my waffle. "There are three in second and one in first," she reported. "Interesting."

"What is?"

"The first-class passenger is *Esantra* Worrbin," she said. "Isn't that one of the Filiaelians on the contract team?"

"Not only one of the team, but one of the team opposed to the contract," I confirmed. "Just like Master Tririn. Do we know what *Esantra* Worrbin's particular condition is?"

"It's listed as Tintial's Disease," she said. "It's a rare form of diabetes that only appeared a few decades ago."

"Of course it is," I said with a cynical smile. "Rare diseases are so convenient when you want to snow a doctor or investigator."

"You think *Esantra* Worrbin and Master Tririn could be working together?"

"It's something we'll want to look into," I said, stacking my two remaining bites of waffle onto the fork and stuffing them into my mouth. It was a stretch, but I managed it.

"So what do we do now?" Bayta asked as I chewed my way valiantly through the mouthful. "Go see if *Esantra* Worrbin can account for all his hypos?"

I swallowed the last of the waffle. "Not quite yet," I said. "Something else occurs to me as a possible reason why Witherspoon and I were jumped last night. Which of the baggage cars is serving as our temporary morgue?"

"The third one back," Bayta said. "There was enough room in there to set up the isolation tanks."

"Okay," I said, taking a last swallow of my tea. "Let's go take a look."

We set off on the long walk toward third class. Three cars behind the dining car we passed the dispensary, and I noted that for the first time in a bad couple of days the room was empty except for the server Spider on duty. I wondered if we would catch the killer before it started filling up again.

The next car back, Bayta informed me, was the one where *Esantra* Worrbin and the two remaining contract team members were seated. I spotted the group at once as we headed through the car: three Fillies with their chairs turned to face each other, a hand of push-pull cards dealt onto their extendable trays. For the moment, though, the game was being ignored, the aliens instead speaking together in low voices. One of them glanced up as Bayta and I passed, but turned back to the conversation without speaking to us. I thought about pausing to introduce ourselves, decided I wanted to check my hunch about the bodies first, and passed them by.

Three cars later we reached the coach car where the late *di*-Master Strinni had had his seat, and where Witherspoon and I had been attacked in the dark of night. My neck throbbed in memory and edgy anticipation as we made our way through the clumps of chairs, my senses alert for trouble.

But no one jumped out at us. We arrived at the rear of the car and I reached for the vestibule release—

"Mr. Compton," a hoarse voice said from somewhere behind me.

A surge of adrenaline shot through my body and straight through my still tender neck and ears. I turned, trying to make the movement look casual, my hands ready to snap up into fighting stance if necessary.

It wasn't. The speaker was merely Rose Nose, or rather *Osantra* Qiddicoj, the Filly Witherspoon and I had been on our way to examine when we were jumped. He was resting in his seat, a blanket spread out across his legs and tucked up around his torso. His face and blaze were still noticeably pale after his bout with the digestive trouble that had killed Givvrac, but he was definitely on the mend. "Good afternoon, *Osantra* Qiddicoj," I greeted him, hoping I was remembering his name right. Fillies hated it when you called them something like Rose Nose to their long faces. "You're looking much improved."

"Thanks to you and your friends," Qiddicoj said, inclining his head. "I'm told I owe you my life. My deepest thanks."

"You're welcome," I said. "But your thanks should more properly be directed to Dr. Aronobal and Dr. Witherspoon.

They're the ones who actually cured you. All I did was point them in the right direction."

"Yet without that direction, their skills would have lain fallow and unused," he said. "Again, I stand in your debt."

"Again, I'm glad I could help in my small way," I said. "Rest now, and continue to heal."

I turned and touched the release, and Bayta and I stepped into the vestibule. "Is extra modesty one of the necessities for detective work?" she asked as we crossed toward the next car.

"It wasn't modesty," I insisted. "I really *didn't* say anything that Aronobal and Witherspoon wouldn't have caught on to eventually."

"Maybe," Bayta said. "But whether they would have or not, the fact is that you *did* save *Osantra* Qiddicoj's life."

"In a small way." I gave her a sideways look. "Besides, it never hurts to be overly modest, especially where potential sources of information are concerned. People who consider themselves in your debt are often amazingly eager to help you out."

"I thought so," Bayta murmured.

We passed through the thirteen second-class cars without talking to anyone and entered third. Dr. Aronobal was seated in the first of the third-class coach cars, dozing in her seat after her grueling night, and I made a mental note to get the Spiders to pass her to first later so that *Osantra* Qiddicoj could give her his thanks in person.

Two cars farther back, we reached the scene of the first two murders.

I found myself looking at Master Colix's seat as we approached, an empty spot between the Juri, whom Bayta had already talked to, and Terese German, whom I was frankly tired of talking to. The Juri looked up as we approached, nodding politely as he recognized us. Terese, her headphones firmly in place over her ears, ignored us completely.

I was starting to pass the row when Bayta nudged me in the side. "Master Colix's storage compartments?" she prompted.

I looked at the upper set of compartments, then at Terese. She had slid down in her seat with her legs stretched all the way out in front of her. Getting to Master Colix's storage compartments would mean stepping over her, and would probably earn me a withering glare at the least. "We'll do it later," I told Bayta.

"You said that yesterday," she reminded me. "Don't you care that someone stole Master Colix's fruit snacks?"

Actually, I didn't. Despite what the Spiders probably claimed, I was pretty sure this kind of petty theft went on all the time aboard Quadrails.

But if it came to facing someone's irritation, it would be safer to deal with Terese's than Bayta's. "Fine," I said, coming to a reluctant halt. "Excuse me," I said to Terese's headphoned ears. Not waiting for a response, or expecting one for that matter, I lifted one leg and stepped carefully over her outstretched body.

Her head snapped up with a quickness and preset glare that showed she hadn't been nearly as oblivious of our presence as she'd been pretending. "You have a problem?" she growled, slipping the headphones down around her neck.

"I just need to get through," I soothed, getting my first foot planted in front of Colix's seat and lifting my other foot over her legs.

"For frigg's sake," she grumbled. "How many times are you people going to do this?"

I frowned as I brought my other foot back to the floor. "I don't know," I said. "How many times *have* we done this?"

"How about just *talking* to each other for once?" she bit out. "They're gone, I didn't take them, and I don't know who did. Can you leave me alone now?"

"What didn't you take?" I asked, sitting down in Colix's seat.

For a second I could see Terese trying to decide whether or not she should just get up and make for the relative sanctuary of the restroom. But Bayta had moved up beside her, blocking easy access to the aisle. "The Shorshian's fruit snacks," she answered me. "Or whatever they were."

"You think they were something else?"

"I don't know *what* they were," Terese snapped back. "All I know is that he never offered to share them, and he kept them right there under his legs where he could watch them until he swapped them out for his special sleepy-time blankie. And *then* he made double damn sure they were locked up tight." Her lip twisted. "I also know that everyone and his dog Rolf seems to want them. You tell *me* what they were."

I leaned over and pulled out the drawer of Colix's underseat storage. There was an assortment of personal stuff under there—a reader and a set of data chips, some headphones, fancier than Terese's, a flexible water bottle, a compact toiletry bag, and the small keepsake box that a lot of Shorshians liked to travel with. All of it was neatly and precisely arranged.

And right at the front left of the drawer was a gap in the arrangement, about fifteen centimeters square. The perfect size for a bag of something.

"Who else has been looking for them?" Bayta asked.

"Well, there was *you* for a start," Terese growled, flicking her a disdainful look. "Then there was that other Human you hang out with. He came by yesterday morning to look for them."

"You mean Dr. Witherspoon?" I asked.

"*No*, not Dr. Witherspoon," Terese growled. "I *know* Dr. Witherspoon's name. It was the other one, the one you were with when you tried to ambush me outside the bathroom."

I frowned. "*Kennrick?*"

"I don't *know* his name," Terese said with exaggerated patience. "Balding, mustache, a little chubby."

"That's Kennrick," I confirmed. "And you're sure he was after Master Colix's fruit snacks?"

"Well, he was after *something*," Terese said. "And he didn't find anything, either. You about done here?"

"One more minute," I promised. Returning my attention to the drawer, I slid my fingers over the lock mechanism. There was no evidence I could find that it had been forced. I stood up and gave the overseat compartment the same check. Again, nothing. Popping the compartment door, I peered inside.

There were two small carrybags in there, plus another toiletry bag, plus a carefully folded blanket. "Did he have the blanket down with him that last night?" I asked Terese as I pulled out the first carrybag and set it onto the seat.

"I don't know," she said. "I went to sleep before he did." She grimaced. "I mean, before he . . . you know what I mean."

"Before he went off to the dispensary to die?" I suggested.

I had the minor satisfaction of watching an emotion other than anger or resentment flicker across her face. "Yes," she muttered.

I looked over at the Juri on my other side. He was half turned toward me, surreptitiously watching the whole operation. "What about you, *Tas* Krodo?" I asked as I opened the carrybag and started sorting through its contents. There was nothing there but changes of clothing. "Did *you* see him with his blanket that night?"

"Yes, he had it," the Juri confirmed. "I distinctly remember him holding it when I returned from my evening ablutions."

"Good—that helps," I said. "Do you have any idea who might have put it back up in his compartment?"

He hesitated. "I'm afraid it was I," he admitted. "The next morning."

"Can you tell me why?" I asked, closing the carrybag and swapping it out for the other one.

"I heard about his death, and I saw his blanket lying crumpled on his seat," he said. "It seemed wrong to leave it there. It had been a relic of his childhood, which he always traveled with as a reminder of home and family. I'm sorry if I did wrong."

"No, it's all right," I assured him, pausing in my search of the second carrybag and pulling the blanket out of the compartment. It was old, all right, with a pleasant scent of distant spices to it. Exactly the sort of keepsake a Shorshian would like. "One could say it was your final honoring for Master Colix. When you put it back, did you happen to see whether or not his bag of fruit snacks was there?"

"It was not," the Juri said firmly. "The blanket would not have fit otherwise."

"Of course," I said, returning the blanket to its place. "I should have realized that. Is there anything else about Master Colix that you can remember?"

"Nothing specific," he admitted. "But he was very kind to me, and kept me entertained with tales of his many interesting journeys."

"And about his precious Path of whatever," Terese muttered. If the moment of maudlin sentiment was affecting her, she was hiding it well. "He talked about that a lot."

I finished going through the second bag—again, there was

nothing there but clothing—and replaced it in the storage compartment. "One final question, *Tas* Krodo. You say that Master Colix was kind to you. Did he ever offer you any of his fruit snacks?"

"He did not," the Juri said. "And I certainly wouldn't have taken one without his permission."

"I'm sure you wouldn't," I assured him. "Thank you for your time."

"You are welcome," *Tas* Krodo said quietly. "I grieve Master Colix's loss to the universe. If I can do anything to help you solve his death, I stand at your disposal."

"Thank you," I said. "If I need you, I'll let you know."

He bowed his head to me. I bowed back, then stepped over Terese's legs out into the aisle again. Typically, she didn't bother to draw up her knees to make the procedure any easier. "And thank you for your cooperation as well, Ms. German," I added as I regained my balance.

She didn't answer, but merely put her headphones back on and closed her eyes.

"A helpful public makes this job so much more rewarding," I murmured. Tririn's seat, I noted, was empty, our lone surviving contract team Shorshian out and about somewhere. That was all right—I hadn't wanted to talk to him right now anyway.

"Do you believe him?" Bayta asked as we resumed our trip toward the rear of the train.

"Who, *Tas* Krodo?" I shrugged. "Assuming he has no connection to Pellorian Medical or the contract team, he shouldn't have any reason to lie." I nodded back over my shoulder. "Actually, I'm more intrigued by Witherspoon's relationship with our helpful Ms. German."

"What sort of relationship?"

"I don't know, but there's *something* going on under the table," I said. "Remember when I confronted him with the fact that he was two cars away when he allegedly noticed all her stomach trouble?"

"But he explained that," Bayta said, frowning. "He said he'd noticed her when he was visiting the three Shorshians."

"That's what he said," I agreed. "But if that was actually true, he should have said it without floundering and fumbling all over himself."

"Maybe he was just nervous," she suggested. "You *did* catch him a little off-guard with those questions."

"True," I said. "But then he should have been caught equally off-guard when I told Kennrick that the good doctor thought I was the killer. But he wasn't. He was quick, decisive, and in complete control of the English language. No, there's something about him and Terese that we still haven't got nailed down."

We walked through the last seven third-class cars in silence, and finally passed through the vestibule into the first baggage car.

The casual passenger wandering into a Quadrail baggage car for the first time might reasonably think he'd accidentally stumbled into a classic English garden maze, with the role of the hedges being played by tall stacks of safety-webbed crates. Add in the silence and dim lighting, and the overall ambience could easily drift from the disconcerting into the spooky. Bayta and I had spent so much time in places like this that I hardly noticed. "Third car, you said?" I confirmed as we made our way through the second car and into the vestibule connecting it with the third.

"Yes, near the back." She shivered. "I don't like looking at dead bodies."

"They tell me you get used to it," I said.

"Have *you* gotten used to it?"

"Not really."

We were halfway down the car when I caught a subtle shift in lighting and shadow somewhere ahead. "Hold it," I murmured, catching Bayta's arm and bringing us both to a halt.

"What is it?" she murmured back.

For a moment I didn't answer, wondering if I'd imagined it. I stood motionlessly, staring at the stacks of crates and the meandering aisles between them.

And then, I saw it again.

So did Bayta. "Frank?" she whispered.

"Yeah," I said grimly.

We'd come way back here to examine the victims' bodies. Apparently, someone else had beaten us to it.

TWELVE :

"What do we do?" Bayta whispered tensely.

I watched the shifting shadows, thinking hard. Chances were good that our intruder was unaware of our presence—the fact that he was still moving around argued that assumption. If we kept it quiet, we might be able to sneak the rest of the way to the bodies and catch him in the act. Whatever that act turned out to be.

On the other hand, sneaking up on a murderer carried its own set of risks. But standing here in nervous indecision would be to lose by default. "Let's take a look," I said, slipping the *kwi* out of my pocket. It was tingling with Bayta's activation command as I settled it into place around the knuckles of my right hand. Tucking Bayta close in behind my left side, where she'd be partially protected and out of my line of fire, I started forward.

We were nearly to the gap where I'd estimated the earlier movement had come from when I realized that the motion had ceased. In fact, as I thought about it, I realized it might have stopped up to a minute or even a minute and a half earlier.

I stopped, turning to put our backs against the nearest stack of crates as I searched for some clue as to where he might have gone. Nothing. Whoever this guy was, he was quick and smart.

But then, I was quick and smart, too. And I had a huge advantage he didn't know about: I had a weapon. Resting my thumb on the *kwi*'s activation button, I gestured Bayta to follow and headed in.

No one jumped us before we reached the gap. Pressing my shoulder against the side of the last stack, I eased a cautious eye around the corner.

Wedged into the narrow space between crate stacks were four coffin-sized tanks. The lid of the nearest was cracked open, while the other three appeared to still be sealed. The intruder himself was nowhere to be seen. Touching Bayta's arm, I slipped around the corner into the impromptu mortuary.

"What do you think he wanted?" Bayta asked quietly as I stopped beside the partially-open tank.

"For starters, not to be caught," I said, getting a grip on the lid and experimentally pushing it closed.

It latched with a loud click that could probably have been heard fifteen meters away. "Which is why he left it open instead of closing it and trying to pretend no one had been here," I went on, popping the lid open again. It made the same loud click as it had when I'd closed it.

And then, from somewhere near the front of the car, I heard an answering sound. Not another click, but the thud of someone bumping into one of the crate stacks. Our intruder, it appeared, was making a run for it.

"Stay close," I murmured to Bayta, and headed at a dead run back toward the vestibule.

Or at least, I tried to make it look and sound like a dead run. But I knew this trick, and I wasn't about to be taken in so easily. The suspicious-noise ploy was a classic way to get the hunter charging off in the wrong direction while the prey slipped away through the dark of night to freedom.

Here, with only a single exit from the baggage car, slipping away for more hide-and-seek was pretty much a waste of effort. Hence, the prey had opted for suspicious-noise variant number two: lure the hunter into ambush range and clobber him.

Which was why my dead run wasn't nearly as reckless as it looked. I was in fact carefully checking every side aisle as I ran toward and past it, my *kwi* ready to fire in whichever direction it was needed. Between aisles I kept a careful watch on the tops of the stacks in case the intruder had scaled one of them in hopes of pulling a Douglas Fairbanks on me.

And with my full attention shifting between right, left, and up, I completely missed the low trip wire that had been stretched out across the aisle in front of me.

I hit it hard, catching my right foot and launching myself into an unintended dive across the dim landscape. I barely managed to get my hands under me before I slammed chest-first into the floor. Even with my arms absorbing some of the impact I hit hard enough to see stars.

For a long, horrible second I couldn't move, my brain spinning, my lungs fighting to recover the air that had just been knocked out of them. Then, through the haze, I felt someone grab my upper arms. I tried to bring the *kwi* around to bear, but my arms weren't responding and my wrists burned with pain. The hands gripping me pulled me up and half over, and

I saw to my relief that it was Bayta. "Where is he?" I wheezed at her.

"He's gone," she said, fighting to drag me over toward the nearest crates. I got my legs working enough to help push, and a moment later was sitting more or less upright with her crouching beside me. It was, I reflected grimly, the perfect time for an ambusher to attack.

Only no one did. Apparently, he really *was* gone. "Are you all right?" I asked Bayta, still working on getting my wind back.

"I'm fine," she assured me, eyeing me warily. "The question is, are *you* all right?"

"Aside from feeling like an idiot, sure," I said sourly, experimentally flexing my wrists. They still hurt, but they were starting to recover. "No chance of catching him now, I guess."

"Do we need to actually catch him?" Bayta asked. "Or do we just need to know who he is?"

I peered up at her. "You have a plan, don't you?"

She nodded toward the front of the car. "I've moved a conductor into the last passenger car," she said. "He's watching to see who comes out of the baggage section."

"Nice," I complimented her. "I don't suppose you and the Spiders have figured out yet how to relay images back and forth."

"Our communication doesn't work that way," she said. "But he doesn't have to send me an image or even a description. The conductors know who's assigned to which seat. All we have to do is see where he lands, and we'll have him."

"Sounds like a plan," I agreed. "But warn him not to get too close. We don't want our friend to know he's being followed."

"He won't *be* followed," Bayta said. "The conductor in the

rear car will stay there and merely pass him off to a Spider who's already in place ahead. In the two cars after that, if they're needed, there will be some mites working inside the ceiling systems who will watch his movements. The next car after that has another conductor, and so on."

"Sounds good," I said. "All those dit rec mysteries I've been pushing on you have obviously done you a world of good." I nodded toward the trip wire behind her. "Let's have a look at our friend's handiwork."

Successful booby traps, in my fortunately limited personal experience, tended toward one of three main flavors: simple, elegant, or opportunistic. This one managed to be all three.

The intruder had cut a section of safety webbing from the base of one of the crates, picking a strand about ankle height, and had continued his cut all the way around the stack until he'd freed enough slack to reach twice across the most likely aisle for us to take when we came charging after him. He'd stretched the line straight across the aisle, looped it through the webbing on the stack on that side, then run it back to the original stack at about a thirty-degree angle.

The result had been a pair of trip wires with a continually varying distance between them, the sort of arrangement that would be perfect for use against two pursuers with different stride lengths. Odds were very good that at least one of us would hit at least one of the lines, which was precisely what had happened. "Nice work," I commented. "This guy's definitely a pro."

"But how did he set it up?" Bayta asked, frowning as she poked experimentally at the taut line. "He couldn't have had more than a couple of minutes once he knew we were here."

"Which means he *didn't* set it up then, at least not completely," I told her. "He must have done all the cutting as soon as he came back here, leaving the loose cord wadded up against the base of the crate where we wouldn't notice it. Once he spotted us and slipped away around the back of the crate stacks, all he had to do was loop the end through here and tie it down back here."

"And then lure us into running after him," Bayta said, grimacing. "We should have known better."

"We *did* know better," I assured her. "I was just expecting a different sort of trap, that's all."

"Wait a minute—there he goes," Bayta said, staring suddenly into space. "He's left the baggage car and is heading forward."

"What species is he?" I asked. I knew Spiders usually couldn't distinguish between individuals, but a species identification would at least get us started.

Bayta frowned in concentration. "He can't tell," she said, sounding rather nonplused. "He's wearing a sort of hooded cloak that's completely covering his head, arms, and torso."

"What about his height? His build? *Anything?*"

"He's tall enough to be a medium-sized Filiaelian, a tall Human, a slightly overweight Fibibib, or a slightly underweight Shorshian," Bayta said, sounding rather annoyed herself. This was *her* plan, after all, that he was outthinking us on. "All the Spider can tell for sure is that he's not a Pirk, Juri, Bellido, or Cimma."

I mouthed a foul word one of my French-born Westali colleagues had been overly fond of. "Fine," I growled. "He wants to play games? We can play games, too. Have the Spiders keep an eye on him. Sooner or later, he'll have to take off the party outfit."

"Do you want the conductor to try to pull aside his hood when he passes?" Bayta asked.

"No," I said. "If he doesn't already know about our close

association with the Spiders, I don't want to tip our hand. Just have them keep an eye on him."

"All right," Bayta said. "What now?"

"We go do what we actually came here for," I said. Pulling out my multitool, I cut the trip-wire cord and pushed the ends out of the way. Then, getting a grip on the safety webbing behind me, I pulled myself carefully to my feet. "Let's go look at some dead bodies."

I had hoped there would be a way of telling which and how many of the storage tanks our intruder had broken into. But no such luck. There were no locks on the tanks, nor were there any breakable—or broken—seals. The four bodies lay quietly and peacefully in their temporary coffins, each wrapped like a mummy in wide strips of plastic. "I guess we'll start here," I said, gesturing to the coffin which had been ajar when we'd arrived. Swiveling the lid all the way up, I started gingerly un-wrapping the corpse.

"What exactly are we looking for?" Bayta asked, her voice sounding a little queasy. "Needle marks?"

"Mostly," I said. "I'm thinking one of the needle marks may have something different about it."

The wrapping came free of the head, and I saw that it was Master Colix's rest I'd disturbed. "Here we go," I said, working the plastic free of his shoulders. "You want to start on one of your own, or shall we both work on this one?"

"You go ahead," Bayta said, making no move toward the other coffins. "I'll just watch."

"Okay, but this is the really fun part of investigative work," I warned. Forcing my mind into clinical Westali mode, I leaned into the coffin and got to work.

I'd expected the job to take a while, with a lot more un-wrapping necessary before I got anywhere. But as seemed to be happening more and more these days, I was wrong.

"There we go," I said, pulling Colix's tunic back to reveal the tiny needle mark a few centimeters below the top of his collar and just to the left of his corrugated spinal ridge. "One needle mark, comma, hypodermic. Definitely fresh."

"How can that be?" Bayta objected. "The Spiders have ac-counted for all the hypos the passengers brought aboard."

"Which means it was either Aronobal or Witherspoon, or else someone managed to smuggle a spare aboard," I said.

Bayta shook her head. "That shouldn't be possible."

"Possible or not, here it is," I said, gesturing to the body. "Take a look."

Bayta shuddered, but gamely leaned in a little closer. "Seems like an odd placement," she commented. "How could someone make an injection back there without him notic-ing?"

"Actually, it's a perfect spot," I said. "Generally speaking, in order for poison to be injected without the victim noticing, he or she has to be asleep, comatose, or drunk. Those third-class nighttime privacy shields have openings at the top for ventilation. All our killer needed to do was go up to Colix's seat, reach in with his hypo—"

"Did Master Colix use his privacy shield?" Bayta inter-jected. "A lot of Shorshians don't."

I stared at her, then down at the needle mark I'd felt so proud about finding ten seconds earlier. Damn it, but she was right. And if Colix's whole skin surface had been available, surely the murderer could have picked a more out-of-the-way spot for his injection.

Had it happened at dinner, then? The mark was also in the

right spot for someone who'd sneaked up behind him and surreptitiously poked a hypo into his back.

Only that brought us back to the question of how that little trick could have been performed without Colix noticing. A brief twinge of pain he'd passed off and immediately forgotten? A close encounter, moreover, that his dinner companions hadn't even noticed? "Good point," I told Bayta. "Let's think about it a minute."

Gingerly, I slid my hand down inside the plastic wrappings to Colix's chest and started feeling around the vicinity of his tunic's inner top pocket. "What are you doing?" Bayta asked.

"Looking for this," I said, pulling out Colix's Quadrail ticket. "I guess the murderer didn't steal it after all."

"Then how did he get into Master Colix's storage compartment?" Bayta asked, frowning at the card.

"Two possibilities," I said. "One is that he didn't need the ticket because Colix's compartments were never locked that night." I wiggled the ticket between my fingers. "The other is that that's precisely what our intruder was doing back here just now. He'd taken the ticket, used it to open the compartment and steal Colix's goodies, and was hoping to return it to its rightful owner before we came looking for it."

"That has to be it," Bayta said. "Master Colix was very possessive of those snacks. He wouldn't have left them unlocked where they could be stolen."

"Not so fast," I warned her. "We also know that the compartment was unlocked the next morning, when *Tas* Krodo returned Colix's blanket."

"Which only means the killer must have left it unlocked after he stole the snacks," Bayta countered.

"Or else that Colix was already feeling too sick to bother locking it after he got out his blanket," I said. "But that brings us to another interesting point." Sliding Colix's ticket into my own pocket, I reached back down to the body, loosened the braidings tying up the front of his tunic, and pulled the collar all the way down. "As the French say, voilà," I said, pointing to the faint parallel scars running lengthwise along his throat on either side of his larynx. "Twenty to one those are the marks of the infamous Gibber Operation."

"The what?" Bayta asked, frowning as she leaned over for a closer look.

"It's an operation the Shorshians don't talk much about," I explained, resisting the temptation to point out how unusual it was for me to have found a gap in her otherwise encyclopedic knowledge of the galaxy. "It creates enough range in the Shorshic vocal apparatus to allow them to speak languages other than their own."

"Oh," she said, her face clearing. "You mean the *Kilfiriaso* Operation."

"Ah . . . right," I said, feeling slightly deflated. Not only did she know about the operation, she even knew its real name. "I don't know how fast Shorshians heal, but I *do* know that the Gibber Operation isn't supposed to leave any permanent scars. The fact that we can still see something implies the work must have been done fairly recently."

Bayta frowned at me. "You mean it was done on *Earth*?"

"So it would seem," I said. "And given the typical Shorshic view of aliens, I imagine there would be a hefty percentage of them who would find it offensive that Colix would let a bunch of primitive Humans cut into him that way." I gestured. "Which may explain both why he wouldn't share his fruit treats, *and* why they were stolen."

"Because they weren't treats, but fruit-flavored postoperative throat lozenges?" Bayta asked.

"That's the first part," I agreed. "The second is that the facility that issued him the lozenges undoubtedly had their name or logo on the bag. Best explanation for the theft is that the killer didn't want it known where Colix had his operation."

Bayta was gazing down at Colix's throat. "And since we know Mr. Kennrick also tried to find the bag," she said slowly, "that suggests Master Colix had the operation at Pellorian Medical."

"Exactly," I said.

"But the rest of the contract team surely also knew about it," Bayta objected. "Stealing the lozenges wouldn't have kept the secret from getting out—" She broke off. "Are you suggesting . . . ?"

"That that's why the team members are dropping like dominoes?" I shrugged. "It certainly fits. The problem is, it fits a little too neatly. Especially when we add in that spare first-class pass. It could just as easily be that our murderer latched on to Colix's operation as a convenient smokescreen."

I smoothed Colix's collar back into place. "But that's just grist for the hopper at the moment. Come on—let's check out the other bodies."

It was a few minutes' work to open the other three containers and unwrap their occupants to the shoulders. Both Bofiv and Strinni had the same suspicious needle marks as Colix, and in similar places. Givvrac, in contrast, seemed to be unmarked, at least down to his waist, which was as far as I was willing to take this particular exercise.

"But we already knew that *Usantra* Givvrac died because of the antibacterial spray," Bayta reminded me as I closed his coffin again.

"We assumed that, anyway," I said, moving back to Strinni's body. "It was still worth checking. Shine the light in here, will you? Right here, on the needle mark."

"What are we looking for?" she asked, taking the light and directing the beam onto Strinni's neck.

"You'll see." Pulling out my multitool's thinnest probe, I began peeling away the skin at the edge of the needle mark.

"You probably shouldn't be doing that," Bayta warned. "If someone from the Path of Onagnalhni finds out we disturbed his body they won't like it."

"They're welcome to file a grievance," I said. My probe hit something solid, and I teased a little harder at the edges of flesh until I exposed the end. Putting the probe away, I pulled out my most delicate set of tweezers and gave a gentle tug.

And with a brief moment of resistance, the two-millimeter-long hypo tip that had broken off in Strinni's skin slid out.

"And now we *really* know why the murderer jumped Witherspoon and me last night," I said, holding up the tip for Bayta's inspection. "He managed to smuggle a hypo aboard, but unfortunately ruined it when he broke off the tip. He already had his cadmium, so he didn't need anything from Witherspoon's collection of drugs, but he hoped he could make off with a new hypo without anyone noticing."

"Only we did," Bayta said, her voice odd. "Did Dr. Witherspoon have anything in his bag that could kill?"

"Probably," I said. "Painkillers in particular tend to be lethal if you overdo the dosages. But our friend obviously prefers more subtle ways of offing his targets."

"I was just thinking," Bayta said slowly, staring at Strinni's needle mark. "Why did he just tie you into the chair instead of killing you?"

"That's a cheery thought," I said, an unpleasant chill running through me. Normally, it didn't do a murderer much good to kill the cop who was after him, since there were always more cops where the first one had come from.

But at this immediate point in time and space, that comforting logic didn't apply. As far as cops aboard this train were concerned, I was it. "Luckily for me, he didn't."

"No," Bayta murmured. "Not this time."

"This time was all he had," I told her firmly. "He won't get another shot. Not at me."

She shivered. "I hope you're right."

"Trust me." Pulling out a handkerchief, I carefully wrapped the needle tip and put it in my pocket. "Come on, let's put everything back the way it was," I said as I started rewrapping Strinni's body. "I think it's time we sat Mr. Kennrick down in some nice first-class bar seat and found out what other little secrets he and Pellorian Medical are sitting on."

THIRTEEN :

As it turned out, we didn't have to go all the way to first to confront Kennrick. We found him sitting in the late Master Bofiv's seat, conversing earnestly with Master Tririn. "There you are," Kennrick said, standing up as Bayta and I stopped beside them. "I was looking for you earlier."

"And now you've found me," I said. "What can I do for you?"

Kennrick hesitated, then looked down at Tririn. "Master Tririn, with your permission, I'll get back to you later on this."

[As you wish, Mr. Kennrick,] the Shorshian said with a polite nod. [Mr. Compton, have you any further information on the tragic deaths of my colleagues?]

"We're making progress," I said. "As soon as we have anything solid, I'll let you and the rest of the contract team know."

[Those of us who remain, at least,] he said heavily.

"Yes," I conceded. "Regardless, you *will* be informed." I raised my eyebrows to Kennrick. "Mr. Kennrick?" I said, gesturing for him to step out.

Carefully, Kennrick stepped past the Nemut in the aisle seat and joined us. "Shall we try the bar?" he suggested. "I don't know how your head feels, but my ribs could use a drink."

I gestured. "Lead the way."

We walked past Terese German, who was playing her usual oblivious self behind the social barrier of her headphones, and continued forward. "You looked like a man in full fire-control mode," I commented to Kennrick as we walked through the next car.

"You have no idea," he said grimly. "*Esantra* Worrbin is calling for a binding vote on the contract, even though the terms explicitly state that such a vote can't be taken until we reach Rentis Tarlay Birim and the team presents its findings to the Maccai Corporation controllers. *Asantra* Muzzfor and *Asantra* Dallilo are insisting we follow the terms as written. *Esantra* Worrbin has countered by threatening to pull rank on them and possibly even revoke their *santra* status if they don't go along with him."

"Can he do that?"

"A simple *esantra*? Of course not. But that doesn't mean he wouldn't try."

"And you were back here trying to talk Master Tririn onto your side?" I suggested.

Kennrick exhaled loudly. "I'm not sure I even have a side anymore," he said ruefully. "Like you said, from here on it's pure fire control. I'd settle for calming things enough that the Filiaelians and Shorshians don't put Pellorian Medical on eternal blacklist."

"Not much of a payoff for all the time and money you've put into this thing," I sympathized.

"Hopefully, my bosses will understand," Kennrick said

grimly. "Frankly, I'm more worried about Dr. Witherspoon than I am about myself."

"Really?" I asked. "Why?"

Kennrick gave me a sideways look. "Nothing," he said. "I shouldn't even have mentioned it."

"Well, now that you have, you might as well give us the rest of it," I said.

He grimaced. "I suppose it doesn't really matter now. The fact of the matter is that Master Colix had some work done while the contract team was on Earth. Medical work."

"You mean the throat job?" I asked.

He stared at me. "You knew about that?"

"We were told he and his seatmates were chattering up a storm," I said. "What does Dr. Witherspoon have to do with it? He wasn't the surgeon, was he?"

"Good God no," Kennrick said. "But he was the one who talked Master Colix into having it at Pellorian instead of waiting until he got back home."

"Why did he do that?"

"Which he?" Kennrick asked. "Master Colix or Dr. Witherspoon?"

"Both," I said.

"Witherspoon wanted to show the contract team how competent Humans were at surgical work. Master Colix liked the idea of getting the work done for free." Kennrick grimaced. "Free. It only cost him his life."

"Those freebies will get you every time," I murmured. So Kennrick was also thinking that Colix's demise had to do with the dishonor of his Gibber Operation. Interesting. "Any of his colleagues in particular take offense at his decision?"

"None of the other three Shorshians liked it, I can tell you that," Kennrick said. "Master Bofiv, in particular, was quite vocal in his objections." He grunted. "But I suppose he doesn't qualify as a suspect anymore, does he?"

"Not unless his return ticket covers more options than the Spiders currently offer," I said.

Kennrick grunted again. "Yeah. The Spiders."

Beside me, I felt Bayta stir. This wasn't the first time that Kennrick had mentioned Spiders in a disparaging way. Bayta hadn't liked it then, either. "You have a problem with the Spiders?" I asked.

"That depends," he said. "But let's not discuss that until we have some more privacy."

"This'll do," I said, gesturing to the third-class dining car just ahead.

He frowned. "*Here?* First class has a better selection."

"First class is twenty-four cars away," I pointed out. "I'm thirsty right now."

He grimaced. "Fine."

The bar was reasonably crowded, but we were able to snag a two-person table and a spare chair. "So what exactly is your problem with the Spiders?" I asked after we'd ordered our drinks and the server had left.

Kennrick's eyes shifted to Bayta. "Actually, this particular conversation is probably more for Bayta than for you," he said. "She's the one who seems to have an in with the Spiders."

"I'm listening," Bayta said evenly.

"I want to ask them a favor." Kennrick seemed to brace himself. "I wondered if they'd be willing to accept some of the responsibility for the four deaths."

Bayta stiffened. "*What?*"

"Just as a formality," Kennrick hastened to assure her. "A

public relations thing. I just want something that'll deflect a little of the blame away from Pellorian."

"And onto the *Spiders*?"

"It's not a big deal," Kennrick insisted. "The victims' families or organizations aren't going to bring the Spiders to court or anything. I'm just trying to salvage something out of this mess."

"And why do you think the Spiders should be giving you that cover?" I asked. "What have they done to deserve taking that kind of PR hit?"

"What has Pellorian Medical done?" Kennrick retorted. "Nothing, that's what. But you can bet your pension someone's going to try to blame us anyway."

"Not if we catch the murderer first," I said.

He snorted. "If there even *is* a murderer," he growled. "As far as I can see, this whole mess can be explained by purely natural causes." He looked pointedly at Bayta. "Or rather, *unnatural* causes."

"Meaning?" I asked.

"Meaning food poisoning," he said bluntly.

"How do you explain someone poisoning their food without them noticing?" I asked.

"*I'm* not convinced anyone did," Kennrick said. "I'm thinking the cadmium was in the food to begin with."

"Quadrail food isn't contaminated," Bayta said flatly.

"Then it must have been in the air," Kennrick persisted. "Food and air are the only ways to get something into a person's system."

"Really?" Bayta said icily. "As it happens—"

"As it happens, we've already checked the food *and* the air," I interrupted, gripping Bayta's knee warningly under the table. "However the cadmium got into their systems, it wasn't because of anything the Spiders did wrong."

"Maybe, maybe not," Kennrick said. "But they can't tap-dance their way out from under liability for *Usantra* Givvrac's death. *They're* the ones who let in whatever that damn antibacterial spray was that ended up killing him."

"People carry antibacterial sprays aboard Quadrails all the time," I reminded him. "This is the first time in seven hundred years that it's caused a problem."

"Do we really know that?" he asked. "Or do we just have the Spiders' word for it?"

He looked at Bayta, clearly challenging her to respond. I gripped her knee a little harder, and she remained silent. "Right," Kennrick said, turning back to me. "So here's the deal. Either the Spiders voluntarily step up to the line and accept some of the responsibility, or I'll step them up to that line myself."

"By spreading rumors?" I asked.

"By spreading truth," he said. "Slanted a little, maybe. But truth just the same."

"You could start a panic," I warned. "With the train still over three weeks from Venidra Carvo, that would be a very bad idea."

"Like you walking around talking about murder isn't just as bad?" Kennrick countered.

"Yes, but I've got facts on my side," I pointed out. "All you've got is innuendo." I cocked an eyebrow. "*And* a fair chance of getting locked up somewhere if the Spiders decide you're scaring the passengers."

"They'd better not," Kennrick bit out. "If they even *think* about—" He broke off. "Look. I'm trying to be reasonable about this. I really am. But I'm between the rock and the grinder here, and my whole future is on the line. All I want is for the Spiders to acknowledge that they *might* maybe have a little responsibility for what's happened. Just enough to lift some of the weight off Pellorian. Come on—what can it hurt?"

"Okay, you've presented your case," I said. "Was there anything else?"

There was a flicker of something in Kennrick's eyes. Maybe he didn't like being talked to like he was my underling. "No, that's it," he said.

"Fine," I said. "We'll take your request under consideration. In the meantime, I trust you'll keep your private rumor mill shut down."

His lip twitched. "For now," he agreed. "But *only* for now. And only if there aren't more deaths."

"Fine," I said again. "Nice talking to you."

Bayta stirred as if preparing to get up. I again squeezed her knee, and she subsided. I also stayed put, and after a few seconds Kennrick got the message. "Right," he said. "See you later." He picked up his drink and strode out of the bar, heading forward toward the upper-class sections and their better selection of drinks.

I watched until he had disappeared from view. "Nice guy," I commented, letting go of Bayta's knee and taking a sip of my iced tea.

"If he thinks the Spiders are going to take any responsibility for this, he's crazy," Bayta said stiffly. "Why didn't you let me tell him about the hypo marks?"

"Partly because it wouldn't have done any good," I said. "He could claim those marks came from the medical treatments Witherspoon and Aronobal gave the Shorshians before they died."

"The doctors would say otherwise."

"They *could* say otherwise," I corrected her. "The question is, *would* they? Especially Witherspoon—don't forget that as a fellow Pellorian employee he's in the same leaky boat as Kennrick. But the more important reason not to mention the marks is that Kennrick doesn't need to know about them. Information is leverage in this game, Bayta. Never give people more of it than they need."

"Even if it means letting someone get away with murder?"

"A temporary situation only," I promised. "Patience is a virtue."

Her eyes were still burning, but she reluctantly nodded. "I know."

"Good," I said. "Meanwhile, what's happening with our mystery guest?"

She gazed off into space. "He's gone into a restroom," she said. "Three cars ahead, the car just behind the second/third dispensary."

A bad feeling began to rumble through me. "How long ago was that?" I asked.

"About ten minutes."

The bad feeling grew stronger. "Has anyone come out during that time?"

"Two Filiaelians and a Human," Bayta said, a dark edge starting to come into her voice. "Oh, no. You don't think—?"

"Yes, I think," I growled. "Can you get a mite into the ceiling over that restroom?"

"It won't help—he won't be able to get into the lighting or ventilation grilles," Bayta said tightly. "I could have a conductor go in and take a look."

"Don't bother," I said, trying not to sound as angry as I felt. Damn stupid non-initiative-taking Spiders. "If by some miracle he hasn't flown the coop, that would just tip him off. If he has, it's already too late, and having a conductor charge in there would just start all the rest of the passengers wondering."

"I suppose," Bayta said, sounding miserable. "I'm sorry, Frank. I should have told the Spiders to alert us at once if he went out of sight."

"Yes, you probably should have," I agreed, a little more sharply than I should have. "But even if they had, you could hardly have said anything. Not with Kennrick sitting right there listening."

"But I could at least have let you know something was wrong," Bayta said. "We could have made an excuse and gotten away." She grimaced. "I *did* warn them he might take off his cloak and hood and so to pay particular attention to everyone's shoes."

"And did they?"

"Yes," she said. "But they insist none of the passengers who came out were wearing the same style of shoes as our attacker."

"He was probably wearing oversilks," I said. "Very thin, very light covers you can wear over other clothing. A good quick-change artist can get them off in seconds, even faster if he's got them tear-threaded to a magician's pull. He can then either flush everything down the toilet or else drop the pull into his pocket and stroll innocently back to his seat. The cloak and hood were probably made of the same stuff."

"Sounds very neat," Bayta said sourly.

"Very neat, and very fancy," I agreed. "And it tells us something new about him."

"That he's a professional?"

"No, we knew that from the trip wire," I said. "What we know now is that he knows about our chummy connection with the Spiders."

She frowned. "We do? How?"

"Because the only reason to wear a disguise out of the baggage car is if he thought we might have a partner watching for him. But if he was assuming a *Human* partner, he should have pulled his quick-change as soon as he was out of sight inside the first vestibule."

"How is that better than changing in a restroom?"

"Because that way he could either have continued forward out of the vestibule and plopped down into the first available seat, or he could have reversed direction and headed back the way he'd come," I told her. "Either way would have given him a good look at our presumed partner, who would be hurrying after him. The restroom change, in contrast, gives a normal pursuer a chance to settle into an empty seat of his own, which makes that pursuer harder to identify when the quarry *does* emerge."

"Only he *did* change in the restroom," Bayta said slowly, tracking through the logic. "Because he knew the Spiders didn't have to actually follow him in order to keep track of him?"

"Exactly," I said. "The vestibule change is useless if your tracker has watchers on both sides of the gap who can instantly compare notes. Since comms don't work inside Quadrails, the only ones who can do such an instant comparison are Spiders."

"All right," Bayta said. "How does that help us?"

"Because it shortens the suspect list from the entire train down to seven individuals," I said. "Witherspoon, Kennrick, and Aronobal, plus by extension the three remaining Fillies and one remaining Shorshian of the contract team."

"Plus everyone in the car where we disassembled the air filter," Bayta reminded me. "They all saw us talking to the Spiders."

I shook my head. "People talk to Spiders all the time. The key here is that after I tripped over his little booby trap our friend knew we could still get a message ahead of him. That means your special relationship with the Spiders, and that means one of those seven people I mentioned."

"Along with any secret allies any of them might have," Bayta said. "You *did* say he might have an accomplice."

"I did say that, didn't I?" I admitted, grimacing. Seven suspects had been such a nice, neat, manageable number. "Still, there's a good chance the primary murderer's ally or allies will also be from our same suspect pool."

"But you can't promise that."

I snorted. "I can't even promise we'll make it to dinnertime before someone else snuffs it." I drained the last of my iced tea. "Come on. Break's over—time to get back to work."

"Where are we going?" Bayta asked as she took a last sip of her lemonade and stood up.

"It's time we got to know the rest of the suspect list," I said. "Let's go talk to some Fillies."

We found the three Fillies right where we'd left them, with their seats formed into a circle and a hand of cards dealt out in front of them. This time, though, they were actually playing. I was wondering if we dared interrupt them when one of them looked up at us. "You are Mr. Compton?" he asked.

"I am," I acknowledged. "And you?"

"*Asantra* Muzzfor," he said. "Fourth of the Maccai contract team." His eyes seemed to cloud over. "I correct: *second* of the contract team."

With the late *Usantra* Givvrac and *di*-Master Strinni having been the team's original first and second ranking members? Probably. "My condolences on your loss," I said. "May I inquire as to which is your new first?"

"I am he," one of the others spoke up, his voice dark and unfriendly. "*Esantra* Worrbin."

"I greet you, *Esantra* Worrbin," I said. I shifted my eyes to the third Filly. "And you must therefore be *Asantra* Dallilo."

"I am," Dallilo said.

"Do you wish something of us?" Worrbin asked in that same unfriendly tone.

"A moment of your time only," I assured him.

Worrbin tilted his head. "We are otherwise occupied," he said.

"I would speak with him," Muzzfor said, setting down his cards. "Perhaps he has further information on *Usantra* Givvrac's death." He rose to his feet. "If you would accompany me to the dining car, Mr. Compton?"

"Reseat yourself, *Asantra* Muzzfor," *Esantra* Worrbin growled, leaning a little on the *asantra* part as if to remind Muzzfor of his lower status in the group. "Very well, Mr. Compton. You may speak." He cocked his head in challenge. "Concisely."

"Of course," I said, letting my gaze drift across them as I took a moment to organize my thoughts. Like many upper-class Fillies, especially those of the *santra* classes, these three showed the subtle and not-so-subtle differences spawned by their species' penchant for genetic manipulation. Muzzfor in particular seemed to have been the recipient of a number of treatments, sporting an odd-shaped nose blaze, an interesting speckled eye coloration, and the kind of extra-large throat Filly high-opera singers often got to extend their vocal range. Dallilo's customized body had extra-thick hair, flatter ears, and a two-tone blaze that shaded a dark brown into a lighter tan.

Esantra Worrbin, in contrast, seemed to have skipped all external improvements except the long, slender fingers prized by the artist and surgeon classes. Judging from the extra-large glass of the god-awful Filly drink *dilivin* resting in his seat's cup holder, I guessed he'd also opted for a strengthened digestive system. Given Givvrac's fate, that might turn out to have been an especially wise use of his money.

"You of course know about the tragic deaths of *Usantra* Givvrac and three of the Shorshians on your contract team," I said. "My question for you is simple and twofold. First, do any of you know any reason, professional or personal, why anyone would wish any of those four people dead? And second, do you know any reason how anyone would profit, financially or in terms of honor, from any of their deaths?"

"Well and concisely stated," Worrbin said with somewhat grudging approval. "It appears Humans can be efficient, after all."

"We're individuals, just as are the members of the Filiaelian Assembly," I reminded him.

He snorted, his eyes pointedly flicking back and forth between Bayta and me. "With such minor genetic variants? You don't even approach *asantra* class."

"That's all right," I assured him. "We like ourselves just the way we are."

"Then why does Pellorian Medical seek Filiaelian genetic manipulation equipment?" Dallilo put in. "If you don't seek to improve yourselves, what *do* you seek?"

"You'd have to ask Mr. Kennrick or Dr. Witherspoon about that," I told him, ducking a question that I sensed could only get me into trouble. "I know too little about the contract to either support or oppose it. I seek merely to find the murderer and bring him to justice."

"Then look to Mr. Kennrick," Worrbin said. "If there was indeed murder, I have no doubt he is the one you seek."

"Nonsense," Muzzfor put in before I could respond. "Mr. Kennrick is a fine Human."

"Nonsense doubled and returned," Worrbin retorted. "I am convinced he seeks to destroy the contract from within for his own ends. That leaves him alone with a motivation for murder."

"That's very interesting," I said. "What are these private ends you speak of?"

"How would I know?" Worrbin retorted. "He is a Human, with motivations beyond the understanding of civilized beings."

"Then what makes you think he's trying to sabotage the contract?"

"Because he displays incompetence at every turn," Worrbin said with a contemptuous sniff. "He deliberately ignores the finer points of dealing with superior peoples."

"His slights are not deliberate," Muzzfor insisted. "He is merely ignorant of proper procedure."

"And yet you stand ready to defend him?" Worrbin challenged.

"Competent or not, he *is* only a Human." Muzzfor looked sideways at me. "No offense to you personally, Mr. Compton."

"No offense taken," I assured him. First we'd had Master Tririn back in third class, whose profession of surprise at my understanding of alien ways had carried an implied dig at Kennrick, and now we had *Esantra* Worrbin singing the same tune. Either Kennrick had an outstanding knack of rubbing people the wrong way, or he really *wasn't* very good at his job.

Which brought up a possibility I hadn't thought of before. "Do any of you happen to know whose idea it was for Mr. Kennrick to represent Pellorian Medical to the contract team?" I asked the Fillies.

"That is hardly information we would have been given," Worrbin pointed out.

"True," I said. "But there was a chance you might have been so informed."

"Then you agree with *Esantra* Worrbin?" Dallilo put in. "That Mr. Kennrick or someone in league with him seeks to destroy the contract?"

"It's a possibility that can't be ignored," I said. "Especially given that three of the four deceased were in favor of the contract."

"Mr. Kennrick would never be a party to such a conspiracy," Muzzfor said firmly. "I know and understand this Human. He truly seeks only what is best for his corporation."

"Yet he could be involved without his knowledge," I pointed out. "Perhaps someone put him into this situation knowing he wasn't properly equipped to handle it, in hopes that his bumbling would ruin the contract as *Esantra* Worrbin suggests. In such a case, Mr. Kennrick could be perfectly sincere about doing his best, yet nevertheless still be helping to bring down the contract."

"And when his fumblings failed to turn all members against the contract, the evil one turned to murder?" Dallilo suggested thoughtfully.

"Then the murderer must be Dr. Witherspoon," Muzzfor jumped in. "He's the only other Pellorian representative aboard."

"Or at least he's the only Pellorian representative that we know of," I said, my mind flashing to the spare first-class pass floating loose aboard our train. "Do any of you have any idea why someone would wish to sabotage the contract?"

"An irrelevant question," Worrbin said. "The contract is dead. As dead as *Usantra* Givvrac himself."

The other two Fillies stirred uncomfortably in their seats. It *was* a rather offensive comment. "As I said, I know too little about the contract to comment one way or the other," I said diplomatically, skipping over Kennrick's earlier claim that none of the team had the authority to make such a pronouncement.

"Yes, I'm quite certain of that," Worrbin said loftily. "Have you any further questions?"

It was obvious he was fully expecting the answer to be no. "You still haven't answered my first one," I said. "Do any of you know of a reason why someone would want *Usantra* Givvrac and the others dead?"

"No," Worrbin said shortly. "In that I speak for all."

I looked at Muzzfor and Dallilo. But if they had dissenting opinions, they were keeping them to themselves. "Then I have only one further question," I said. "*Esantra* Worrbin, if we checked with the Spider at the dispensary, would the number of your visits correspond to the number of hypos used?"

"Yes," Worrbin said without hesitation.

"You're certain of that?"

"I brought twenty aboard," he said stiffly. "I have visited the dispensary seven times this journey. You may confirm for yourself that there are thirteen remaining." His eyes bored into mine. "As I'm certain you already have."

I inclined my head to him. "Then we'll take our leave of you," I said. "Thank you for your time. And yours," I added, nodding to the other two.

We left them to their cards and headed forward. "What do you think?" I asked Bayta as we stepped into the vestibule.

"*Esantra* Worrbin doesn't seem to like Mr. Kennrick very much," Bayta said. "But I find it hard to believe someone in Pellorian Medical would deliberately try to sabotage his own contract."

"I've seen political moves that were equally crazy," I told her. "But usually when there's someone trying to pull down the barn, the rest of the power structure learns about it quickly enough to counter the maverick's moves. I suppose this could be an especially clever maverick, though."

"Do you think we should tell Mr. Kennrick about *Esantra* Worrbin's animosity?" Bayta asked, lowering her voice as we emerged from the vestibule into the next car.

"I would guess Mr. Kennrick is fully aware of *Esantra* Worrbin's opinion of him," I said. "Still, I suppose it's only fair to get his side of the story. Let's wander up to his compartment and see what kind of reaction we get out of him."

FOURTEEN :

Kennrick's reaction was pretty much what I'd expected.

"Ridiculous," he snapped. "Which one of them made a boneheaded suggestion like that?"

"I don't think we need to name names," I said, giving his compartment a quick glance. It was about what I'd expected given the occupant: neat and tidy, no messes, no surprises. A few hangers' worth of clothing hung together in the clothes rack/sonic cleaner, a reader sat on the computer desk, and the luggage rack held the three bags I'd seen him board with at Homshil Station. "Incidentally, if *bonehead* is your typical characterization of non-Humans, I can see why you don't get along very well with them."

"Don't start, Compton," he warned, glaring at me. "I'm not in the mood. You have *no* idea what I've been through with these people."

"I'm sure it's been difficult," I said, again cranking up my diplomacy level. "Still, at least one of the team is solidly on your side."

"*Asantra* Muzzfor," Kennrick said, nodding. "Yes, he's been the one bright spot in all this."

"He'd certainly make a good sidekick, if you're ever in the market for one," I said. "So how exactly *did* you get hired?"

He shrugged. "The usual way. A matcher put my résumé with an opening at Pellorian, and next thing I knew I was on the payroll."

"Any idea why you were chosen for this particular job?"

"Obviously, my legal background," he said. "I was at Shotoko Associates, remember, and we were heavily into Filiaelian and Shorshic contract law."

"I suppose that makes sense," I said. "Strange that Pellorian didn't also send along an expert on Filly and Shorshic cultures."

"Not when you consider the price of Quadrail tickets," Kennrick said. "But you see now what I was talking about earlier. These people are bound and determined to dump this whole mess squarely on Pellorian's shoulders. That's why I want—that's why I *need*—the Spiders to take a little of the heat."

"No."

The word was so flat, so cold, and so unexpected that it took me a second to realize it had come from Bayta. Apparently, it hit Kennrick that way, too. "What did you say?" he asked.

"I said no," she repeated. "The Spiders aren't to blame for any of this, and they're not going to take any of the responsibility. *Any* of it."

I looked at Bayta, then at Kennrick, then back at Bayta. Suddenly, my quiet, emotionless, self-effacing assistant had caught fire. A slow fire, maybe, volcano rather than cooking-surface deep. But it was fire nonetheless.

And it wasn't hard to figure out why. There was a murderer running loose on the Quadrail—*her* Quadrail—defying not only us but the Spiders who had made these trains the safest mode of transportation in the history of the galaxy. Kennrick was pushing for Spider admission of responsibility, and if he was thinking such things it was a safe bet other passengers were thinking them, too.

And anything that reflected badly on the Spiders also reflected badly on their Chahwyn masters, including the Chahwyn bonded to Bayta within her own body.

For Bayta, this had become personal.

"Fine," Kennrick said. "Whatever. I just thought—never mind. Fine."

"Then let's hear no more about it," Bayta said darkly, the fire in her eyes slowly fading into watchful embers. "Have you anything else to add about your appointment to this job?"

"No, I think that's been covered," Kennrick said. He was still trying to be contrary, but his heart didn't seem to be in it anymore.

"Then I believe we're finished here," Bayta said, her tone stiffly formal. She looked at me, and I could tell she was belatedly remembering that I was supposed to be the one in charge.

But I wasn't about to undercut her. Not after that performance. "Thanks for your time," I said to Kennrick as I took a step backward toward the door.

And as I did so, my eyes drifted again to the clothing hung neatly on the sonic rack. The clothing, and the considerably larger capacity of the three bags sitting on the luggage rack. "We may have more questions later, though," I added.

"Feel free," he said sarcastically. "My door's always open."

We left, Kennrick closing and undoubtedly locking his door behind us. "Where to now?" Bayta asked.

"Dining car," I told her. "I'm hungry. Did you happen to notice the clothing hanging on Kennrick's rack?"

"Not really," she said, her voice suddenly hesitant. "Frank—"

"Interesting thing is that there wasn't much of it," I said. "Not nearly enough to fill all three of those carrybags."

"Maybe the rest of his clothing is in the drawers," Bayta suggested.

"I doubt it," I said. "I've seen what sort of outfits he typically wears, and I'm guessing the drawers are no more than half full. But even if they were loaded to the gills, he should still be able to cram everything into the two larger bags." I cocked an eyebrow. "Which leads to the intriguing question of what he's got in the third one."

"You have a theory?"

"Of course," I said. I might be rotten at solving actual murders, but theories I had by the truckload. "Remember when we asked Kennrick why the contract-team Fillies had come aboard our compartment car even though they had regular coach seats?"

"He said they had documents they wanted to store in his compartment."

"And since at least some of those documents might have concerned the Pellorian contract, I'm guessing they wouldn't want Kennrick snooping through them any more than they would want random citizens doing so," I said. "Which suggests that one of Kennrick's bags may in fact be a portable lockbox."

"How does that explain why they came aboard in our car?" Bayta asked. "Shouldn't the documents have already been inside the lockbox?"

"They should indeed," I agreed. "The only logical explanation is that the Fillies came aboard with Kennrick because he couldn't heft the thing up onto the luggage rack by himself. Which immediately implies that it's not just a simple lockable file case, but a genuine monster of a metal or layered-ceramic safe."

"Kennrick could have asked a conductor to help."

"And yet he didn't," I said. "He didn't put the papers into a standard Spider lockbox, either. That tells me Kennrick and the papers' owners didn't want the Spiders knowing what they've got, or having access to them."

"Considering Mr. Kennrick's attitude toward the Spiders, I'm not really surprised," Bayta said stiffly. "Where does that leave us?"

"I'm not sure," I said. "But if there's something in Kennrick's safe that somebody wants, and if *Usantra* Givvrac was the one carrying the key—" I shrugged. "We might have yet another possible motive for our murders. Like we needed one."

"Yes." Bayta wrinkled her nose. "Are all murder cases this messy?"

"Hardly ever, actually," I said. "We're just lucky."

"I suppose." She hesitated. "Frank . . . about the way I talked to Mr. Kennrick back there. I'm sorry if I was out of place."

"You weren't out of place, and I'm not sorry at all that you slapped him down," I assured her. "The whole idea of trying to pin any part of this on the Spiders is ridiculous. It was about time he heard that in a format he could understand."

We reached the dining car and went in. "I suggest you eat well," I advised Bayta as we seated ourselves at one of the tables. "I have a feeling we're in for another long night."

"You think someone else is going to be murdered?"

"Our killer didn't clobber Witherspoon and me and take that hypo just for the exercise," I reminded her grimly. "One way or another, he's going to use it."

We had our dinner, discussed the case without making any discernible headway, and retired to our compartments for the night. I hit the sack immediately, hoping to get at least a couple of hours of sleep before the inevitable alarm sounded.

Only the inevitable alarm never came.

I hardly believed it when I woke up eight hours later and realized that my rest hadn't been interrupted by emergency calls from doctors, Spiders, or dying passengers. I checked with Bayta, confirmed that the Spiders hadn't spotted any problems during the night, and grabbed a quick shower before taking her back to the dining car for breakfast.

The car's acoustics prevented me from eavesdropping on my fellow passengers as we ate, but there was nothing to interfere with my eyesight. If there was any fresh tension out there, I couldn't read it in anyone's face. On the contrary, it was as if the rest of the travelers had also noted the passage of a quiet night, and were equally relieved by it.

After breakfast Bayta and I set off on a leisurely tour of the train. The three remaining contract team Fillies were back at their card game, giving the impression they'd never left it. Possibly they hadn't. *Asantra* Muzzfor, the sole team member still on Pellorian Medical's side, nodded gravely as we passed. *Esantra* Worrbin and *Asantra* Dallilo, in contrast, ignored us completely. Three cars beyond them, *Osantra* Qiddicoj also nodded in greeting as we passed. He was still a little pale after his brush with gastrointestinal death, but was definitely on the mend. A small victory, I noted cynically, floating bravely along amid a sea of defeats.

We passed through second class, where we didn't know anyone, and reached third. *Logra* Emikai, the white-knight Filly who'd come to Terese German's aid a couple of days ago, was ensconced in the bar, where I'd noticed he seemed to spend a lot of his time. He spotted us about the same time as I spotted him, and I could see his eyes following us as we passed by. Possibly he was thinking about his offer of a bribe for inside information on my air filter analysis and wondering if he should follow through on that. But I made a point of not slowing as we passed the bar, and he apparently thought better of it and returned to his half-finished drink.

Three cars farther back we passed Emikai's damsel in distress herself, who ignored us as usual. Terese's Jurian seatmate, *Tas* Krodo, had his hawk beak buried in his reader, while two rows back Master Tririn was again staring moodily at the display window beside him. Still in private mourning for his late contract-team companions, I guessed, or else quietly plotting his next victim's death. I didn't spot either Dr. Witherspoon or Dr. Aronobal during our journey, but with the dining and entertainment cars up and running, there were a lot of passengers away from their seats.

And with our casual tour of suspect and acquaintance completed, we slipped back into the baggage cars for another look at the victims.

"Why exactly are we here?" Bayta asked as I started undoing Master Colix's mummy wrappings.

"Trying to find something we might have missed," I told her.

"Like what?"

"I have no idea." I finished unwrapping Colix, this time going all the way down to his waist, and set off on a careful, square-centimeter-by-square-centimeter search of the body.

And in the end, after half an hour, I found nothing.

"Two hypo marks, exactly," I reported, wincing as I straightened my back out of the crouch it had been in for most of the examination. "The killer's, and the one Dr. Aronobal made while he and Witherspoon were trying to save his life."

"Are you sure?" Bayta asked.

I looked down at the body. "Did you see something I missed?"

"No, I meant are you sure they were trying to save his life," Bayta corrected. She was gazing at the hypo mark in Colix's arm, an intense look on her face.

"Meaning?"

"I was just thinking," she said slowly. "After Master Colix died, Mr. Kennrick suggested that neither Dr. Aronobal nor Dr. Witherspoon actually knew what was in the vials they were using."

"I assumed the Spider read the labels for them."

"Actually, the way it works is that the doctor asks for the drug he or she wants and the server pulls those ampoules from the cabinet," Bayta said. "But what if Dr. Witherspoon had another drug with him that he added to the hypo when no one was looking?"

I scratched my cheek and tried to pull up the memory of the scene as Bayta and I had come charging in. It would have been tricky, but not impossible, particularly if Witherspoon picked his moment carefully.

Witherspoon *or* Aronobal. Now that I thought about it, I realized I hadn't actually seen that injection take place, mainly because Kennrick had popped his face into and out of the dispensary and I'd gone charging off after him. "Did you see Aronobal give Colix the injection?" I asked Bayta.

"I saw her remove the needle from Master Colix's arm," she said. "But not the actual injection."

"Because you were watching me take off after Kennrick," I said thoughtfully. "Interesting timing."

"It could just be coincidence."

"True," I agreed. "Especially since we know that Colix was showing symptoms long before the doctors started working on him." I frowned at Colix's body. "But there *is* something else here, Bayta. Something significant. I just can't put my finger on it."

"Maybe when we reach Venidra Carvo and can have a proper autopsy done," Bayta suggested.

"If it's even still there," I growled. "I'm sure the Spiders did their best, but after three-plus weeks of less-than-perfect preservation some of the more subtle evidence will almost certainly be gone."

Bayta sighed. "And even if it hasn't, the killer himself will be long gone by then."

"With probably a new identity and maybe even a new face to go with it," I agreed. "Possibly new DNA, too. We *are* headed for Filly space, after all, land of the lunatic gene-manipulators."

"We'll get him," Bayta said firmly, an edge of fire creeping back into her eyes. "And then we'll prove—to *everyone*—that the Spiders had nothing to do with it."

"Absolutely," I said, wishing I believed that. The farther we got into the mess, the more elusive proof of any sort seemed to be. "Well, nothing more for us here," I added, starting to re-wrap Colix's body. "Give me a hand, will you?"

The next few days passed quietly. No one else even got sick, let alone died, and life aboard the train settled back a bit gingerly into its normal low-key routine.

We reached the three-week midway point without incident and passed on to the back half of our journey. Bayta told me the next morning that Kennrick and Tririn had gone ahead and held their halfway-celebration meal, the one Kennrick had been discussing with Colix the night of the first two deaths.

Under the circumstances, I suspected the event was somewhat more subdued than originally planned.

I spent most of those days in my compartment, coming out only for meals, exercise, and occasional flybys of my primary suspects. Most of the compartment time was devoted to reexamination of the spectroscopic data I'd taken from the air filters and the bodies. But it was all just wheels spinning in mud. If there was anything in there aside from the bald fact of the cadmium poisoning, I reluctantly concluded, it would take someone better trained than me to spot it. All I could do now was wait for the other shoe to drop.

Two nights after the journey's midpoint, it finally did.

I had just taken off my shoes in preparation for bedtime when the divider opened and Bayta hurried into my compartment. "The Spiders say Dr. Aronobal is calling for you," she said tautly.

"What's the problem?" I asked, grabbing my shoes and starting to put them on again.

"They don't know," she said. "They just say she needs to see you right away. She's in the second/third dispensary, staring at the medications in the drug cabinet."

"Maybe she's thought of something relating to the murders," I suggested, finishing with my shoes and standing up. "I'll be back soon. Feel free to eavesdrop via the dispensary's server."

"What are you talking about?" she asked, frowning as she started for the door. "I'm coming with you."

"No, you're staying here," I corrected, getting to the door first. "Aronobal asked for *me*, remember?"

Her face had gone very still. "You think it's a trap, don't you?"

That was, in fact, exactly what I was thinking. "I just think she might feel more comfortable talking to me alone," I lied.

I reached for the door control, paused, and instead dug into my pocket. "Here," I said, handing Bayta the *kwi*. "This won't do me any good out there."

She took it, her eyes going even darker. "Frank—"

"Besides, if there's a problem and I have to fight, I'd rather you be here and not right in the middle of things where I have to worry about you," I cut her off. "I'll be back soon."

I escaped into the corridor before she could come up with a suitable retort.

The corridors of the compartment cars were deserted, most of the other passengers probably having turned in for the night. The first-class coach car just beyond had the same settled feel about it, though there were still a few reading lights showing.

I went past the dining car and its usual contingent of late-night diners and drinkers, then trekked through the storage, shower, and exercise/dispensary cars into the next coach car. I walked through it and into the first-class entertainment car, where reflected flickers of light showed that a few viewers were still finishing up their dit rec dramas and comedies, and entered the next coach car. One more, and I would finally be finished with first class.

After which would come the long walk through second class and then finally to third. After all this, I told myself darkly, Aronobal had better have either one hell of a significant breakthrough to offer, or else have one hell of an innovative ambush to spring.

I was nearly to the end of the last first-class coach when I heard a quiet voice call my name.

I looked around. The only passenger anywhere nearby who should even know my name was *Osantra* Qiddicoj. He was slumped in his seat, his eyes closed, apparently sound asleep.

And then, as I watched, his eyes opened. "Go back," he said, his voice soft and raspy.

I felt a sudden tightness in my chest. Qiddicoj's open eyes were slightly unfocused, his long jaw slackened, and even in the dim light of the compartment I could see his rose-colored nose blaze had gone a little darker.

Which meant that it wasn't Qiddicoj who was speaking to me.

I took a deep breath. For the past three weeks I'd been wondering whether the Modhri had a presence aboard our train. Occasionally, way back in the back of my mind, I'd also wondered if he might have something to do with our rash of mysterious murders.

Now, at least the first of those two questions had been answered. "Hello, Modhri," I said. "I've been wondering when you would pop up."

"Go back, Compton," the Modhri said again. "He's in your compartment car."

"Who is?" I asked. "What are you talking about?"

"He was hiding in one of the shower stalls," Qiddicoj's voice rasped, a sense of urgency creeping into his voice. "He waited until you'd passed, then moved forward. He has a device with which he hopes to gain access to your compartment."

The tightness in my chest went a little tighter. The double compartment, where I'd left Bayta waiting all alone. "Who is he?" I demanded. "What does he look like?"

"I don't know," the Modhri said. "He's wearing a hooded robe that obscures his features and his build."

So our baggage car intruder hadn't flushed his disguise down the toilet after all. The thrifty type. "What does he want?" I asked.

"How should I know?" the Modhri retorted. "Perhaps the deaths of us all. Do you wish to stop him, or not?"

I cursed under my breath. If this was a trick to get me to miss my appointment with Aronobal, the doctor could likely be facing some death of her own.

But Aronobal wasn't my responsibility, and on a personal level I didn't really care what happened to her. Bayta was, and I did. "You have any walkers up there?" I asked.

"I have an Eye in the bar and one in the first coach car," the Modhri said. "That's how I saw the intruder making his way forward."

There were a dozen other questions I needed to ask, starting with how this intruder thought he could get though a Spider-designed lock and ending with why the Modhri was giving me this warning in the first place. But those questions could wait. "Let me know if he starts back or goes to ground somewhere," I said.

I was ten cars back from our compartment car. I retraced the first nine cars' worth of steps at a dead run, slowing to a quieter and more energy-conserving jog for the last one. A well-dressed Juri in that first coach car watched me as I came through, his eyes bright and preternaturally aware. Almost certainly he was the walker the Modhri had mentioned, and I raised my eyebrows in silent question as I passed him. He gestured toward the car ahead in silent response. I nodded, and slipped through the door into the vestibule.

I crossed the vestibule, taking in huge lungfuls of air as I did so to try to restore my blood oxygen level after my mini-marathon run. I got to the front and reached for the door control.

And paused, my memory flicking back to the trip wire the intruder had left for me in the baggage car. This guy was a professional, and professionals didn't set themselves up for key jobs in the middle of exposed corridors without taking precautions against unexpected company.

Which meant there was probably a booby trap waiting on the other side of the door.

It wouldn't be a trip wire. That was fairly certain. I was the unexpected company he would be most worried about, and he would assume I wouldn't fall for the same trick twice.

On the other hand, given the lengths he'd already gone to in order to keep anyone from seeing who he was . . .

It was a gamble, but I had no time to think it through any further. Squeezing my eyes tightly shut and holding my breath, I hit the door release.

And as I charged through, a burst of cold air threw a choking cloud of dust squarely into my face.

I bellowed with feigned surprise, the sharp exhalation serving to blow the powder away from my nose and mouth. A simple talcum powder, I gathered from the taste. Simultaneously, I threw up my left forearm over my face, hopefully hiding the fact that my closed eyelids had protected me from the blinding effects of the powder. I staggered a couple of steps forward, feeling wildly around with my right hand as I watched the floor in front of me beneath the concealment of my left arm.

He fell for it like an egg from a tall chicken. Three seconds later a pair of feet entered my truncated field of view as he hurried toward me, clearly intent on putting me down for the count.

Instantly, I shifted my hands and body into fighting stance. I caught a glimpse of a billowing cloak and a dark-filled hood, then caught one of his outstretched arms at the wrist, levered it at the elbow, and turned his forward motion into a backward arc to slam his back hard onto the corridor floor.

With the average opponent, that would have ended the fight right there. But this one was tougher than average. Even as his shoulders hit the floor he was twisting his torso around, swinging one leg in a horizontal sweep straight at my ankles.

I managed to get one leg out of his way, but I didn't have the time or the balance to get the other one clear, too. His leg caught me just above the ankle, and I toppled over, the move forcing me to let go of his wrist so that I could use both hands to break my fall. Luckily, he was similarly unable to get his sweeping leg completely out of my way, and I landed partially on top of it, hampering his effort to regain his feet.

We made it back to vertical at about the same time, with me making sure I ended up standing between him and the door to the rear of the train. "Had enough?" I asked, still panting a little.

The intruder didn't reply. His hood, which I could see now had been wired to stay firmly in place around his head, had nevertheless slipped enough during the tussle to reveal the tip of a Filly nose. "I didn't think so," I went on. "You know, you're taking this contract thing way too seriousl—"

Without warning, he leaped forward, his hands grabbing my left shoulder and shoving sideways in an attempt to push me far enough out of the way for him to get past. I was ready for something like that, and responded by grabbing one of the arms and trying a repeat of my earlier aikido move.

Unfortunately, this time he was waiting for it. He spun around on one foot as I made my grab, the movement twisting my arm instead of his and breaking my grip. With his escape path now open, he made a break for the door.

He got exactly one and a half steps before I slammed a kick hard into the back of his leg, once again sending him sprawling.

I leaped for him, hoping to pin him down long enough to

get a wrist lock on him. But he was too quick. He bounced up off the floor and spun around, and as I grabbed his left wrist he gave me a shove with his free hand that threatened to break my hold and send me to the floor in my turn.

But I wasn't giving up, either. I hung on grimly, overbalancing him and bringing him tumbling after me. With the alternative being to let him land on me full-weight, I brought my left leg up and planted it into his lower torso. As I hit the floor I straightened my leg, executing a stomach toss of the sort so beloved of early dit rec thrillers and so nearly impossible to pull off in the real world.

Apparently, my opponent had never heard of this one. The toss actually worked, and he went sailing over my head to once again slam onto his back on the floor. Rather surprised myself at the move's success, I nevertheless had the presence of mind to execute the proper follow-through, using the momentum of my backward roll to somersault over him into a position where I would be sitting on his chest with my knees pinning down his upper arms.

Then again, maybe he *had* heard of this one. I was still in mid-somersault when he rolled over onto his side, giving a hard sideways yank to the hand I still had on his wrist. Pulled off my planned trajectory, I landed off balance. He twisted my wrist as I hit the floor, breaking what was left of my grip. I grabbed for the arm again, missed, and he bounded to his feet, heading for the rear of the car. Still off-balance, I threw myself at his feet, and by sheer luck got one hand on his ankle. He stumbled, nearly fell, and half turned. As I tried to get a grip with my other hand, out of the corner of my eye I saw his arm windmill as if he was throwing something at me.

An instant later, a patch of something black slapped across my face.

I inhaled sharply from the sheer surprise of it. That was a mistake. The stuff was some kind of clingcloth, of the kind sported by teenaged show-offs, and inhaling against the thing merely sucked the last bit of remaining air from beneath it and plastered it that much tighter against my skin. I tried exhaling, but I didn't have enough air to do more than temporarily puff out the middle of the cloth.

And with that move I was now completely out of air. I let go of the intruder's ankle, scrabbling with both hands to try to get a grip on the edges of my new blindfold. Clingcloth was legally required to be porous enough to breathe through, but my current oxygen needs were far greater than any level the regulators had anticipated. If I didn't get the damn stuff off, and fast, I was probably going to pass out.

Someone grabbed my arm. I shrugged violently against the hand, my fingernails still trying to locate the edges of the cling-cloth. "Hold still," Kennrick's voice came in my ear. The grip on my arm vanished, and I felt another set of fingers pulling at the edges of my face. "Mm!" I grunted, jabbing a finger down the corridor. I could get the clingcloth off by myself—what I needed Kennrick to do was get to my assailant before he could escape from the car and melt back into the Quadrail's general populace.

Only with my mouth covered, I couldn't say that. "*Mm!*" I tried again.

"Relax, it's covered," he said. His fingernails worked their way under the cloth and pulled it away from my face.

I blinked, gasping for breath as I looked around. On both sides, compartment doors were beginning to open as other passengers looked to see what all the noise and commotion was about. Between me and the far end of the car I could see that Bayta had also emerged from her compartment. She was facing away from me, but as I refilled my lungs I saw she was backing toward where Kennrick and I still huddled on the floor. She glanced behind her to double-check my position, then veered a little to her left and dropped down on one knee beside me.

And as she moved out of my line of sight, I saw that my assailant had not, in fact, escaped. He was lying in the middle of the corridor, his hooded cloak flapping like a wounded bird as he writhed in agony.

"You all right?" Bayta asked anxiously, her eyes flicking to me and then back to the thrashing Filly. Gripped in her hand, I saw, was the *kwi* I'd left with her.

"I'm fine," I assured her, still breathing hard. "Nice work."

"And then some," Kennrick put in, his voice sounding stunned. "Special relationship with the Spiders, huh?"

I focused on him, to discover that he was gazing at the *kwi*. Terrific. "Nothing special about it," I said, putting an edge on my tone, acutely aware of all the other eyes and ears gathered around us. "She got in a good gut punch, that's all."

Kennrick tore his gaze from the *kwi* and locked eyes with me. A flicker of something went across his face— "Ah," he said. "Right."

I held his eyes a moment longer, just to make sure he'd gotten the entire message, then looked back at the Filly. "Want to make any bets as to which of your three Filly friends is inside that hood?" I asked as I levered myself back to my feet. "My guess is that it's *Esantra* Worrbin."

"No bet," Kennrick said grimly. "Let's find out."

We headed down the corridor, and I noticed in passing that there was a small gray box lying on the floor beside my compartment door. I reached the Filly and leaned over him. "You going to cooperate?" I asked politely. "Or do we need to make sure you'll hold still?"

The Filly didn't answer. But he was clearly in no position to give any serious resistance. Straddling his torso, I slipped my hands inside his hood, found and disengaged the stiffening wires that had held it in place, and threw it back.

It was a Filly, all right. But it wasn't any of the contract-team members, as I'd assumed. It was, instead, *Logra* Emikai: barstool warmer, protector of Human maidens in distress, and attempted briber of Spider agents.

"Huh," Kennrick grunted from my side. "I guess I *should* have taken that bet."

"Hilarious," I growled, grabbing one of Emikai's arms. "Come on—help me get him into my compartment. He has some explaining to do."

FIFTEEN :

Emikai was pretty heavy, and his legs still weren't functioning all that well. But between Kennrick, Bayta, and me we got him into my compartment and seated more or less comfortably on the curve couch. Our next task was to remove his cloak and search for any other goodies or semi-weapons he might have on him. We confiscated another patch of clingcloth, a squeeze bulb filled with talcum powder like the booby trap he'd set up on the vestibule door, and, for good measure, the extra unlimited first-class pass that we'd known was wandering loose on our train.

We also confiscated the gadget he'd left lying by my door.

"So what now?" Kennrick asked when we'd finished our frisking.

"We start by calling in a couple of Spiders," I said. "Bayta, I need a conductor and two mites. Have them wait out in the corridor until I need them."

She nodded, her eyes unfocusing as she sent the message.

I watched Emikai closely during the silent communication,

searching for signs of surprise or interest. But there was neither. Clearly, he already knew all about Bayta's special relationship with the Spiders.

"They'll be here in a few minutes," Bayta reported.

"Thank you," I said. "So, *Logra* Emikai. How are you feeling?"

"I have been worse," he said stiffly.

"I'm sure you have," I said, looking him over. His convulsions had mostly ceased, but he was still twitching occasionally from the aftereffects of the *kwi*. I wondered which of the three pain settings Bayta had used, but I wasn't about to ask that question with Kennrick standing there listening. He knew way too much already. "I suppose we should first offer you the easy way. Would you care to make a statement as to what the hell you've been up to lately?"

For a moment Emikai gazed at me, possibly trying to decide which lie would be the most believable. "Several days ago I asked you for information about the air filter analysis you claimed you would be performing," he said. "You never returned with that information."

"So you thought you'd stop by and help yourself to the data?"

"I stopped by merely to inquire on your progress," he corrected.

"Of course," I said. "You must have forgotten that I'd already told you that if there was anything relevant the Spiders would inform everyone at the same time."

"Perhaps," he said. His eyes drifted around the room, pausing on the two carrybags sitting together on their rack above my bed. "But perhaps they fear to reveal the truth."

"Has anyone else dropped dead?" I asked, watching his eyes. He was definitely interested in my carrybags. Probably wondering which of them held my alleged spectroscopic analyzer. "Has anyone else even gotten sick?"

"Not to my knowledge," he admitted, shifting his gaze back to me. "But the two Shorshians were in equally good health for over two weeks before their sudden deaths."

"Why are you even interested about the air in that car?" Kennrick asked. "I spent a fair amount of time back there with my associates, and I never once saw you put in an appearance. Is that even your car?"

"Should not one be concerned about the welfare of others?" Emikai countered. "Especially if one has the ability to guard that welfare?" He looked back at me. "Or claims to have that ability."

"Are you suggesting I don't actually have the spectroscopic analysis equipment Dr. Aronobal told you about?" I asked mildly.

His nose blaze lightened noticeably in reaction at Aronobal's name. More aftereffects of the *kwi*—normally he probably would have tried to suppress such a giveaway. "The Filiaelian physician?" he hedged. "I have not spoken to her about any such equipment."

"Oh, please," I scoffed. "It's painfully obvious that Aronobal's midnight call just now was to get me out of the way so you could use your little first-class pass to come up here and burgle my room." I gestured to the carrybags. "By the way, if you were hoping for a look at my analysis equipment, forget it. It's not actually here at the moment."

Again, his nose blaze lightened briefly. He'd been scoping out my bags, all right. "That may be," he said, an edge of challenge in his voice. "In my view, until I have evidence of its existence, I also have no belief."

"Wait a second," Kennrick said, looking back and forth

between Emikai and me. "Wait just a damn second. This guy has a *first-class pass*? I thought he was riding in third."

"He is," I confirmed. "Apparently, he likes slumming."

"Why, you son of a—" He jabbed a finger at the Filly. "It's him. It has to be. *He's* the one who's been killing off our contract team."

"I have harmed no one," Emikai insisted, his blaze lightening again in reaction. "I give you my word."

"Like your word means camel spit," Kennrick snarled, taking a step toward him. "Compton, this is the guy. It all fits."

"Calm down," I soothed, putting a restraining hand on his arm. "We're a long way yet from accusing him of mass murder."

"Are we?" Kennrick countered. "Who else had access to both third *and* first?"

"Well, for starters, everyone in first," I reminded him.

He stopped in mid-tirade, his lip twisting. "Oh. Yes, I suppose . . ." He trailed off.

"But attempted breaking and entering is another story," I went on, hefting the flat gray box we'd found outside my door. On the outside, it looked like a standard bypass mimic, the sort used by locksmiths when people lock themselves out of their apartments or cars. But I was betting its guts were considerably more sophisticated than that. "You have a license for this, I assume?"

"That device is not mine," Emikai insisted. "I never saw it before."

"Of course not," I said. "And you attacked me why?"

"I did not attack you," he said. "I saw something on the door explode into a white powder in front of you, and I was coming to offer my aid."

"You mean this kind of white powder?" I asked, holding up the squeeze bulb.

"I do not know what kind of powder it was," Emikai said, an edge of wounded indignation in his tone. "My powder is for relief of a painful rash from which I suffer."

"Ah," I said, nodding. With the effects of the *kwi* wearing off, he was proving himself a decent actor and liar both. I would have expected nothing less from the professional who'd snookered me into that trip wire in the baggage car.

The question was, what had he been looking for back there? And what had he hoped to find in my compartment?

But whatever the answers, we weren't going to get them tonight. I'd seen Emikai's type enough times to know that he was going to require a lot more persuasion, or the right lever, before he would give anything up. "Whatever," I said. "You realize, of course, that you're going to have to be locked up pending a full investigation."

"Nonsense," he said stiffly. "You have not reached the required legal bar for such action."

"Maybe not by Filiaelian standards," I said. "But in case you haven't noticed, we're aboard a Quadrail. Quadrails run under Spider rules."

Emikai looked at Kennrick, then Bayta, then back at me, and I could see that the full nature of his situation was starting to sink in. "The Filiaelian Assembly will not tolerate the mistreatment of its citizens," he warned.

"Oh, I don't think they'll have too much of a problem with it," I said, waving him to his feet. "In general, Filiaelians dislike criminals every bit as much as Humans do."

Slowly, Emikai stood up. His eyes flicked again to Bayta, probably checking on her alertness. Having been shot from behind, he couldn't know what exactly she'd done to lay him out on the corridor floor that way. But from his expression and cautious movements it was clear that he wasn't interested in having another go at it. "Where do you intend to take me?" he asked.

"Well, we don't have a proper brig," I said consideringly. "So I guess we'll have to put you in the morgue."

"The *morgue*?"

"Yes," I said. "Unless you're ready to have a serious talk?"

He drew himself up. "There is nothing to talk about," he said. "Show me to my prison."

"As you wish," I said. "Bayta, let the mites in, will you?"

She crossed to the door and opened it, and a pair of the little Spiders came in. "What do you want with those?" Emikai asked, a hint of apprehension creeping into his voice as the mites skittered toward us on their seven slender legs.

"Unfortunately, wristcuffs aren't allowed on Quadrails," I said. "So we're going to have to improvise. Turn around, please, and cross your wrists behind your back."

I actually wasn't at all sure this was going to work. But Bayta had caught on to the plan, and with a little experimentation—and probably a lot of silent communication—we got the mites wrapped solidly around Emikai's arms, their slender legs interlocked to keep them in place. "I'll have to remember this one," I commented to Bayta as we headed out the door into the corridor.

Bayta nodded toward the waiting conductor. "What did you want him to do?" she asked.

"He's to keep an eye on our compartments while we're gone," I said. "Just in case *Logra* Emikai and Dr. Aronobal have another friend aboard."

"I am not associated with Dr. Aronobal," Emikai insisted.

"Right—I keep forgetting," I said. "By the way, Bayta, is the good doctor still waiting for me in the dispensary?"

"Yes," she confirmed.

"Have the server tell her that I'm not coming and to go back to her seat," I said. "He can tell her I'll come by in the morning and talk to her then."

"All right." Bayta said doubtfully. "You sure you don't want to deal with this tonight?"

"Positive," I said. "This way, by the time we get back there, she'll hopefully have her privacy shield up and won't see us march Emikai past her. She'll then have a few hours to miss her friend and wonder what went wrong before I go see her." I nudged Emikai in the side. "Get moving—we've got a long way to go."

It was a long, but fortunately quiet, walk back to the rear of the train. Emikai, probably still aching from the *kwi* blast, had apparently opted for the fight-another-day strategy and gave us no trouble along the way. I half expected him to stumble, cough, or otherwise try to signal Aronobal as we passed the doctor's privacy-shielded seat, but he didn't even try that.

I'd had Bayta send instructions on ahead, and by the time we reached the third baggage car I found the Spiders had set up everything just as I'd requested. There was a chair, a small table holding a box of emergency ration bars and bottled water, and a spare self-contained toilet the Spiders had scrounged from one of the storage cars, everything laid out neatly in front of one of the stacks of cargo boxes. We settled Emikai on the stool, and using the pieces of safety webbing he'd cut earlier, I tied his wrists to opposite ends of the crate stack. I adjusted the lengths carefully, leaving him enough slack to be able to reach his food tray and to shift himself over onto the toilet, but not enough for either hand to reach the other hand's rope. With Humans or Shorshians I would also have had to keep him from biting through his bonds, but Filly teeth weren't configured for that sort of thing.

"There we go," I said, stepping back to examine my handiwork. "Enjoy the quiet, *Logra* Emikai. We'll be checking on you every once in a while, in case you decide you want to tell us what you and Dr. Aronobal are up to."

"Dr. Aronobal and I have nothing to do with each other."

"Right," I said. "Well, pleasant dreams. I hope you can sleep sitting up."

Ushering Bayta and Kennrick in front of me, we left Emikai to his new home. "Aren't you going to leave a guard?" Kennrick asked as we reached the vestibule and crossed into the next car forward.

"No need," I assured him. "He's not going anywhere." I carefully avoided looking significantly at Bayta who, I was sure, was similarly smart enough not to look significantly at me. There *was* a guard team on duty, in fact: a pair of twitters, lurking in nearby shadows where they could watch for visitors or escape attempts.

"I suppose not," Kennrick muttered. "Anyway, even if he gets loose, it's not like he can jump from a moving train. You still going to wait until morning to brace Dr. Aronobal about this?"

"Why? You think I should do it now?"

"It might not be a bad idea," Kennrick said. "She has to know that something has gone wrong. If you wait until tomorrow, she'll have had all those extra hours to come up with a good story."

"She'll also have had those same hours to sweat about what's happened to her accomplice and wonder what went wrong," I pointed out.

"I still think it'd be better to do it now," Kennrick said. "If you're too tired, I could run the interrogation while you watched. I trained in law, remember—I know all the techniques for getting witnesses to say the wrong thing."

"I'll keep that in mind," I said. "It's still not happening tonight."

Kennrick hissed out a sigh. "Whatever." He sent me a sideways glare. "Just remember that it was *my* contract teammates who were killed. Whenever you're ready to try and get a confession—out of either of them—I want to be there."

"You'll be at the top of the visitors list," I promised.

"Fine," he said. "By the way, do you think I could have a look at that bypass mimic of his?"

"What for?"

"Just curious," he said. "Early on in my career I handled a high-level corporate espionage case, and I ended up learning a lot about gadgets like that. I might be able to figure out if his would actually work."

"So you can duplicate it?" I asked mildly.

"So I can find out whether I can sleep for the next three weeks," he retorted. "Once Emikai and his buddies have finished off the rest of the contract team, who's to say they won't come after Dr. Witherspoon and me, too?"

"An intriguing thought," I agreed. "Maybe after the Spiders have checked it out they'll let you take a look."

We walked the rest of the way in silence. When we reached our car, I sent Bayta through her compartment door, nodded a good-night to Kennrick as he and I reached mine, and opened my door as he continued forward to his.

I'd barely closed the door behind me when the divider opened and Bayta came in. "How long do we wait?" she asked briskly.

"How long do we wait for what?" I asked.

"To go back and confront Dr. Aronobal," she said, frowning. "We *were* just dropping off Mr. Kennrick so he wouldn't be there, weren't we?"

"No, we were dropping off Mr. Kennrick so that we could all go to bed and get some sleep," I said.

Her face fell a little. "Oh," she said. "I thought . . ." She trailed off.

"You thought I was blowing smoke," I said. "And under other circumstances, I might have been. But not this time."

"Oh," she said again. "Well, then . . . I'll see you in the morning. Good night."

"Good night," I replied. "Sleep well."

She disappeared back into her compartment, and the dividing wall between us again closed.

With a tired sigh, I checked my watch. Twenty minutes, I decided, would be enough for her to finish her bedtime preparations and fall asleep.

It wasn't like I'd just lied to her, I reminded myself firmly. I really *wasn't* going back to third to confront Aronobal.

The Modhri had clued me in on Emikai's attempt on my compartment. Why he'd done that I didn't know.

But twenty minutes from now I was going to find out.

My first plan was to go back to the rear first-class coach car, where the Modhri had spoken through Qiddicoj to warn me about the intruder. But the Modhri was a group mind, after all, which meant that talking to one walker was the same as talking to another. On a hunch, I stopped by the bar.

Sure enough, the Juri I'd seen earlier was still there. He'd collapsed onto his table, his head pillowed on his folded arms, obviously sound asleep.

Back when I'd traveled third-class for Westali I'd seen occasional passengers sleeping that way. Up to now I'd never seen a first-class traveler who hadn't managed to make it back to his or her much comfier seat. The implications, and the invitation, were obvious. Walking over to the sleeping figure, I sat down across the table from him. "Hello, Modhri," I said quietly.

"Hello, Compton," the Juri replied instantly. "I see you were able to stop him."

"Yes, thanks to your timely information," I confirmed. "Why did you do it?"

"I hoped to prove myself trustworthy." He hesitated. "I need your help."

I felt my eyebrows creeping up my forehead. The Modhri as someone trustworthy was novel enough. The idea that he needed—and wanted—help from me was right off the scale. "To do what?" I asked.

"To find the murderer aboard this train," he said. "*Is* the intruder you stopped that murderer?"

"It's possible," I said. "He's got a first-class pass, and those don't come cheap, which means this guy has some serious financial backing." I grimaced. "But my gut says no."

"Then the killer is still at large," the Modhri said grimly. "And may kill again."

"Fair chance of that, yes," I agreed. "Why do you care?"

Again, he hesitated. "Because as he kills those aboard this train, he is also killing me."

I stared down at the sleeping face. "He's *what?*"

"He has killed four and tried to kill two others," the Modhri said. "Two of the dead were my Eyes."

I looked over at the server Spider standing behind the counter, out of range of our conversation, my brain swirling as everything about this case tried to realign itself. Could the as-yet-unexplained motive for these murders be something as simple as an attempt to kill off this particular Modhran mind segment? "Which two?" I asked.

"The first and third to die," he said. "Master Colix and *di*-Master Strinni."

"And what makes you think you can trust me?" I asked. "I'm your enemy, remember?"

"But you have destroyed my Eyes and Arms only in battle," he said. "Never have you engaged in direct murder." The sleeping Juri's mouth twitched. "And you have already saved one Eye that would also have been lost without your intervention."

He was right on that one, anyway. Qiddicoj would almost certainly have died of the same intestinal ravages that had killed Givvrac if I hadn't come up with the solution. "Of course, I didn't know *Osantra* Qiddicoj was a walker at the time," I reminded him.

"Would that have made a difference?"

I thought it over. The worst thing about fighting the damn Modhri was that most of his pawns were both unwilling and innocent. You couldn't go around slaughtering them for crimes they didn't even know they'd committed. You couldn't stand by and let someone else knock them off, either. "Not really," I conceded.

"As I thought," the Modhri said. "At first I feared you might be the person responsible for the deaths. But I'm now convinced otherwise."

"Glad to hear that," I said. I was, too. About the only thing that could have made this situation worse would have been to have a paranoid Modhran mind segment also gunning for me. "But just because I'm not going to let people get murdered doesn't mean I'm ready to jump on board as your ally."

"Yet I may be of assistance in your investigation," the Modhri pointed out. "And recall that two others who were not associated with me have also been killed. Do you not seek justice for them?"

I chewed the inside of my cheek. After all I'd been through with the Modhri, the thought of cooperating with him had all the skin-crawling unpleasantness of being offered lunch by a high-ranking member of the Inquisition.

And yet, the detached Westali investigator in me could see the possibilities here. One of the most frustrating roadblocks of the investigation so far had been my inability to nail down the last few hours of Master Colix's life. But if he'd been a Modhran walker, all those details were suddenly available to me, as clear and precise as if his whole life had been copied onto off-site backup. Which, in a sense, it had. "Let me get this straight," I said. "You're suggesting that we work together—you and I—to catch the murderer aboard this train."

"Correct."

"And afterwards?"

"You will have my thanks," the Modhri said.

"That's not what I meant," I said. "What's the rest of the Modhri going to say when he finds out you joined forces with someone he'd like to see dead?"

For a moment the Modhri didn't answer. I looked at the server again, wondering if he was even now informing Bayta that I was having a heart-to-heart with a sleeping passenger. "As with all beings, my first duty is to survive," the Modhri said at last. "Clearly, this murderer has found a way to bring weapons of death aboard a Quadrail. If he is permitted to escape undetected and unpunished, then none of us will ever be safe. Not you, and not I."

That was something I'd also thought about lately. I'd

thought about it a lot. "Let's hope the rest of the mind will also see it that way," I said. "So the plan is that we team up, catch this joker, then go our separate ways?"

"Yes," he said, and there was no mistaking the relief in his voice. "Thank you."

"Hang on," I warned. "Before you go all grateful, there are a few ground rules. First of all, how many walkers do you have aboard?"

"Three remain," he said.

Three out of an original five, kicking the mind segment down by forty percent. No wonder he was panicked enough to ask me for help. "Their names and species?"

He hesitated. "Why do you ask?"

"Because I need to know who, what, and where you are," I told him. "Partly for operational purposes; mostly because I don't like having potential surprises at my back."

"I have sworn to cooperate with you."

"And I'm pleased to hear that," I said. "Their names and species?"

He sighed, exactly the sort of sound a sleeping person might make. "First is *Osantra* Qiddicoj, the Filiaelian you saved from death," he said reluctantly. "Second is Prapp, a Tra'ho government oathling. His seat is in the first coach car. This Eye's name is *Krel* Vevri. He sits in the second coach car, the one between the dispensary and the entertainment car."

The same car, I noted, that the rest of Kennrick's contract-team Fillies were in. That could be useful. "Good," I said. "Ground rule number one: I call the shots. All of them. You can report to me, and you can recommend action, but nothing happens unless I explicitly sign off on it. Understood?"

"Understood," he said.

"Ground rule number two: when we do catch him, I'm the

one who'll interrogate him," I continued. "This guy is smart and well funded, and there will be some fairly ugly layers we'll need to dig through to get where we're going. You can sit in on the conversation and offer suggestions, but I'm the one who'll handle all the actual questioning."

A shiver ran through the Juri's body. "I have heard stories of Human interrogations. I will not interfere."

"Good." I hadn't actually been talking about torture, but it probably wouldn't hurt to let the Modhri think that I had. It probably wouldn't hurt to remind the killer of humanity's bloody past, either, when the time came. "Ground rule number three: I decide what to do with him after we've finished putting him through the spin cycle. I doubt the Spiders are set up for either executions or long-term prisoner storage, and there are already two different governments that have legitimate claims on his scalp. Depending on who and what he turns out to be, we might end up with three. Based on the interrogation, I'll make the decision as to who gets him."

"Agreed," the Modhri said. "How do we begin?"

I yawned. "With some sleep," I said. "The rest of the train's already settled down for the night, so there's no point trying to find anyone to question. And I'm way too tired to think straight, anyway." I gestured to him. "Sleeping on the table that way isn't doing your walker any good, either."

"Very well," he said. "*Osantra* Qiddicoj practices meditation several times a day. During those times, he allows his mind to empty itself."

I felt my stomach tighten. "And you're conveniently there to refill it?"

"It will be an opportunity for us to discuss matters and formulate a plan," the Modhri said. Apparently, he'd missed the irony in my tone.

"Fine," I said. "I'll have a couple of other things to deal with first tomorrow—mainly following up on tonight's little adventure—but I should be able to touch base with you by early afternoon at the latest."

"And if the killer strikes again this night?"

"He's been lying pretty low since *Usantra Givvrac's* death," I reminded him. "There's no particular reason for him to come out tonight."

"No reason that you know of."

"True," I conceded. "If it's any consolation, I don't think he's specifically targeting you." I stood up. "But I've been wrong before. Pleasant dreams."

SIXTEEN :

I half expected Bayta to be waiting for me when I returned to my compartment, her eyes blazing, her arms folded across her chest, demanding to know what I'd been off doing. But she wasn't. Apparently, the server Spider at the bar hadn't sold me out. Yet. Five minutes later I was climbing into bed, sleep tugging at my eyelids and my brain.

But even as I adjusted the blankets around my shoulders, I had a nagging sense that something significant had happened this evening. Something so subtle that I hadn't picked up on it on a conscious level.

For a minute I fought against sleep, trying to get a handle on the feeling and whatever it was that had sparked it. But it was an uphill battle, and after that single minute I knew it was hopeless. Tomorrow, when I'd caught up on my sleep, I would make another effort to track it down.

★ ★ ★

Once again, tomorrow arrived earlier than I'd expected it to.

And yet, at the same time, it nearly didn't arrive at all. At least for me.

I'd been asleep barely two hours when I was jarred awake by something soft and vague; a distant, eerie whistling sort of sound that was as much felt as it was heard. For a handful of heartbeats I lay still, my eyes wide open in the darkness, my ears straining against the silence as I waited for the noise to come again.

But it didn't. I'd just about decided it had been an artifact of my sleeping brain when I heard another sound.

Only this one wasn't vague and ethereal the way the first had been. This one was real, solid, and very close at hand.

Someone was scratching on my door.

I rolled silently out of bed and into a crouch on the floor, fighting against the mental cobwebs as I tried to figure out just what in hell was going on. There was a perfectly good door chime out there, not to mention equally good hard surfaces all around that anyone with working knuckles could knock on. There was no reason why whoever was out there should be scratching away like a pet malamute who wanted back into the house.

Unless he was too weak or too sick to do anything else.

I slid my hand along the floor until I found my shoes. I picked up one of them, getting a good grip on the toe. Holding it over my head like a club, I walked silently to the door and keyed the release.

To find that no one was there.

Frowning, I stepped out into the corridor and looked both directions. No one was visible along the car's entire length.

But someone *had* been there. At the rear of the car, the vestibule was just closing.

My first thought was that whoever this was, he must have

exquisite timing to have been able to get out of sight just as I was opening my door. My second thought was that whatever game he was playing, it probably boiled down to being a trap.

My third was that there was no way in hell he was going to get away from me.

I ducked back into my compartment, grabbed my other shoe and my shirt and headed out after him, making sure my door closed and locked behind me. I got my shoes on as I jogged down the corridor, and by the time I reached the vestibule I had my shirt on as well. Bracing myself, I keyed the door release.

The vestibule was empty. I crossed it and opened the door to the next compartment car, again preparing myself for whatever lay beyond it. But again, the corridor was empty. Hurrying past the closed compartment doors, I went through the vestibule and into the first of the first-class coaches.

Compartment cars didn't really lend themselves to ambushes, given that the only place you could launch one from was one of the compartments themselves. But coach cars were another matter entirely, as I'd already learned the hard way on this trip. Most of the seats scattered around the car were canopied, their occupants long since in dreamland, though there were a couple of quiet conversations still going on in various corners. But none of the conversationalists were near my path, and in fact didn't seem to even notice my presence, and I continued on through and into the dining car.

And nearly ran into my old Modhran pal *Krel* Vevri as he staggered out into the corridor from the bar end. "Compton," he breathed as he stepped into my path.

"Did you just scratch on my door?" I demanded, coming to a halt in front of him.

For a moment he just stared at me in silence, his body weaving a little, his eyes apparently having a hard time focusing on me. To all appearances he was as drunk as a goat. "Compton," he said again. "There's trouble."

I felt a tingle go up my back. Drunk Juriani nearly always slurred their words. Vevri wasn't doing that. Stepping close to him, I leaned forward and sniffed his breath.

One whiff was all it took. Any alcohol he might have poured into his system earlier that evening had been burned away hours ago. Whatever had put Vevri into this state, it wasn't anything the Spiders had served him.

Our poisoner had struck again.

"Understood," I said, taking his arm and trying to turn him around toward the dispensary three cars back. "Come on—we'll get the Spiders to call a doctor—"

"No doctor," he interrupted, throwing off my grip with an unexpected burst of strength. "Hypnotic—dizzy, but not in danger."

"We should at least try to figure out what it was," I insisted, trying to get a grip on his arm again. "Or wasn't it you?" I added as it belatedly occurred to me that Vevri himself might be completely unscathed, that the hypnotic or whatever might have been administered to one of the other walkers and merely be affecting the Juri via their shared mind.

But once again, he pulled away from my grip. "Not in danger," he insisted. "The prisoner. He's the one in danger."

I stared at him. "Emikai? What does the killer want with him?"

"Don't know," Vevri said. He wobbled suddenly and had to grab the edge of the archway to regain his balance. "Don't call Spiders. Warn him—warn him off. Never find him then."

I looked over his shoulder down the corridor. "Did you see the killer?" I asked Vevri. "The killer, *Krel* Vevri. Did you see who he was?"

Vevri shook his head. "He's on his way. Already on his way. You must stop him."

"Yeah," I said, gazing hard into the Juri's face.

And not believing it for a second, because this whole thing stunk to high heaven. Even if I actually trusted the Modhri—which I damn well didn't—it would still smell like a setup.

But I had no choice but to play along. If the killer really did want Emikai silenced, for whatever reason, the Filly was a sitting duck back there. The two twitters on duty might get a glimpse of the killer, but that would be pretty small comfort to Emikai himself.

Besides, knowing it was a setup gave me certain advantages, especially if the killer didn't know I knew. "Okay, I'll go take a look," I said to Vevri. "You stay here and keep an eye out in case he doubles back."

Vevri nodded. "I will. Good luck."

Slipping past him, I continued on my way. Knowing you were walking into a trap could definitely be helpful in beating that trap.

But it never hurt to also hedge your bets.

I had covered another two cars and was passing the line of shower compartments before I finally ran into a conductor tapping his way along on some errand or another. "Hey—you," I said, catching up to him. "You—Spider."

"Yes?" he said.

"I want you to call Bayta," I said. "Tell her I've had word that *Logra* Emikai is in trouble, and I'm heading back to check on him—"

"Bayta is asleep."

"Then wake her up," I snarled. "Tell her I want her to do a running track on me—conductors, servers, mites, and anyone else who's available. You got that?"

"Yes," he said.

"Good." I started to go, then turned back. "And she's to stay put," I added firmly. "Whatever happens, she's to stay in her compartment and not open the door. For anyone."

"Yes," he said.

I gazed hard into his silvery globe for another moment, the way you might underline the seriousness of an order if you were talking to a real, actual person, then turned and resumed my jog. If Bayta could mobilize enough of the Spiders to monitor the action, we had a chance of bringing this thing to an end right here and now.

The baggage car seemed quiet enough as I slipped through the vestibule doorway into the gloom. Setting my back against the nearest stack of crates, I paused for a moment to take stock of the situation. No shadows seemed to be moving out there, at least none that I could see from my current vantage point, and I could hear nothing above the muted clickity-clack of Quadrail wheels.

Was the killer still here? Or had he been and gone, leaving a fresh corpse where I'd earlier tied up a prisoner?

Only one way to find out. Taking a deep breath, I headed off through the maze of stacked crates.

The attack came without any warning, in spite of all the care I had been taking with corners and crate tops. An arm suddenly appeared from behind me, snaking around my neck and yanking me backward. I tried to twist sideways, to get my throat turned into the crook of his elbow where there was a little extra space, but he was already on it, his other hand snapping up to link into his choking arm and simultaneously push the back of my head forward.

Reflexively, I kicked backward. But my foot hit only air, and before I could bring it back for another try a foot slapped into the back of my other knee, just hard enough to break my balance.

And barely a second after the attack had begun, I found myself kneeling on the floor, the tiny prickly hairs of a Filly snout pressed against my right cheek, his chokehold ready to squeeze the life out of me.

I tried to reach up toward his head, in hopes of reaching his eyes or ears. But the arms wrapped around my throat and head blocked any such path. I switched direction and jabbed backwards with my elbows, landing solid blows against his torso. He grunted with the impact, but his grip didn't loosen.

So this is how it ends, the thought flitted through my mind as I continued my futile efforts to break my attacker's grip. I wondered distantly what Bayta would do without me, and what the Chahwyn and Spiders would do after I was dead.

It was only then that it belatedly dawned on me that the arm pressed against my throat, which should have been squeezing ever tighter, cutting off my air and choking the life out of me, was doing no such thing. In fact, it wasn't all that tight even now, more of a controlling hold than a killing one.

Was he just waiting so that I would sweat some more? Or did he genuinely want to keep me alive, at least until he could get something else out of me?

Bracing myself, painfully aware that if I was wrong, it would be the last gamble I ever made, I brought my pummeling hands and elbows to a halt.

He didn't press his attack. But he didn't let go, either. He just stood there, towering silently and motionless behind me.

I cleared my throat, which turned out to be a lot harder in my present condition than I'd expected. "If you're trying to make a point," I croaked out, "consider it made."

"What point is that?" he asked.

I grimaced as I recognized his voice. My assailant was none other than *Logra* Emikai himself. "That you're the greatest escape artist since Houdini?" I suggested.

"That I could have killed you," he corrected. Abruptly, the pressure against my throat disappeared as he let go of me and stepped backward. "And that I did not," he added.

I turned my head, massaging my throat as I looked up at him. He was just standing there, his arms hanging loosely as his sides, gazing back at me. "Interesting demo," I commented, getting back to my feet. "Of course, as has already been noted, you're on a super-express Quadrail with nowhere to run. Killing me would be kind of stupid."

"Agreed," he said. "But he who freed me apparently was not concerned with such questions of logic." He paused. "He who freed me, then ordered me to kill you."

"Did he, now," I said as casually as I could. So our killer was starting to sharecrop his business. "Did this helpful passerby have a name or face?"

"I'm certain he had both," Emikai said grimly. "Unfortunately, I was asleep when he freed me."

"*And* when he gave you your marching orders?" I asked, frowning. "What did he do, leave a voice message in your dreams?"

"You are actually not far off," Emikai said, for the first time seeming a little uncertain. "The words came to me in . . . it's hard to describe. It was a distant, whistling sort of voice. I'm afraid I cannot explain it more clearly than that."

"That's okay," I assured him, a prickling sensation running up my back. A distant, eerie whistling sort of sound was the way I'd characterized my own recent wake-up call. "How long ago did all this happen?"

He shrugged. "An hour. Perhaps a bit more."

Just enough time, in other words, for someone to make his way back up to the front of the train, dose a sleeping Modhran walker with hypnotic so that he could play shill for me, and call me awake so he could send me to my death.

In fact, with this added bit of information, the late-night conversations I'd noticed as I passed through first class suddenly took on an entirely new aspect. Odds were that one of those conversations had been the killer talking to one of the Modhri's other walkers, getting ready to feed *Krel* Vevri's lines to him by remote control. That was a capability of the group mind that had never occurred to me. "So why didn't you kill me?" I asked.

Emikai snorted. "I do not murder on anyone's demand," he growled.

"Glad to hear it," I said, rubbing my throat again. "So what now? We let bygones be bygones and I let you go back to your nice comfy Quadrail seat?"

He cocked his head. "Do you think that would be wise?"

My estimate of his competence, which had already been pretty high, rose a couple more points. Most citizens would have leaped at the offer. But Emikai was either more thoughtful or more canny than that.

Which led directly to the bigger question of who or what this horse-faced enigma was, and whose side he was on. If anyone's. "Unfortunately—unfortunately for you, anyway—no, I don't," I said. "I'm thinking it could be highly interesting to see what kind of reaction we get when I not only don't turn up dead, but you turn up back in irons."

"I expected you would say that." Emikai looked around us. "I presume this time you will have watchers present in the event that he attempts this again?"

"Absolutely," I promised, keeping my voice even. "If you're ready, let's go ahead and reset the stage."

He eyed me another moment, then nodded. "Very well," he said.

Five minutes later, with Emikai once again tied to his perch, I was on my way back to the front of the train. And this time, I was moving with a lighter, quicker step.

Because though Emikai didn't know it, there *had* been watchers present during his abortive rescue: the two twitters Bayta had left on guard.

It was going to be highly interesting to find out what exactly they'd seen.

What they'd seen, it turned out, was exactly nothing.

"That's impossible," I growled, glaring at Bayta from my seat at her computer desk as she sat stiffly on the edge of her bed. "You left them there. You ordered them to watch. How can they not have seen something?"

"I don't know," Bayta said. Her voice was as stiff as her posture. "They just froze up, somehow."

"How does a Spider freeze up?" I asked.

"I don't *know*," Bayta repeated tartly. "Something happened to them. Something I've never heard of happening before."

I stared at her . . . and then my fatigue-numbed brain finally got it. Bayta hadn't gone all stiff and angry because she was mad at me.

She wasn't angry. She was scared.

"Okay," I said, forcing the frustration out of my voice. This was no time for emotion of any sort. "Let's start at the beginning. When did this blank spot happen?"

"As near as we can tell, just under two hours ago," Bayta said, her voice still stiff but sounding marginally calmer now that I was no longer yelling at her. "About the same time *Logra* Emikai says someone cut him free of his bonds."

"And it knocked out both Spiders so that they didn't see anything?"

"It didn't exactly knock them out," Bayta said hesitantly, frowning out into space as if looking for the right words. "It was more like they had been looking somewhere else and . . . is 'spaced out' a correct English term?"

"It is indeed," I assured her. "Did they notice anything unusual happening just before or during this brain freeze?"

"How could they notice anything *during* the brain freeze?" Bayta asked patiently. "They were incapacitated."

"I know *they* were," I said. "But they're telepathically linked to the rest of the Spiders, and I assume no one else was affected."

"No, no one else was affected," Bayta said, shaking her head. "But the two twitters were somehow disconnected from the rest of the Spiders during that time."

"And no one noticed that?"

She shrugged. "The Spiders aren't a group mind," she reminded me. "They're not connected that tightly."

I grimaced. And even if someone *had* noticed, they probably wouldn't have done anything. That wasn't the way Spiders did things. "Well, it's certainly not the first dead end we've hit in this case," I said. "At least we've proved now that *Logra* Emikai isn't our killer."

"Have we?" Bayta countered. "Couldn't this have just been an elaborate plan on his part to deflect suspicion away from him?"

"Hardly," I said. "The whole story about being ordered to kill me implies that his midnight visitor thought he would be willing to do the dastardly deed, which implies a relationship of some sort with said midnight visitor. That actually puts him closer to the center of this mess than he would have been if he'd just stayed put like a good little prisoner. It's more likely that the real killer was hoping this would muddy the waters by throwing some of the suspicion onto Emikai."

"Or hoped *Logra* Emikai *would* kill you," Bayta said quietly.

"There is that," I conceded. "Fortunately, he couldn't be present to either encourage or assist. He had to be up here pulling Vevri's strings."

"Yes," Bayta said, her voice chilling a bit. "Let's talk about *Krel* Vevri, shall we?"

I took a deep breath. For a while I'd considered keeping my deal with the Modhri private, knowing that Bayta probably wouldn't take the news very well. But down deep, I'd known all along I couldn't do that. Bayta was my ally and my friend, and it would be neither safe nor fair for me to cut her out of something this important.

Besides, I could still see the quiet pain that had flooded into her eyes when she'd learned I'd held out on her about the Chahwyn's new defender-class Spiders. I wasn't about to go through that twice in one trip.

So as she sat still and silent on her bed, I told her all about it.

I was prepared for her to be stunned, or aghast, or outraged. I wasn't prepared for her to be quietly unreadable. "So there *is* a mind segment aboard," she said when I'd finished. "I'd always thought there probably was."

"It seemed a reasonable deal to make," I said, still trying to figure out what was going on behind that emotionless face. "This may be our only chance of getting fresh information on this case."

"And you'd rather work with the Modhri than let a killer escape punishment?"

"This isn't an ordinary killer, Bayta," I reminded her. "He's figured out how to commit quiet, subtle murder on a Quadrail. Not just beat someone to death with his bare hands, which we've seen before, but real, genuine, untraceable murder." I waved a hand. "Not to mention that he's also got a technique for freezing or otherwise incapacitating Spiders. You think the Chahwyn will want him getting away with all that?"

"It doesn't really matter what the Chahwyn wants, does it?" she countered. "You've already made the decision." She eyed me. "But there's a possibility you haven't mentioned. What if it was the Modhri himself who was responsible for what happened with *Logra* Emikai and the twitters?"

"And, what, he committed all the murders, too?" I asked. "Two of the victims being his own walkers? Why would he do that?"

"To get us killed," Bayta said quietly. "To get *you* killed. Maybe the reason he volunteered to help us was to set you up for a thought virus that would make sure you went back to the baggage car after he freed *Logra* Emikai."

I grimaced. There was some sense in that theory, I had to admit. More sense than I liked. Especially when you tossed in Bayta's speculation earlier in the trip that the Modhri might slowly be going crazy. "If that's the case, his reaction tomorrow when I turn up alive ought to be interesting," I said. "His explanation for what happened tonight ought to be interesting, too."

Bayta seemed to draw back. "You're not going to go *on* with this whole thing, are you?"

"I don't see that I have a choice," I said. "No matter who's behind the murders, the Modhri or someone else, the fact remains that *someone* has figured out a way to get poison aboard a Quadrail. If it wasn't the Modhri, he may be able to help us figure out how it was done. If it *was* the Modhri, he might let something slip while he's pretending to assist us. Either way, I have to play it out."

Bayta's throat worked. "I suppose you're right," she said reluctantly. "You won't do anything more until morning, though, will you?"

I thought about pointing out that, technically, it *was* morning. But she didn't seem in the mood for that sort of whimsy. "No," I promised. "No matter who comes scratching on my door."

"And we'll be going together?"

I winced. She hadn't added *this time* to her question, but I could hear it anyway. "Of course," I assured her.

"All right." She took a deep breath. "Then we should probably get some sleep now."

Apparently, the conversation was over. "Agreed," I said, standing up and stepping past the folded-up divider into my own compartment. "I'll see you in the morning." I reached for the divider control.

"Maybe you should leave it partly open tonight," she said.

So that we could be better able to protect each other? Or so that I would have a harder time running off somewhere without her again?

Or had this whole thing so spooked her that she just wanted the sense of a little company close at hand?

"Sure," I said. Touching the control, I let the divider close to about half a meter, then tapped the control again to stop it. "Pleasant dreams," I called through the opening.

"Good night, Frank," she called back.

SEVENTEEN :

I woke up seven hours later, still tired, and with an aching throat where Emikai had delivered his object lesson. The elusive thought that had been nagging at my brain after my first midnight conversation with the Modhri still eluded me, but on the plus side the possibility that our new ally was trying to kill me was looking considerably less likely here in the light of day.

"I don't think the Modhri is the killer," I told Bayta over breakfast. "If he'd wanted me dead, he could have done it when he took me out after all the Fillies started coming down with digestive trouble. As you yourself pointed out, he had Witherspoon's medical bag right there, with hypos and any number of potential overdoses to choose from."

"Except that he wouldn't have had a built-in perpetrator to take the blame, the way he would have if *Logra* Emikai had killed you," Bayta pointed out.

"Right, but why would he care?" I countered. "It would have cost him at most one more walker, whichever one he picked to take the fall. After killing off two other walkers, that hardly seems like a consideration."

"Perhaps," Bayta said. She still didn't seem convinced, but with her professional mask back up I couldn't tell what she was thinking or feeling. "Are we starting with him, then?"

"Actually, I was thinking we'd start with Dr. Aronobal," I said. "She's had plenty of time now to wonder where her pal Emikai's gotten to. Worried people often blurt out things they would keep to themselves if they were calmer."

"That seems reasonable." She took a final bite of her breakfast, her other hand reaching under the table. "Here—you should probably carry this."

I reached under the table, and she pressed the *kwi* into my hand. "Thanks," I said, slipping it into my pocket. "And thanks for the assist last night, too, when Emikai was making a run for it. You were right on top of things."

She nodded, thanks or simple acknowledgment, I couldn't tell which. "You ready?" she asked.

I sighed to myself. This was going to be a very long day. "Sure," I said. "Let's go."

We left the dining car and headed once again on the long walk toward the rear of the train. As usual, *Asantra* Muzzfor nodded politely as we passed the apparently eternal card game he had going with his two contract-team companions, while the other two Fillies, also as usual, ignored us completely. I looked around at the other passengers as we walked through that car, wondering which of them was Prapp, the Tra'ho government oathling the Modhri had named last night as being the third of his walkers. Both Tra'ho'seej in evidence, unfortunately, had the distinctive oathling half-shaved heads and flowing topcuts, which I'd counted on identifying him with.

Neither Tra'ho gave us a significant look as we passed, either, which was the other way I might have recognized him.

Osantra Qiddicoj was similarly preoccupied with other matters as we passed him three cars later. Apparently, the Modhri was keeping to himself this morning. Maybe he was ashamed of his unwitting part in the murder attempt against me last night.

Maybe he was just sulking because it hadn't worked.

Aronobal's seat was in the first third-class coach. We reached her car, to find the doctor herself was nowhere to be seen. She was probably farther back in the train, in the dining car having breakfast, or possibly sneaking back to our makeshift brig for a hurried conference with *Logra* Emikai. That would be the most interesting possibility of all. Passing her seat, we continued on.

We were just entering Emikai's assigned car, two back from Aronobal's, when I began to notice a change in the atmosphere around us.

At first it was nothing I could put my finger on. The passengers seemed quieter than they'd been in either first or second, but not quiet in the sense of peace or comfort. This was the quiet of fresh tension simmering beneath the surface.

Behind Emikai's car was the third-class dining car. Bayta and I took a quick look inside, confirmed that Aronobal wasn't there, and kept going toward the entertainment car.

As we did so, I could feel the quiet tension continuing to grow. More and more, the passengers' eyes turned toward us as we came into sight, and continued to follow us as we passed.

And the expressions on their faces were running the unpleasant gamut from neutral to suspicious to downright hostile.

Bayta noticed it, too. "Something's not right here," she murmured as we passed through the shower car.

"And whatever it is, we seem to be getting the blame for it," I murmured back. "Is anything happening with Emikai?"

"The twitters say he hasn't had any visitors since you left, and that he's still secured," she said. "The conductors aren't reporting anything odd with the rest of the train, either."

"So it apparently is just us," I concluded.

"Do you think we should turn back?"

It was a tempting idea. But we had a job to do, and somehow I doubted the passengers were going to get any less hostile as the day wore on. "Let's at least go as far as the entertainment car," I said. "If we haven't located Aronobal by then, we'll backtrack and wait for her at her seat."

Actually, I wasn't expecting we'd have to go that far back. Just behind the shower car was Terese German's car, and if Emikai, Aronobal, and Terese were in cahoots, there was a fair chance we'd find the latter two members of the troika in urgent consultation together.

For once, I was right. As we exited the vestibule into the car, I saw a small group of passengers gathered around Terese's row, their heads hunched forward the way people do when having intense, semi-private conversations. Two of the group were Halkas, one was a Juri, and the fourth was Dr. Aronobal.

"There she is," Bayta said.

"I see her," I said, the back of my neck starting to tingle. The conversationalists had turned to face us, and their expressions weren't even bothering with the neutral or suspicious areas of today's third-class mood scale. All four were deeply into the hostile end of the spectrum, and every cubic centimeter of that hostility was aimed at Bayta and me. "Maybe you ought to hang back a bit while I go talk to them," I said quietly.

Bayta reached over and got a grip on my left arm. "No," she said in a voice that left no room for argument.

"Stay a step behind me, then," I told her, gently disengaging her grip. "You might want to fire up the *kwi*, just in case."

I started forward again, the *kwi* in my pocket tingling as Bayta activated it. "Good afternoon," I said, nodding to the group as I got within polite conversational range. "Dr. Aronobal, I wonder if I might have a few minutes of your time."

To my surprise, Terese bounded up from her seat, planting herself squarely between me and the rest of them. "What do you want her for?" she demanded, her face dark with emotion.

"I just want to ask her a few questions," I said soothingly.

"And then, what, make *her* disappear, too?" Terese shot back.

I took another look at the group standing silently behind her. "What in the world are you talking about?"

"She speaks of *Logra* Emikai," Aronobal said grimly. "He's disappeared, and no one can find him." She drew herself up. "We've heard reports that you were the one responsible."

"Reports," I said, letting my tone go flat. "You mean rumors."

"Yes, that's what I thought you'd say," Terese said scornfully.

"You protest too glibly," the Juri agreed in a precise, clipped voice. "Rumors always have a basis in fact, a touchpoint with reality. The reality here is that *Logra* Emikai *has* indeed vanished."

I really wanted to ask him how he could possibly know that, given that he and his fellow worriers were all confined back here in third class while their buddy Emikai had a pass that let him roam the entire train at will. But I kept my mouth shut. Those who didn't already know that almost certainly wouldn't believe it anyway. "Maybe he's taking a long shower," I suggested instead. "Maybe the Spiders asked him up to first or second for some kind of consultation."

"Oh, right," Terese bit out. "Far as *I* can see, the only people consulting with the Spiders are you two."

"Let us also not forget that *di*-Master Strinni's final act was to form his hands into the sign-language symbols of your initials," Aronobal added.

I *had* forgotten about that, actually, and I made a mental note to hit up the Modhri later and find out what the hell he'd thought he was doing with that.

Assuming there *was* a later. Most of the nearby passengers were listening intently to the conversation, and their expressions reminded me of sharks at feeding time. They were scared, they were frustrated, and, worse, after nearly four weeks on the road they were bored. If there was no justice in me getting my ears pounded, there might at least be some entertainment.

I came to a sudden decision. Aronobal wasn't going to talk now anyway, not surrounded by indignant supporters who clearly thought I was out to add her to some phantom body count. There would be plenty of other opportunities to hit her up about her relationship with Emikai before we reached Venidra Carvo. "I get the feeling you really don't want to talk right now," I said, taking a casual step backward. "Fine. We'll do this later."

"Don't let him go!" Terese snapped. "If he gets away, we'll never find out what he did with *Logra* Emikai."

She started toward me, and to my surprise I saw she had tears in her eyes. Either she was choking with rage or she really did feel something for the supposedly vanished Emikai. "I didn't do anything with *Logra* Emikai," I insisted.

But it was too late. Behind her, one of the two Halkas—the bigger one, naturally—shouldered her aside and strode toward me, the glow of righteous indignation in his eyes.

"Move it," I murmured to Bayta, crowding backwards

against her as I dipped my hand into my pocket. Unfortunately, while the *kwi* gave me the power to drop the Halka where he stood, I couldn't use it, at least not openly. Kennrick already knew I had brought a supposedly forbidden weapon aboard, and *Logra* Emikai probably suspected it, and the last thing I wanted was for the rest of the train to find out, too.

But if I couldn't use the *kwi* openly, maybe I could use it *not* openly.

The Halka was still lumbering forward as I pulled my hand out of my pocket, the *kwi* in position around my knuckles. The second Halka had fallen into step behind the first, with Terese now third in line. "Take it easy," I said soothingly as I keyed the *kwi* for its lowest unconsciousness setting. "I don't want any trouble here. Neither do you."

The two Halkas merely picked up their pace a little. Knowing Halkas, I'd expected that. I continued to back up, keeping my hands moving in little circles to prevent anyone from getting a clear look at the *kwi*. The lead Halka got to within grabbing distance and reached out a large hand toward my neck.

And I slammed my right fist into his gut.

It wasn't all that hard a slam, actually. In fact, the punch was over ninety percent pure noise, with as little genuine impact as I could get away with while still making it sound real. There didn't have to be any impact, because an instant before my fist hit his torso I thumbed the *kwi*'s firing button.

The weapon worked with its usual gratifying speed, instantly sending the Halka off to dreamland. As his knees started to buckle beneath him I brought my left hand up and made a show of chopping him at the base of the neck. After that, my only job was to get out of his way as he collapsed with an impressive thud onto the floor.

The second Halka came to an abrupt halt. So did the various mutterings and twitterings that had been going on among the onlookers. Our entire end of the car, in fact, went deathly quiet.

And from behind me I heard Bayta give a short, strangled gasp.

I spun around, *kwi* ready, both hands coming up into combat position. But it was only Kennrick, his hands on Bayta's shoulders as he moved her sideways out of his way. "What the hell are you doing back here?" he demanded, his voice taut, his eyes flicking to the line of potential attackers still facing me. "Come on—we've got to get out of here before you get lynched."

I was opening my mouth to tell him that we had every intention of doing exactly that when the second Halka made his move.

Unfortunately for him, the same relative silence that had allowed me to hear Kennrick's non-assault on Bayta also enabled me to hear him coming with his more genuine attack. I spun back around, evaded his pile-driver punch, and dropped him to the floor with a second *kwi* shot and some more martial-arts window dressing.

And then Kennrick's hand was on my shoulder, pulling me backward toward the vestibule. "Come *on*," he repeated urgently. "Let's get the hell out of here."

I took one last look at Terese's stricken, disbelieving, anguished expression, and got the hell out of there.

We reached the next car and Kennrick slipped around past me, putting himself behind Bayta and me and between us and any potential follow-up trouble that Aronobal and Terese might choose to send in our direction. But no one came bursting through the vestibule in hot pursuit. The three of us retraced our steps back through third class, and again I could feel the eyes of the passengers on my back as we hurried forward. Fortunately, none of them did anything but look, and a few minutes later we made our escape from third class into second.

"Whew," Kennrick puffed as we slowed our pace back to a normal walk. The passengers here, I noted, seemed to have no interest whatsoever in us. "That was way too close."

"Close to *what*, I'm not sure," I said, eyeing him over my shoulder. "What was all that about, anyway?"

"What, they didn't tell you?" he asked. "There's a rumor racing through third that you killed *Logra* Emikai during the night."

"That much I gathered," I said. "I was mostly wondering if this rumor has anything more to it. Like why I would do something like that or, better yet, how I managed to dispose of a body from a sealed Quadrail."

"You really think anyone's paying attention to actual logic?" Kennrick said sourly. "Especially when it's a trusted member of the medical profession who's telling you all this?"

"Dr. Aronobal started the rumor?" Bayta asked, frowning over her shoulder.

"Who else?" Kennrick said. "I'm just glad I got back there in time." He grunted. "Not that you seemed to need me. That, uh, asset of yours is really something."

"We like it," I said. "Which isn't to say that reinforcements aren't always welcome. How did you happen to be there, anyway?"

"Pure luck," he said. "*Asantra* Muzzfor went back to third earlier this morning to discuss the contract situation with Master Tririn. While he was there he got wind of the rumor about Emikai's mysterious disappearance, though your name apparently wasn't yet connected to it. He mentioned it to me when I stopped by his seat half an hour ago, along with the fact that he'd seen you heading that direction. I put two and two to-gether and went charging back to try to stop you before you walked into a hornets' nest."

"Why would Dr. Aronobal start such a rumor?" Bayta asked.

"Obviously, to keep you two at bay while she locates Emi-kai and finds out what we know," Kennrick said. "Or, failing that, to come up with another plan."

"But that doesn't make any sense," Bayta insisted.

"Of course it does," Kennrick said. "Like I said, she needs to find Emikai—"

"Why doesn't it make sense?" I interrupted.

"Because if Dr. Aronobal knows *Logra* Emikai well enough to send him to break into your compartment, she should also trust him not to tell us anything," she said. "Especially about whether or not the two of them are working together."

Kennrick snorted. "I think the *working together* part was ob-vious as soon as Aronobal tried to lure Compton out of his compartment so that Emikai could break in."

"Obvious, but not provable," Bayta insisted. "We might sus-pect, but we couldn't know for sure. Given that, wouldn't Dr. Aronobal do better to pretend she was innocent, or had been set up, and try to find out what we know?"

There was an answer for that, I knew. But I kept quiet. Bayta was doing just fine without my help, and I was curious to see how Kennrick would respond.

Not very well, as it turned out. "Look, I'm not here to de-fend her cleverness," Kennrick said stiffly. "All I know is that the rumor is there, and that she's the only one who benefits from it."

"Or possibly Terese German," I suggested. "They seem to have some kind of relationship going, too."

"And the rumor also keeps you away from her," Kennrick said with an air of vindication. "Like I said."

"Yes, you're probably right," I agreed. Bayta frowned at me, and I gave her a small warning shake of my head. She grimaced, but turned back without another word. "So what are your plans for the day?" I added to Kennrick.

"First I need to find out from *Asantra* Muzzfor exactly what he and Master Tririn talked about," Kennrick said. "I was about to do that when I found out you two were in danger and cut the meeting short. After that, depending on what he says, I'll need to sit down with all three of the Filiaelians and discuss the contract status."

"You don't sound very hopeful," I said.

"I'm not," he admitted. "But I have to try."

We reached the rearmost of the first-class cars, and as we entered I casually glanced around. *Osantra* Qiddicoj was seated in a corner by himself, his eyes closed, his breathing slow, his mind presumably emptied.

The Modhri was open for business.

"You go on ahead," I told Kennrick, taking Bayta's arm and bringing the two of us to a halt. "I want to see how *Osantra* Qiddicoj's doing."

"Yes, poor guy," Kennrick said, peering over at Qiddicoj. "I hear those Filiaelian stomach things can drag you down for weeks. He's looking better, though."

"Hopefully, he'll be recovered by the time we reach Veni-dra Carvo," I said. "Thanks again for coming to our rescue."

"Any time." With a nod to Bayta, Kennrick continued on forward.

I could feel the taut muscles in Bayta's arm as I steered us toward Qiddicoj's seat. "You okay with this?" I asked her quietly.

"Would it matter if I wasn't?"

"Sure," I said. "I could take you back to your compartment and do it alone."

She straightened her shoulders. "I'm all right."

There were a pair of empty chairs nearby. I pulled them over to Qiddicoj and we sat down. "Hello, Modhri," I said.

"Good afternoon, Compton," the Modhri said, Qiddicoj's eyes remaining closed. "And to you, Bayta, agent of the Spiders."

Bayta didn't answer.

"Let's start with last night," I said. "I'd like your take on just what the hell happened."

For a long moment the Modhri was silent. "It was very strange," he said at last. "I was . . . I could hear and see what I was doing, and I knew it was a lie. And yet, I could not stop myself."

Which was, I knew, the hallmark of a good hypnotic drug. "At least you were able to slip in the clue about the hypnotic," I commented. "So who was feeding you your lines?"

"I don't know," the Modhri said, a hint of frustration edging into his otherwise emotionless voice. "The voice spoke to my Eye Prapp, but spoke from behind him. I never saw who it was, neither before, during, nor after."

"Did you recognize the voice?" I persisted. "Male, female, species—did you get *anything*?"

"Nothing," he said. "But I do remember that a faint whistling sound seemed to underlie my attacker's words."

I looked at Bayta. I'd heard a whistling sound that evening, and so had Emikai. Now the Modhri had joined the club.

Obviously, that was significant. I just wished I knew how. "I don't suppose you have any idea how the hypnotic got into your system. *Any* of your systems," I amended. "I assume what gets into one walker affects the whole mind."

"It does," he confirmed. "Unfortunately, I have no idea how that was done."

I sighed. If dead ends were money, Bayta and I could retire rich. "You really ought to try to be more alert," I told the Modhri.

"I will," the Modhri promised. "And may I say that I'm pleased you are still alive."

"I'm reasonably pleased about that myself," I said. "Okay, back to the business at hand. What can you tell me about Master Colix's last day?"

"I've been pondering that question since his death," the Modhri said. "Unfortunately, there's little I can tell you that you don't already know. He ate his sunrise and midday meals alone. No one approached his table during either time. Sundown was eaten with Master Bofiv and Master Tririn."

"Master Tririn told us Dr. Witherspoon and Terese German were seated nearby at that latter meal," I said. "Did Master Colix have a good view of them?"

"He did, and neither of them approached the table," the Modhri confirmed. "They seemed interested only in each other." Qiddicoj's nostrils flared briefly. "Perhaps *too* interested."

I felt my ears prick up. Terese, and *Witherspoon*? There was at least a forty-year age difference there. "What makes you say that?" I asked.

"He touched her in a very intimate way," the Modhri said, and I could hear the contempt in his voice for primitive Humans who didn't know any better than to display their affection in public.

"Where exactly did he touch her?" I asked.

A hand lifted limply from Qiddicoj's lap. "Here," he said, his fingertips touching his lower abdomen. "And here," he added, moving the fingers upward a short distance.

I frowned. There wasn't a single Human erogenous zone in either place. "Are you sure?" I asked, holding my hand a couple of centimeters above Bayta's abdomen. "He was touching her right here?"

Qiddicoj's eyes flicked briefly open, then closed again. "Yes," the Modhri confirmed.

"I see," I said, bringing my hand back. "Well, well."

"What is it?" Bayta asked.

"At least one corner of this mess is suddenly making sense," I said. "This dinnertime get-together wasn't a meeting. It was a medical consultation." I tapped my own abdomen. "Remember Terese's stomach trouble?"

Bayta's eyes widened a little. "Are you saying . . . ?"

I nodded. "Our young friend Terese German is pregnant."

Bayta shot a look at Qiddicoj. "What in the world is she doing alone on a Quadrail heading for the far end of the galaxy?"

"That's the question, isn't it?" I agreed. "And it's clear now that our Filly friends Aronobal and Emikai are definitely involved with her."

"Why do you say that?" the Modhri asked.

"Because if they are, a few more of the pieces fall into place," I told him. "Emikai's concern for the air in Terese's car, for starters—air quality would be especially important for a woman carrying a baby. And then there's Dr. Witherspoon's reaction after di-Master Strinni's death, when I asked him about his rendezvous with Terese."

"Yes," the Modhri murmured thoughtfully. "He was very reluctant to speak of her."

I frowned. "*You* remember that?"

"The polyp colony within an Eye lives for a short time after the Eye's own death," he explained.

"Ah," I said, a shiver running up my back. I'd always suspected that was the case, but to have it confirmed in such a coldly clinical manner was a little disconcerting. "What you *couldn't* see was that Witherspoon kept looking at Aronobal during that conversation, as if he wasn't sure how much he was allowed to say. Physician/patient privilege is pretty much a standard of Human law these days, but other species handle it in different ways. And Witherspoon was only brought in as a consultant, after all."

"You think Dr. Aronobal was concerned about Ms. German's stomach trouble?" Bayta asked.

"That's my guess," I said. "I'm sure she knows about morning sickness, but the duration and intensity of Terese's bouts may have thrown her enough to want a Human doctor to take a look."

I looked back at Qiddicoj. "Speaking of death and Modhran afterlife, why did you try to finger me—no pun intended—with Strinni's silly dying clue?"

"My apologies," the Modhri said, a touch of embarrassment in his tone. "At the time I believed you to be the one killing off my Eyes. I wanted to raise that same suspicion in others so that they would keep watch on your future actions."

"That makes sense, I guess," I said. "You have no such suspicions now?"

"None," the Modhri assured me. "To return to Master Colix's sundown meal. His individual was *birrsh*, and the common was *po krem*, which he ate with *prinn* scoops."

"Yes, Tririn's already given me the menu," I said. "Any chance either Bofiv or Tririn spiked any of the food?"

"None," the Modhri said firmly. "I've replayed the memory of the entire meal through my mind many times since then. Neither of the others could have done so."

I nodded. I'd already come to the same conclusion, but it was good to have it verified by a fresh source. "Let's move on to the rest of Colix's evening. He finished dinner and . . . ?"

"He returned immediately to his seat," the Modhri said. "His stomach was starting to bother him."

I frowned. "By the time he reached his seat?"

"Even sooner," the Modhri said. "He was feeling the first twinges before the end of the meal."

"Really," I said, tapping my fingertips on the arm of my borrowed chair. Heavy-metal poisoning hit Shorshians quickly, but not *that* quickly. "Let's back up a bit. Did anything unusual happen that afternoon?"

"And did he have his throat lozenges with him all afternoon?" Bayta added.

I threw a sideways look at her. As distasteful as it might be for her to have to deal with the Modhri, she was obviously intrigued by the chance to access one of the murder victims' memories. "Including during dinner," I added, looking back at Qiddicoj.

"Mr. Kennrick visited him briefly in the early afternoon," the Modhri said. "They discussed the halfway-celebration meal Mr. Kennrick was planning."

I nodded. Kennrick had already told me about that. "And the lozenges?"

"They were locked in his lower storage compartment the entire time, including during the sundown meal." The Modhri considered. "Though Mr. Kennrick *did* handle them later that evening, when he retrieved Master Colix's keepsake blanket for him."

I sat up a little straighter. *That* meeting Kennrick *hadn't* mentioned. "What exactly happened?"

"Mr. Kennrick stopped by to say good night," the Modhri said. "Master Colix was feeling too ill to rise, and asked Mr. Kennrick to obtain his blanket and transfer his lozenges to the upper storage compartment."

"Were either of Master Colix's seatmates there at the time?" I asked.

"The Juri was absent," the Modhri said. "The Human female was already beneath her privacy shield. I believe Master Tririn was absent as well."

Which would explain why neither Tririn, Terese, nor the Juri in the window seat had mentioned the incident. "Did he lock the upper storage compartment after he got the blanket?"

A slight frown creased Qiddicoj's face. "I'm not certain. Master Colix watched as he pulled out the blanket, placed the bag of lozenges in its place, then flipped the blanket open and draped it across Master Colix's torso. Master Colix was looking at the blanket, adjusting its position, when Mr. Kennrick returned Master Colix's ticket."

"Where did Master Colix put the ticket?" I asked.

"In his tunic's inside top pocket."

Which was where Bayta and I had found it when we'd later examined the body. "Did anyone else go pocket-diving in his tunic between then and the time he was brought to the dispensary?" I asked.

"I don't know," the Modhri said, sounding frustrated. "Master Colix was so focused on his internal condition that he wasn't really paying attention to his surroundings."

"And you weren't either?"

"I have only my Eye's senses to work with," the Modhri reminded me. "If those senses are impaired, I'm as helpless as the Eye itself."

"Let's try a different angle," I suggested. "Did Master Colix always keep the ticket in that pocket?"

"Yes."

"Did his seatmates know that?"

"Most likely. Master Colix didn't keep it a secret."

"Master Tririn know it, too?"

"Again, most likely."

I grimaced. In other words, whether Kennrick had locked the compartment or not, way too many people knew where to find the key.

"But *Logra* Emikai was the one we caught in the baggage car," Bayta pointed out. "How would he have known where the ticket was?"

"*Logra* Emikai had Master Colix's ticket?" the Modhri asked, sounding confused.

"Possibly," I said. "We ran into him poking around the bodies a couple of days after the first deaths. He may have been returning the ticket, or he may have been up to something else he didn't want to get caught at. No chance you were still hanging around the morgue, I suppose?"

Qiddicoj shook his head. "Both Master Colix's and *di*-Master Strinni's colonies were dead soon after their bodies were taken there," the Modhri said. "Yet you told me *Logra* Emikai was not connected to the murders."

"I said that was my gut feeling," I corrected. "But that was largely based on the fact that I didn't have a motive for him, barring some deep, dark connection with either the victims or Pellorian Medical that we didn't know about. Now that we know there's at least a tenuous connection between him and Witherspoon via Terese, I may have to put him back on the list."

"At least as an accomplice," Bayta murmured. "He couldn't have created last night's situation by himself."

"Agreed," I said. "All that having been said, he still doesn't feel right for the job."

"I had hoped for more from you than mere intuition," the Modhri said with a hint of disapproval.

"Don't worry, you'll get more," I said, standing up. "Thank you for your assistance. We'll be in touch."

Qiddicoj nodded. "If I can be of further assistance, merely ask."

"I will," I said. "One other thing. One of your walkers shares a car with the three Fillies on the contract team. Have you seen any of them disappear for long periods, or head back toward third class?"

"No," the Modhri said without hesitation. "They leave for meals and hygienic needs, but that's all. All other time is spent sleeping, reading, or playing games together."

"Thank you," I said. "Good afternoon, Modhri."

"Good afternoon, Compton." Qiddicoj took an extra-deep breath, and the skin of his face tightened subtly as the Modhri disappeared back under his rock.

Bayta and I returned our borrowed chairs to their original places, then headed forward toward our compartments. "There, now," I said as we passed through the vestibule into the next car. "That wasn't so bad, was it?"

"He's a monster," Bayta said shortly.

"That he is," I agreed. "But sometimes in investigative work you have to deal with one monster in order to bring down another."

She was silent another half coach length. "Did we at least learn anything useful?" she asked at last.

"Oh, yes," I said softly. "For starters, we learned that Kennrick lied to us. Let's go find out why."

EIGHTEEN :

Kennrick was right where I'd expected to find him: sitting in the bar in earnest conversation with *Asantra* Muzzfor. Both of them looked up as Bayta and I approached, and neither looked especially happy to see us. "Compton," Kennrick greeted me perfunctorily as we got within conversation distance. "Sorry, but this is a private meeting."

"This'll only take a minute," I promised. "I just want to know why you lied to me."

That got his full attention. "What?" he asked, frowning. "When?"

"Perhaps we should step out into the corridor for a moment?" I suggested, inclining my head microscopically toward Muzzfor.

"No," Muzzfor said firmly. "I wish to hear this. Bring a chair for yourself and your companion, Mr. Compton."

I raised my eyebrows at Kennrick. "Kennrick?"

"Go ahead," he said firmly. "Whatever you think you've

found, I can already tell you there's a perfectly reasonable explanation."

I pulled over a pair of chairs from an unoccupied table nearby. Kennrick shifted his seat toward Muzzfor to give us room, and Bayta and I crowded in across from them. "I've been told you had a meeting with Master Colix the night he died," I said without preamble. "I was wondering why you never mentioned that."

"I did," Kennrick said. "I told you I was there that afternoon to—"

"Not the afternoon meeting," I interrupted him. "Later, after dinner, when you swapped out his keepsake blanket and his lozenges."

A muscle in Kennrick's cheek tightened. "Oh," he said. "That meeting."

"Yes, *that* meeting," I said. "Why didn't you tell us about it?"

Kennrick seemed to wilt a little in his seat. "Because I'd been ordered to stay away from him and the other Shorshians."

I flicked a glance at Muzzfor. He was watching Kennrick, his expression set in that neutral mask so beloved by prosecutors eyeing potential witnesses, or lions checking out a herd of elk. "Ordered by whom?" I asked.

"*Usantra* Givvrac," Kennrick said. "He thought I was spending too much time back in third and told me to give it a rest."

"Were you?" I asked. "Spending too much time back there, I mean?"

Kennrick looked sideways at Muzzfor. "I didn't think so," he said. "Others obviously had different opinions."

"You also spent a great deal of time with them aboard the torchliner from Earth," Muzzfor said.

"But not because I was trying to influence their votes,"

Kennrick insisted. "I just happen to like Shorshians, that's all. And Shorshic food, too. It was just natural that the five of us liked to spend time together."

"Especially on the torchliner, where there aren't any travel-class barriers between passengers?" I asked.

"Exactly," Kennrick said, looking back at me. "I was just trying to keep up those friendships here, that's all."

"To the point of defying *Usantra* Givvrac's orders about staying away from them?"

Kennrick grimaced. "The only reason I went back there was to tell Master Colix why I wouldn't be able to share the halfway-celebration meal with them," he said. "It didn't seem right to just disappear without explanation."

"What did he say?"

"Nothing, because I didn't tell him," Kennrick said. "When I got there he wasn't feeling well, and I decided it wasn't the time to drop this on him, too." He winced. "If I'd realized he was dying . . . anyway, I got his blanket down for him and put his lozenge bag in its place, and said good night."

"Did you lock the upper compartment before you returned his ticket to him?" I asked.

"Of course." Abruptly, Kennrick's eyes widened. "I'll be damned. *Logra* Emikai!"

"What about him?" I asked.

"His locksmith's bypass mimic," Kennrick said, his eyes darkening with anger. "*He's* the one who sneaked in and stole Master Colix's lozenges."

"Interesting thought," I said. "Why would he do that?"

"How should I know?" Kennrick growled. "The point is that no one had to have Master Colix's ticket to get in there."

I looked at Bayta, eyebrows raised. "Bayta?" I said.

"*Logra* Emikai's device doesn't work on Quadrail locks,"

she said. "The Spiders have tried it on several, and it won't even read them, let alone duplicate the trip codes."

"Maybe, maybe not," Kennrick said. "Do you have it?"

"At the moment, yes," I told him. "Why?"

"I'd like to take a look at it," he said, holding out his hand.

"Why?" I repeated, making no move toward my pocket. "You heard her—the Spiders have already concluded it's useless here."

"That assumes the Spiders actually know the mimic's whole potential," Kennrick countered, his hand still outstretched. "But there could very well be another tech layer below the surface that you can't reach unless you punch in an access code."

"And you know what *Logra* Emikai's code might be?"

"I already told you, I know a little about these gadgets," Kennrick replied. "Give me an hour, and I'll bet I can find the next level down."

"Interesting thought," I said again. "I'll ask the Spiders to have another go at it."

For a moment Kennrick and I locked eyes. Then, reluctantly, he withdrew his hand. "Fine," he said. "Whatever. But if you want my opinion, you've got the thief *and* the killer already tied up."

"Let's hope you're right," I said. "Thanks for clearing that up. We'll let you get back to your meeting now. Good day, *Asantra* Muzzfor."

"And to you, Mr. Compton," Muzzfor said, inclining his head. His face, I noted, still had that lion/elk expression.

Bayta waited until we were out in the corridor before speaking again. "Do you believe him about *Usantra* Givvrac's order?"

I shrugged. "It's plausible enough, I suppose, especially if Givvrac thought Kennrick was trying to unduly influence the three Shorshians back there."

"I wonder if Mr. Kennrick really does like Shorshians and their food that much," Bayta murmured.

"That part does seem a little thin," I agreed. "And of course, with Givvrac now inconveniently dead, there's no way to confirm any of it."

"I also find it strange that he disobeyed *Usantra* Givvrac and then didn't even tell Master Colix what he'd supposedly gone back there to say." Bayta hunched her shoulders. "You think we should ask the Modhri what they actually *did* talk about?"

"I don't think that'll be necessary," I told her. "Besides, there's also the possibility Kennrick thought he might be able to change Givvrac's mind enough to at least let him host the halfway celebration they were planning. In that case, he also wouldn't mention his new marching orders." I glanced behind us to make sure no one was within earshot. "Personally, I'm more interested in Kennrick's ideas about Emikai's mimic. *Could* it have another programming layer to it?"

"I suppose that's possible," she said. "I'll have the twitters look into it."

"Thanks," I said. "By the way, it sounded earlier like you were having doubts about Aronobal starting that rumor about us clobbering Emikai and throwing him off the train. That still true?"

She looked suspiciously at me. "Why?"

"Because I agree with you," I said. "More intriguing is the fact that Kennrick's IQ seems to have dropped a few points today."

"What do you mean?"

"I mean he's being remarkably slow at picking up on the obvious," I said. "First there was your suggestion that Aronobal should be trying to find out what we know instead of starting a rumor to keep us away from her. The obvious counterargument is that Aronobal is the amateur part of the team—amateur in the skullduggery aspects, anyway—and hasn't got the chops to brazen out a role like that. That should also have occurred to Kennrick, only apparently it never did."

I nodded back over my shoulder. "And now it only just occurs to him, after a whole bunch of hours, that Emikai's mimic is the perfect solution to the mystery of Colix's vanishing lozenges."

"Maybe he's just not as good at this as you are," Bayta suggested.

"Or maybe there are other reasons," I said. "Such as hoping we'll think of the mimic ourselves so he doesn't have to look like he's grabbing on to the first diversion that comes along."

Bayta pursed her lips. "So if Dr. Aronobal didn't start the rumor, who did? And why?"

"Not sure about that," I admitted. "On the surface, I can't see what sense it makes."

"Maybe it doesn't make sense because there's no sense to be made," Bayta said hesitantly. "Maybe *Usantra* Givvrac was right, that the killer is just insane."

"He's not insane, and it does make sense," I said firmly. "We just have to find the right way to put the pieces together."

She sighed. "I'm sorry I'm not being more help," she said. "Putting people's motives and thoughts under a microscope— that's not something I'm good at."

I stared at her, my stomach tightening as a memory abruptly popped into my mind: Emikai, still twitching from the after-effects of the *kwi*, studying my luggage as if he could see through it to the spectral analysis equipment he assumed was inside.

There it was, the nagging feeling I'd been wrestling with. And with it, the clue I hadn't even known I'd been missing. Not what had been done, but what *hadn't* been done.

And suddenly, I had it. I had it all.

"Too bad *Korak* Fayr isn't here—" Bayta broke off with a muffled gasp as I grabbed her arm and picked up my pace, dragging her forward. "Frank?"

"Come on," I told her grimly. "We've got work to do."

"You've figured it out?" she asked, a flicker of hope in her voice.

"I think so," I said, my mind flashing back to the very beginning of our journey. Bayta had called it, all the way back then. She'd called it exactly.

My past had indeed come back to haunt me.

"It's the Modhri?" she asked, her arm tensing inside my grip.

"No," I said. "Actually, it's worse."

We spent the rest of the afternoon discussing the case, and laying out the facts to test against my new theory. By the time we broke for dinner, I was ninety percent convinced I was right.

With luck, I would get that final ten percent tonight.

I waited until two in the morning by the train's clocks, when even the most dedicated night owls among the passengers were probably thinking about turning in. Bayta offered to come with me, but I told her to go back to bed. There was nothing that could put the damper on a heart-to-heart, off-the-record conversation like having a third party present.

And so I made my solitary way back through first, through second, and through third, until I was in the baggage car by the dead bodies, standing in front of *Logra* Emikai.

I'd left the Filly in a fairly awkward and uncomfortable position when I'd retied his bonds, mainly because with my limited resources I hadn't had a lot of alternatives. To my mild surprise, I found he'd risen to the challenge of his situation. With strategic repositioning of the chair, toilet, and table, he'd been able to stretch out instead of having to sleep sitting up-right. His head was pillowed, hammock-style, on one of his pinioned arms, while the other hung free. It looked tolerable, even marginally comfortable.

Of course, if he turned over in his sleep he would instantly roll off his makeshift three-point bed and land on the floor, which would snap him fully awake as well as possibly giving one or both of his arms a nasty sprain. Still, it was an ingenious use of resources. One more indication, I reminded myself, of the kind of person I was dealing with.

"Are you here to watch me sleep?"

Mentally, I tipped him a salute. His eyes still appeared closed, but I could see now the small slits he was watching me through. Professional, indeed. "Sorry—just me," I said. "I gather you were hoping for someone else?"

"Indeed," he said, opening his eyes all the way and shifting back up to a sitting position on the chair. "Still, a clever perpe-trator seldom tries the same trick twice on the same person."

"You know something about perpetrators, do you?" I suggested, pulling out my multitool and flicking out the small knife blade as I walked toward him. "I thought you probably did."

He drew back as he watched me approach, his eyes on the knife. "What do you do?" he asked cautiously.

"Not what you're thinking," I assured him. Setting the blade against the safety webbing tying his left wrist to the crate stack, I carefully sliced through it. "I think I know what's go-ing on," I said as I stepped to his other side and cut his right arm free, too. "But I need your help and expertise to prove it."

"What expertise is that?" he asked suspiciously as he massaged his wrists.

"The kind I'd expect," I said, "from a fellow cop."

He stiffened, just enough to show I'd hit the mark. "You misread," he said. "I am not an enforcement officer."

"Former cop, then," I said. "Come on—we both know I'm right. Back in my compartment you talked about not believing something until you had evidence of its existence, and of needing to reach the required legal bar for action. Those are both phrases I've heard before from Filiaelian security officers."

"That hardly constitutes compelling evidence."

"We Humans are pretty good with hunches," I said. "And of course, your current evasiveness just adds weight to my conclusion."

For a moment he eyed me. "Very well," he said. "I was indeed once an enforcement officer. But no longer. I am retired, with no official authority from any Filiaelian governmental body."

"Close enough," I said. "Let me try another hunch on you. Before your retirement, you were a forensic investigator."

His nose blaze darkened with surprise. "That was indeed my specialty. Remarkable. May I ask how you reached that conclusion?"

"It was a combination of things," I said. "You seemed very interested in my technique as I was taking samples from the air filter in Terese German's car. You also didn't fall for that 'congenital disease after-elements' soap bubble I spun for the rest of the passengers, either. More interestingly, you knew roughly how big a standard spectroscopic analyzer was, which was why you were studying my luggage last night in my compartment. You were trying to figure out if I'd lied about that, too."

I gestured behind me. "But mostly because Bayta and I

nearly caught you snooping around back here a couple of days ago. My first thought was that you were returning Master Colix's ticket to him after having used it to steal the lozenges from his storage compartment."

"The tablets were medicine?" Emikai asked, looking surprised again. "Ms. German said they were foodstuffs."

"Ms. German is not the most observant person in the galaxy," I said dryly. "Though to be fair, Master Colix wasn't exactly advertising it, either. Speaking of Ms. German, what exactly is going on with her, anyway?"

He shook his head. "I cannot tell you."

"Come on, *Logra* Emikai," I cajoled. "This is just between two ex-cops, remember? By the way, what kind of title is *logra*? It obviously doesn't come from *lomagra*, as my partner thought."

"It is a new rank, a title given me by my current employers," he said. "It refers to the ancient Filiaelian name for a *bulwark*, or a protector of the people."

"Ancient Filiaelian, eh?" I commented. "We have people who like mining old languages, too. Anyway, the point is that I already know Ms. German is pregnant, which is why you were concerned enough about the air quality in her car to try to break into my compartment to see what I'd found out about that. I also know that you and Dr. Aronobal are escorting her from Earth to Filiaelian space. I just want to know why."

He gazed at me for a long moment. I waited, keeping my best encouraging expression in place. Finally, he shrugged. "I suppose it cannot hurt. Several weeks ago Ms. German was assaulted near her home in the Western Alliance and impregnated by her attacker. Dr. Aronobal and I were already on Earth, seeking Human subjects for genetic testing, and we received orders to offer her our assistance and invite her to accompany us back to the Filiaelian Assembly for medical treatment and study."

"Who exactly did these orders come from?" I asked.

"One of Dr. Aronobal's superiors, I presume," he said. "I was never shown the actual message. We offered Ms. German our assistance, which was accepted, and we are now returning to the Filiaelian Assembly with her."

"Interesting timing, you being right there in the vicinity of this attack and all," I commented. Actually, the timing struck me as more suspicious than interesting, but this wasn't the time to go into that. "Dr. Aronobal's part I understand, kindly physician and all that. Where exactly do you come into it?"

"To be honest, I am not entirely certain," he said hesitantly. "I was asked to come out of retirement and accompany Dr. Aronobal to Earth as assistant and protector."

"Someone thought she needed protecting?"

"Apparently so." Emikai smiled suddenly. "It was apparently thought that I had the necessary skills for the position."

"And correctly so," I assured him, rubbing my throat. "So what kind of genetic testing are they planning for Ms. German?"

"That I also do not know," he said. "But it must be highly urgent for us to have been hired to bring her all the way across the galaxy."

"So it would seem," I agreed. And that, I sensed, was all I was going to get out of him on this subject. Time to move on. "But as I was saying, my first assumption was that you were returning Master Colix's ticket. But I know now that you stole neither the ticket nor the lozenges. Ergo, you must have come here for some other purpose." I raised my eyebrows. "You were examining the bodies, weren't you?"

He inclined his head. "I was attempting to do so," he said. "You interrupted me before I could complete my investigation."

"I presume you got far enough to notice the needle marks

on the three Shorshians," I said, mentally crossing my fingers. *Ninety percent sure . . .* "Anything interesting about them?"

He smiled tightly. "You would not ask unless you already knew," he said. "Your unstated hunch is correct: the needle marks were made *after* the victims' deaths."

I felt my stomach tighten. "You're absolutely sure about that?"

"I am," he said. "I also suspect the tip of the needle is still buried within *di*-Master Strinni's skin."

"Not anymore, but it was," I said. There it was, the last ten percent of doubt. "Thank you, *Logra* Emikai. I believe you've just helped me identify a killer."

His eyes locked hard into mine. "Who?"

I reached into my pocket and tossed him his first-class pass. "Come to the first-class dining car tomorrow at ten o'clock," I told him. "I'll introduce you."

"Thank you," he said softly as he slid the pass into a pocket. "I will be there."

"Good." I gestured in the direction of the bodies. "In the meantime, I have a couple of final tests to run on the bodies. I was hoping you would assist me."

He inclined his head. "I would be honored."

An hour later, our tests completed, we left the baggage car. I dropped Emikai off at his seat among the sea of privacy-shielded sleepers and continued on forward. I hoped he would get a good night's rest.

I hoped I would, too. But I still had one more task to perform.

I found *Osantra* Qiddicoj sleeping in the open, without his sleep canopy deployed. Qiddicoj himself was sound asleep, but the Modhri inside him was awake and alert and obviously waiting up for me. Our conversation took another hour, and when I finally dragged myself back to my own bed I had the whole, bloody story.

Back when I worked for Westali, the hours leading up to a high-profile arrest were generally cluttered with a million last-minute details. There were warrants to get, backup to arrange, logistics to plan, loopholes to anticipate, and bolt-holes to plug. If you did everything right, the arrest itself was almost anticlimactic. If you did anything wrong, the whole event was likely to blow up in your face.

But here on the Quadrail, where Spider authority was absolute and bureaucratic red tape nonexistent, none of those details was relevant. As a result, I got to spend eight of those final hours asleep. A more restful sleep than I'd had since Bayta and I had first been summoned to the second/third dispensary to watch Master Colix die. It was finally almost over.

I really should have known better.

It was ten minutes to ten, and Bayta and I were just finishing a light breakfast, when Emikai arrived. "I trust I'm not overly early?" he asked, glancing around the dining car as if he expected the killer to be wearing a sign announcing his identity.

"Not at all," I told him, standing up and offering Bayta my hand. She didn't need my help, of course, but Filly cops were genetically engineered toward courtesy, and my show of politeness toward my partner might buy me a few points when it came time to shake him down for more information. "The rest of the group should be assembled," I added as I gestured to the entryway. "Shall we go?"

I led the way four cars to the rear. Kennrick and the three remaining contract-team Fillies were indeed there, sitting in a circle and talking earnestly. For once, there were no dealt cards sitting in front of the group. "Greetings to you, *Esantra* Worrbin," I greeted the head of the group. "And to you, *Asantra* Muzzfor, and you, *Asantra* Dallilo," I continued, nodding to each in turn. "I appreciate your giving me a few moments of your time."

"What's *he* doing here?" Kennrick growled, eyeing Emikai darkly.

"I asked him to join us," I said.

"And he got free how?"

"It was actually pretty easy once I'd cut his ropes," I said. "The reason I asked you all here—"

"Without consulting any of us first?" Kennrick interrupted. "Our opinions and concerns don't matter?"

"Actually, no, they don't," I said. "The reason I asked you all here was so that you could bear witness to the end of the ordeal. I finally know the identity of the murderer."

Muzzfor sat up a little straighter. "You've found him?" he asked, an edge to his voice. "Why did you not say so earlier?"

"Because until last night I wasn't a hundred percent sure," I told him. "I thought—"

"Last *night*?" Muzzfor echoed. "And yet you waited until now to speak? How many more of us might have died in the dark hours because of your lack of haste?"

"You aren't in any danger," I assured him. "Not anymore. The contract team was indeed the target, but not for the reasons we all thought."

"A moment," Worrbin spoke up. "If this matter concerns the contract team, all members should be present. Master Tririn and Dr. Witherspoon must be summoned."

"He's right," Kennrick seconded. "And as long as you're

going to get them passed up from third, you might as well go the whole dit rec mystery route and have the rest of the suspects join us, too."

"Which suspects are those?" I asked.

"All of *his* friends," Kennrick said, nodding toward Emikai. "Dr. Aronobal and that Human girl, Terese whatever."

"Terese German," I said. "Actually, she's not a suspect. Never was, really, if you think about it."

"Why not?" Dallilo asked, gazing down his long Filly nose at Emikai.

"Because *di*-Master Strinni and *Usantra* Givvrac were killed here in first class," I said. "Ms. German didn't have access to this part of the train."

"Dr. Aronobal did, though," Kennrick persisted. "She and Dr. Witherspoon were making the rounds between here and third all the time."

"True," I agreed. "Still, I think we can dispense with their company for the present." I raised my eyebrows at him. "So, Kennrick. You want to tell everyone why you killed them? Or shall I?"

NINETEEN :

I'd said it so casually that for the first couple of seconds no one seemed to get it. Then, almost in unison, Worrbin and the others turned to look at Kennrick. "You're not serious," Worrbin said, sounding stunned. "Mr. *Kennrick?*"

"Absolutely serious," I assured him, watching Kennrick closely. His eyes were just starting to widen with shock as the words sank in. Exactly the correct reaction, with exactly the correct timing. The man was good, all right. "Would you like to make a statement, Kennrick?"

"Yes," Kennrick said, coming out of his pretended paralysis. "I want to state that you're completely and certifiably insane. Where in *hell* do you get off making outrageous accusations like that?"

"Truth is never popular, is it?" I said regretfully. "Fine—if you don't want to tell them, I will. The point is—"

"Just a moment, Mr. Compton," Worrbin interrupted me. "I have no great personal affection for Mr. Kennrick, but you cannot simply make public statements like that without proof in hand. *Have* you such proof?"

"Let's take this one step at a time," I suggested. "The point is—"

"I knew it," Kennrick muttered under his breath. "I *knew* you didn't just quit Westali. Loose damn cannon—they fired your butt, didn't they?"

"The point is," I said, raising my voice a little, "and the point we all missed, was that the murders had nothing to do with the contract itself. They were, in fact, an experiment. A field test to see if a new kind of murder technique could be slipped through Spider security and used aboard a Quadrail."

Around us, the car was starting to quiet down as more and more passengers tuned in on our conversation. "What is this technique?" Muzzfor asked.

"Nothing I care to talk about in the open," I said. "But trust me, it works."

"And I presume you've got an explanation for how *Usantra* Givvrac and the three Shorshians died in entirely different ways?" Kennrick demanded. "Come on, Compton. Playing detective can be fun, but you're way over the line with this one."

"Actually, I believe *Usantra* Givvrac's death was mostly accidental," I said. "Collateral damage, as it were, from *di*-Master Strinni's murder."

Muzzfor stirred in his seat. "*Esantra* Worrbin, I submit that this is not the proper venue for such a sensitive discussion," he said, looking significantly around the car.

"Agreed," Worrbin said grimly. "We must find a place with more privacy."

"We can go to my compartment," Kennrick offered. "There's enough room there."

"Or you can just confess and surrender now," I suggested.

"Once you're properly secured, I can go over the details with the others at their convenience."

Kennrick snorted. "If you think I'm going to confess to something I didn't do, you're crazy."

"I further submit that if there is to be a medical discussion that Dr. Witherspoon be asked to join us," Muzzfor continued.

"And Dr. Aronobal, too," Kennrick added. "She and Witherspoon are the only ones with access to hypos."

I felt a surge of relieved affirmation. I'd hoped he would fall for that one. "And how exactly did you know the three Shorshic bodies had hypo marks in them?" I asked.

If this had been a proper dit rec mystery, Kennrick would have inhaled sharply as he belatedly realized the folly of his revelation. Unfortunately, here in the real world, he was right on top of it. "How else could the poison have gotten into their systems?" he retorted without hesitation. "Besides, whoever jumped you and Witherspoon wanted that replacement hypo for *something*."

"He's correct," Muzzfor said. "Such obvious deduction is hardly proof of any wrongdoing."

"No, the murderer wanted the hypo for something, all right," I confirmed. "But not as a replacement. Kennrick knew I was sniffing around the other possible methods for introducing poison into someone's system, and he decided he needed to send me off in the wrong direction."

Worrbin grunted. "You make no sense."

"Actually, I make perfect sense," I countered. Kennrick's expression, I noted, was still walking that realistic path between bewilderment and outrage.

But there should have been something else there, too, a hint of concern as I backed him slowly into a corner. Only there was no such concern that I could detect.

What did he know that I didn't?

"His best shot at a wrong direction was to make me think the cadmium that killed Master Colix and the others had been injected," I continued. "So the night I was attacked he hid under the sleep canopy in *di*-Master Strinni's vacant seat, knowing either Dr. Aronobal or Dr. Witherspoon would eventually show up in answer to *Osantra* Qiddicoj's call for medical help. It was just my bad luck I decided to stick with Dr. Witherspoon that night. Kennrick waited until we'd passed, clobbered both of us, and stole the hypo."

"I was in my compartment," Kennrick said in a tone of strained patience. "The Spider who came for me will testify to that."

"By *then* you were, sure," I said. "After you got the hypo, you slipped past the activity in the dispensary and beat it back to your compartment so you could pretend to be asleep when we sent for you."

I looked back at the three Fillies. "But later that night, once things had calmed down, he went back to the morgue and made needle marks in the bodies. He also made sure to break off the needle tip in *di*-Master Strinni to make us think that was the reason the murderer needed a replacement hypo. After that, he probably just dumped the rest of the hypo down the toilet into the reclamation system."

"You say he wanted you to think the poison had been injected," Muzzfor said. "What makes you think it wasn't?"

"Because I availed myself of the services of *Logra* Emikai," I told him. "He's a former law enforcement officer who specialized in forensic investigations, and he confirmed that the hypo marks had been made postmortem."

The three Fillies looked questioningly at each other. "Is that the sum of your evidence, Mr. Compton?" Worrbin asked.

"Isn't it enough?" I countered.

"No, it is not," Worrbin said flatly. "I'm not convinced."

I grimaced. That wasn't really surprising, I conceded, given that Kennrick had avoided all my guilty-reaction traps and I couldn't afford to give them my actual evidence. "I'm sorry to hear that," I told Worrbin. "But that's certainly your privilege. This was just a courtesy call anyway."

"What do you mean, a courtesy call?" Worrbin demanded, his blaze darkening ominously.

"I mean that I really don't have to convince any of you of Kennrick's guilt," I said. "Here inside the Tube, the Spiders are in charge. Thank you for your time—we'll take it from here."

"Like hell you will," Kennrick said, standing up.

"Don't try it, Kennrick," I warned, motioning Emikai to step in a bit closer. "It's two against one, and we're both former cops."

"This has gone far enough," Worrbin said, his voice suddenly gone lofty and imperious with the weight of thousands of years of Filiaelian history and thousands of planets of Filiaelian geography. "This Human is associated with us, and through us with the Filiaelian Assembly. I forbid you to imprison him without incontestable proof of guilt." He pointed to Emikai. "I further call upon this former enforcement officer to support my decision."

"*Logra* Emikai is with me," I reminded him.

"Not any more," Emikai said softly.

I turned to look at him, a sinking feeling in my stomach. "We're not in Filiaelian territory, *Logra* Emikai," I reminded him carefully. "You're not required to obey their orders."

"Unfortunately, I am," Emikai said. He looked decidedly unhappy about it, but there was no wavering in his voice. "He is an *esantra* of the Filiaelian Assembly. No matter where in the galaxy we find ourselves, I have no choice but to uphold his legal decisions." His eyes flicked to Worrbin, then back to me. "It is what I am," he added.

And so it was. Retired or not, he'd been genetically engineered to be a cop, and the absence of his badge and gun didn't change that.

I looked back at Kennrick. His arms were crossed over his chest, a righteously indignant expression plastered across his face, a hint of a smirk lurking behind his eyes. Was Worrbin's interference the back door he'd been counting on? "You want proof, *Esantra* Worrbin?" I asked. "Fine." I held out my hand toward Kennrick. "Your reader, please."

Kennrick's expression didn't change, but the subtle smirk was suddenly gone. "Why?" he asked.

"Give it to me and I'll show you," I said.

"Not a chance," he said flatly. "All my personal records are on it."

"Consider this a subpoena," I said. "Let's start by showing them who Whitman Kennrick really is."

Kennrick looked at the Fillies. "*Esantra* Worrbin?"

Worrbin looked at him, then at me, then back at Kennrick. "Give him your reader," he ordered.

Kennrick's lips puckered, but he nodded. "Fine," he said. "But let it be noted that this is under protest." He reached his right hand into his jacket, got a grip on something, and started to pull his hand back out.

And without warning, he leaped in front of Bayta, his left fist snapping in a short punch from the hip into her solar plexus.

She gasped and bent forward, grabbing for her stomach. Kennrick kept moving, sidestepping around behind her, and I saw now that he was holding a pair of small cylinders in his right hand. As he turned back to face me he flipped one of the cylinders to his left hand, his hands tracing a quick pattern over and around Bayta's head. As I belatedly started toward them, he jerked both hands back toward his face, Bayta's head snapping backward in perfect synchronization.

And as her hands grabbed at her neck, I saw the glint of the thin wire wrapped around her throat.

"Careful, Compton," Kennrick warned, his voice quiet and deadly, as I came to an abrupt halt. "That goes for the rest of you, too."

"Do as he says," I croaked out through a suddenly dry mouth, my heart pounding in my throat. Oh, no. God, no. "Take it easy, Kennrick."

"Take it *off* easy, did you say?" Kennrick asked. He twitched the cylindrical handles of his garrote a little, making Bayta twitch in response.

"*Damn* it—" I broke off, clenching my teeth, fury and terror bubbling in my throat. Bayta's face was tight and pale, a hint of pain in her eyes from Kennrick's gut punch, her fingers trying uselessly to force their way between the wire and her throat. "Don't hurt her."

Kennrick smiled, a cold, evil thing. "Say please."

I took a deep breath. "Please don't hurt her."

"Good," he said, his voice brisk and almost businesslike. "Well, this is awkward, I must say. Any suggestions as to how we should proceed?"

"You want trouble, I'm available," I said, holding my arms away from my sides. From the positioning of his hands, a detached part of my mind noted, the garrote wire had to cross itself behind Bayta's head, meaning the loop completely encircled her neck instead of just pulling against the front and sides. It also meant that all Kennrick had to do was pull his hands apart to kill her. "Let her go, and you can do whatever you want to me."

"Oh, I know," he said brightly. "That handy little gadget of yours, the one you used on *Logra* Emikai two nights ago. Where is it?"

"I have it," Bayta croaked.

"Where?"

"Here." She reached for her right front pocket.

And gasped, her hand darting back up to her throat as Kennrick twitched the garrote again. "No, you just hold still," he ordered. "I'll get it."

I felt a surge of adrenaline. In order to get into her pocket, he would either have to let go of one end of his garrote or else hold both handles in a single hand. Either way, it would mean a brief chance to get to him before he could use the wire against her. If I was quick, and lucky, I might be able to get to her in time.

But he was already ahead of me. Watching me closely, he slid the wire around Bayta's throat, adjusting the positions of the handles, until the one in his right hand was back by his own throat. A quick twitch of his fingers, and he'd clipped the handle to his jacket collar. With his left hand still applying pressure against Bayta's throat, he reached with his right around her hip and pulled the *kwi* from her pocket. "There we go," he said, deftly wrapping it in place around his knuckles before unclipping the other garrote handle. "I think that officially leaves me holding all the cards."

"What do you want?" I asked.

"For now, to go back to my compartment," he said. "The lady goes with me, of course."

"Take me instead," I offered again.

He smiled tightly. "I'd rather bed down with a Malayan pit viper," he said. "Don't worry, I won't hurt her. Not unless you force me to."

I focused on Bayta's face, searching desperately for inspiration. The last thing I wanted was to let him get Bayta behind locked doors, with access to whatever other tricks he might have smuggled aboard. But with the wire pressing against Bayta's throat, there was nothing I could do without risking her life.

"Patience is a virtue," Bayta murmured.

"She's right," Kennrick seconded. "Your move, Compton."

I took another deep breath. "Go," I said.

"We'll talk later," he promised. He glanced once over his shoulder, making sure the path was clear. Then, holding Bayta close, he started backing toward the front of the car. I watched them go, my hands curled into helpless fists at my sides, still trying to come up with something—anything—I could do.

They were halfway to the vestibule when *Krel* Vevri quietly detached himself from the wall where he'd been standing and began moving silently to intercept.

I felt my breath catch in my throat. Vevri's eyes were shining with determination, a slight but unmistakable sag in the scales around his hawk beak. It was the Modhri who was currently in command of that body, coming to Bayta's rescue.

And about to get her killed.

I watched the unfolding drama, my brain and muscles paralyzed by indecision. Should I warn Kennrick of the approaching Juri, thereby temporarily protecting Bayta's life but destroying any chance the Modhri might have of stopping him? Or should I keep quiet, cross my fingers, and hope the Modhri's million-to-one shot actually came through?

I was still frozen in uncertainty when the decision was taken out of my hands. Abruptly, Kennrick spun halfway around, swinging Bayta around with him like a full-body shield as he lifted his right hand over her shoulder. I saw his thumb shift its grip on the garrote handle and squeeze the *kwi*'s firing switch.

Without even a twitch, Vevri collapsed to the floor with a thud and lay still.

Before anyone else could react Kennrick swung himself and Bayta back around to face me. "I'll be charitable and assume that wasn't your idea, Compton," he said. "If it happens again, there'll be consequences." He lifted the *kwi* again slightly. "This really *is* a handy little gadget."

And abruptly my spinning mind caught the tracks again, my eyes shifting to the unconscious Juri Kennrick had just shot with the *kwi*. The *kwi* that could only be activated by Bayta or one of the Spiders.

How the hell had Kennrick gotten the damn thing to work?

If any of the other passengers had it in mind to intervene, Vevri's failure convinced them otherwise. No one else so much as blinked as the killer and his hostage backed into the vestibule and vanished from sight.

The door had barely closed before Emikai started toward the door, a glint of fire in his eyes. "No—let them go," I said quickly.

"We cannot let him get to his compartment," Emikai said.

"How are you going to stop him without getting Bayta killed?" I demanded.

"He will not harm her," Emikai insisted. "Without a hostage, he is dead."

"So he kills her and grabs someone else," I snarled, my legs literally shaking with the overwhelming urge to go after Kennrick myself. "Don't you understand? This man is a professional, and he's clearly thought this through. We can't just go charging in after him. We have to figure out what his plan is, and outthink him."

Emikai looked at the door where Kennrick and Bayta had vanished. "And if we cannot?"

"We can," I said grimly. "We will."

For a long moment Emikai and I just stared at each other. Then, his shoulders slumped a little and he nodded. "She is your assistant," he said. "He is of your people. I yield to your authority."

"Thank you," I said. I squeezed my hands into fists to force out some of the adrenaline flooding my system and tried to think. "Okay, here's what we do. First of all, we need to make sure not to spook Kennrick again. Go find a conductor and tell him to alert any Spiders between here and Kennrick's compartment to make sure none of the other passengers tries to play hero."

"What if the conductor won't listen to me?"

"He will," I said. If he didn't, he would surely check telepathically with Bayta, who would just as surely confirm the order. "Next, we need to isolate Kennrick from other potential hostages. Tell the Spider to start figuring out where we can temporarily put the rest of the passengers in that car."

"I will obey," he said. "What about you?"

"Someone needs to talk to Kennrick and find out exactly what he wants." I squared my shoulders. "I guess that's me."

I forced myself to take my time, not wanting to come within sight of Kennrick before he reached his goal lest he think I was crowding him. I passed through the exercise/dispensary, shower, and storage cars, bypassed the dining car with its mostly oblivious patrons, and reached the first coach car.

I'd made it barely five steps inside when a hand darted in from my right, grabbed my arm, and spun me around.

And I found myself staring into the angry eyes of a Tra'ho government oathling. "What did you do?" he demanded.

I took another look at his face, with its sagging jowls and the slight flatness of the eyes. "Later, Modhri," I said shortly, reaching over to pull his hand off my arm.

"Not later," he insisted. "Now. What did you do?"

"What did *you* do?" I countered. "That stunt could have gotten Bayta killed."

"And so you allow the weapon to work?" he shot back. "How does that benefit either of us?"

"What makes you think *I* control the weapon?" I growled, glancing surreptitiously around the car. Fortunately, the rest of the passengers were already gathered in small knots, talking quietly but nervously among themselves, with little attention to spare for us. Kennrick's passage must have made quite an impression.

"Do not lie," the Modhri bit out. "I know the weapon must be activated. There was no Spider present. The agent herself would not have done so. That leaves only you."

"And since when do I have—?" I broke off, a jolt of understanding abruptly hitting me. "No, you're wrong," I said. "Bayta *did* activate it."

"Why would she foil my attempt to rescue her?"

"Because your attempt didn't have a chance," I told him. "And because she was thinking ahead."

"To what?"

"To the next real chance we have, whenever that is," I said, smiling tightly. "Don't you get it? *Kennrick now thinks he has a functional weapon.*"

The other's face worked as he thought it through. Then, slowly, the anger faded from his eyes. "Indeed," the Modhri murmured. "So the next time he thinks to use the weapon, it will fail?"

"Or at least the next time he tries to use it when Bayta judges we have a real chance of success," I said. "That doesn't mean one of us won't get zapped if we try something stupid again."

"Understood," the Modhri said. "What's our next move?"

"I'm going to go talk to him," I said. "Try to find out what he wants, how he expects to get it, and hopefully find a chink in his armor that we can exploit."

"Dangerous," the Modhri rumbled. "But necessary. What do you wish me to do in your absence?"

"For the moment, just hang back and let me work," I said. "If the *kwi* was still on its lowest unconsciousness setting, your Jurian walker should recover in an hour or two." I leveled a finger at him. "But I mean that about letting me work. We *will* nail him, but we'll do it my way. Understand?"

"I'll await your instructions," the Modhri promised reluctantly. "Good hunting to you."

"Thanks." I nodded. "In the meantime, if you really want something to do, you could help soothe your fellow passengers. You might also start getting them mentally prepared for some changes in their traveling conditions. We're going to evacuate the rest of that car's compartments, which will mean an influx of displaced travelers settling down in here and the other coach cars."

"I can do that." The Tra'ho's eyes shifted to the front of the car. "What is this?"

I turned to look. Maneuvering his way awkwardly through the vestibule door was a pale, frail-looking Nemut in a Shorshic vectored-thrust-powered support chair. His truncated-cone-shaped mouth had a slight distortion in it, and one of his angled shoulder muscles seemed frozen in a permanent off-center hunch. I'd seen him a few times since we left Homshil, mostly eating solitary meals in the dining car. "Trouble?" I asked quietly.

"I don't know," the Modhri said. "His name is Minnario, journeying to a Filiaelian clinic in hopes of finding a genetic cure for his congenital difficulties. But I've never seen him leave his compartment except for meals, which he always takes alone."

Something pricked at the back of my neck. "Do you know which compartment he's got?" I asked.

"No," the Modhri said, his oathling topcut wobbling back and forth as the Tra'ho shook his head. "None of the conversations I've overheard has mentioned that."

Minnario finished getting through the door and started down the center of the car, his head turning slowly back and forth as he studied the passengers. His eyes passed me, then paused and came back. His fingers shifted on the chair's control box, and he altered course in our direction.

"Wait here," I told the Modhri, and moved ahead to intercept. "Are you looking for me?" I asked as we neared each other.

Minnario looked down at a plate that was fastened to the chair's control box by a slender stem. [Are you the Human who chases the other Humans?] he croaked in slightly lisping Nemuspee as he brought the chair to a halt.

"I am," I confirmed. "You have a message for me?"

There was another pause as he again studied the plate. I took a final couple of steps toward him and saw that it was running him a transcript of what I'd just said. Apparently, deafness was another of his congenital defects. [I was told to give you this,] he croaked. Reaching to a pouch in his lap, he carefully extracted a Quadrail ticket. [The key to my compartment.]

"Let me guess," I said grimly. "Your compartment connects to the male Human's?"

[I don't know where the male Human goes,] he said. [I was asked to give you my key, and told I could move into this one.] He held up another ticket, this one glittering with the diamond-dust edges of a first-class, unlimited-use pass. Bayta's ticket. [Is that all right?] he croaked. [Should I remain here instead?]

"No, that's all right," I said, taking his ticket from him. "Go ahead and make yourself comfortable. I may ask to come in later to collect some of the female's personal effects."

[Certainly,] he said when the transcript had finished scrolling across the plate. [Is there trouble? The female seemed frightened.]

"There is, but it doesn't concern you," I assured him. "Thank you for this." Stepping past him, I continued forward.

The corridor of the rear compartment car was empty. I made my way through it, then entered the equally deserted corridor of the middle car. I located Minnario's compartment and used his ticket to open the door. "Hello?" I called carefully.

"There you are," Kennrick's muffled voice came back. "Don't just stand there—come on in."

I stepped into the compartment, letting the door slide shut behind me. The room was a typical Quadrail compartment, to which strategically placed grips and bars had been added to assist Minnario with his physical challenges. At the front of the room, the dividing wall between compartments had been opened about ten centimeters and a soft light was showing through. "Okay, I'm in," I called.

"Come over to the divider and take a look," Kennrick's voice came through the gap. "But carefully, please. Very carefully."

I crossed the compartment, stepping past the curve couch frozen midway into its collapse into the divider. I reached the opening and eased an eye around the edge.

Kennrick was all the way across the room, sitting cross-legged on the bed and turning the *kwi* thoughtfully over in his hands. Between him and me, sitting with unnatural stillness in the computer desk chair, was Bayta, a pair of wire loops wrapped around her neck.

"Let me explain the situation," Kennrick said. "You'll note the usual control on the wall beside you that will open the divider the rest of the way. I'd strongly advise you not to bump it."

"Because if I do, one of those wire loops will strangle her?" I suggested.

"It might," Kennrick said. "These are actually thinner wires than the garrote I pulled on you a few minutes ago, so it's possible the loop would slice her head clean off instead of just strangling her. Me, I'm not all that anxious to find out for sure. But if you're curious, be my guest."

"No, that's all right," I said. "I suppose the other loop is fastened to the corridor door?"

"You suppose correctly," he said. "Rather clever, if I do say so myself."

"Oh, it's brilliant," I assured him. I'd wondered how he thought he would be able to hold out another two and a half weeks without falling asleep and thus leaving himself open to attack. With this setup, he could sleep until noon every day without worrying about anyone charging in on him. "Your boss will be proud."

"Thank you," he said. "Incidentally, what exactly gave me away? Assuming something *did* give me away, and that you weren't just blowing smoke out there."

"Oh, no, I'm on to you," I assured him. "You're my replacement, the man who's supposed to figure out how to take control of the Quadrail from the Spiders."

I cocked my head. "So tell me. How *is* our good friend Mr. Larry Cecil Hardin?"

TWENTY :

"I was right," Kennrick said, shaking his head in admiration. "The minute I saw you getting on my Quadrail I knew you were going to be trouble. So again: what gave me away?"

"Several things," I said. "Though it wasn't until I'd collected enough of them that I started to see the pattern. For starters, Colix wasn't even room temperature when you were blaming the Spiders for incompetence or worse. Given their seven-hundred-year spotless operational record, it was a strange attitude to take. In retrospect, I can see it was just part of the plan to undermine confidence in their ability to run the Quadrail."

"Yes, I thought you seemed surprised by that," Kennrick conceded. "I suppose it was a bit of a risk, but with Aronobal and a couple of Shorshians in the room I really couldn't afford to pass up the chance to start planting seeds."

"And it was a theme you kept coming back to the whole trip," I said, trying to visually backtrack the wires around Bayta's neck. But my field of view was too limited for me to see where and how either of them was attached at the far end. "You also were way too incompetent for the liaison job you'd supposedly been hired for. Quite a few members of your team agreed on that."

"I thought I already explained that," he reminded me.

"Yes, and rather badly, too," I said. "There must be hundreds of people on Earth who are competent at both the legal *and* the social aspects of Filly and Shorshic cultures. Surely Pellorian could have hired one of them in your place, if that was actually the job you were supposed to be doing."

"I'm starting to think Mr. Hardin could have hired someone better than me for the real job, too," Kennrick said calmly. "Fortunately, it's too late for him to reconsider."

"If I were you, I wouldn't make assumptions like that," I warned. "Not with Hardin. And of course, there was the near-riot you sparked by starting the rumor back in third class that I'd done away with *Logra* Emikai. That whole thing made no sense until I realized its purpose was to maneuver Bayta and me into a situation where you'd get to see the *kwi* in action again."

"Now, *that* one you shouldn't have caught," Kennrick commented. "Excellent. I can see why Mr. Hardin was so complimentary about you."

"He was complimentary about *me*?"

"Within the context of hating your guts, yes," Kennrick said. "Anything else? Come on—honest criticism is how we learn to do better the next time."

Only there wouldn't be a next time, I knew. The last thing the Spiders could afford   the last thing *any* of us could afford— was for him to make it to the next station and send a report back to Hardin on the success of his ghoulish little mission. One way or another, Kennrick was going to have to die aboard this train.

Even if Bayta had to die along with him.

"Compton?" Kennrick prompted. "You still there?"

"I'm still here," I assured him.

"Anything else?"

"Just one more," I said. "The bit that finally caught my attention. Remember when we hauled Emikai in here two nights ago and he was looking around trying to figure out if I really had a spectroscopic analyzer? He spent a lot of that time looking at my luggage, because obviously something like that would have to take up a lot of space."

"Obviously," Kennrick said. "So?"

"It got me thinking about the morning after Colix's death, when you barged into my compartment also wanting to see the results of my tissue analysis," I said. "Only unlike Emikai, you never even glanced at my luggage. Your eyes went instantly to my reader. My one-of-a-kind, high-tech, super-spy-loaded reader." I cocked my head. "Only it isn't one-of-a-kind anymore, is it?"

"Not anymore, no," he agreed. "You know, I never even thought about that. *Damn*, but you're good."

"You're too kind," I said. "Yours must be even more interesting than mine for you to have sacrificed your high-ground bluff to keep it out of my hands."

"Oh, it's probably no more advanced than yours," Kennrick said. "But I could hardly let you go poking around the encrypted files where my detailed report was hidden. Not with your familiarity with the thing."

"Interesting," I said. "Actually, my plan was just to show them that your reader was gimmicked like nothing they'd ever seen before. It never occurred to me that you'd be careless enough to actually have the data sitting in there where someone could find it."

"You're kidding," Kennrick said, looking chagrined. "Well, *damn* it all. I guess I should have stood my ground a little longer."

"It wouldn't have made a difference," I said. "We already knew enough about the killings to put you on ice, with or without Worrbin's approval."

"Speaking of which, what do you think of the method?" Kennrick asked. "Pretty clever, eh?"

"Hellishly clever," I agreed, my stomach tightening. Back in my Westali days, I reflected, I could actually sit back and dispassionately discuss techniques for murder and torture without qualms. Not anymore. Not with Bayta's life in this lunatic's hands. "Where did you come up with a bacterium that could pack away that much heavy metal, anyway?"

Kennrick barked a laugh. "You want the real irony? That strain was originally designed with an eye toward *curing* heavy-metal poisoning. You inject the bacteria into the patient and let the little bugs spread out through his system, gobbling up every heavy-metal atom they happen across. Since their own biochemistry actually needs the stuff for reproduction, they multiply like crazy, but only up to the point where the metal's all been found and locked up. All you do then is flush them out of the system, and voilà—patient's cured. Send him home and charge his account."

"Only here you reversed the process," I said. "You spent the torchliner trip from Earth feeding the Shorshians bacteria that were already loaded to the gills with cadmium. You gave it a couple of weeks on the Quadrail to settle into their deep tissues, then uncorked a bottle of that really high-power antiseptic spray we found in the air filter. The bacteria die, in the process dumping their supplies of cadmium into the Shorshians' bodies, and we've got three impossible murders."

"Beautiful, isn't it?" Kennrick said, a disturbing glint in his eyes. "There are no warning symptoms because the bacteria have the metal solidly locked up. The Spiders' sensors won't notice anything, because the bacteria themselves are perfectly benign and the detectors aren't keyed for anything as low-level as basic elements. You can pick your time and place—hell, you don't even have to be anywhere near your victim when he's supposedly poisoned. It's the perfect crime."

"Only if you make sure there aren't any Fillies around," I pointed out.

His lip twisted. "There is that," he conceded. "I didn't realize how potent that spray really was, or that it would go deep enough to kill off Filiaelian gleaner bacteria. Too bad about Givvrac, really. I kind of liked the old coot. He was so—I don't know. So old-world calcified, I guess. Wanting everything to be just like it had always been."

"As opposed to the new world order you and Hardin are trying to make?"

"Not *trying* to make, Compton," he corrected me softly. "*Going* to make."

"Right," I said. "So why let Tririn live? And why steal Colix's throat lozenges that last night, when he thought you were putting them away for him?"

"Oh, come now," Kennrick chided. "What's a good murder without a suspect or two? Tririn's annoyance over Colix's throat operation made him the perfect patsy. I figured all I had to do was make the lozenges mysteriously disappear, to make it seem like Tririn was trying to cover up what Colix had done, and you'd fall all over yourself burying him in circumstantial evidence."

"Without nailing down the method?" I shook my head. "Not a chance."

"It was still worth a try," Kennrick said. "Besides, this was an experiment, remember? I wanted to see what effect distance from the antiseptic spray had on the bacteria's demise. Apparently, Master Bofiv was right on the edge—that's why it took him longer to croak—and Master Tririn was just past it." He picked up his reader from beside him on the bed and held it up for me to see. "It's all in my report," he added, a mocking edge to his tone.

"What about Strinni?"

"What about him?" Kennrick asked. "Oh—you mean the extra necrovri-laden bacterial strain I put in his food?" He shrugged. "I thought that as long as I was at it I might as well test the bacteria that had been designed to carry more complex molecules. Strinni was the perfect candidate for that one, sitting isolated from the others up in first class and all." He snorted gently. "Also the perfect candidate because he didn't usually eat with the other Shorshians aboard the torchliner. Made it easy to feed him his special servings without getting it mixed in with the others' dosages."

"As well as making him look like a drug addict to his fellow Quadrail passengers?" I suggested.

Kennrick shrugged again. "I never liked him anyway."

"And the thing with *Logra* Emikai and *Osantra* Qiddicoj?"

He frowned. "What thing?"

"Cutting Emikai loose and pumping Qiddicoj full of hypnotic," I said. "How did you pull that one off?"

He frowned a little harder. "Sorry, but you've lost me," he said. "But enough reminiscing. You ready to take a few orders?"

"Not yet," I said, frowning in turn. If Kennrick hadn't been involved with Emikai's mysterious midnight visitor . . . but there was no time to worry about that now. "I want to know first what's going to happen to Bayta," I said. "She obviously can't sleep sitting up in that chair."

"Don't worry, I've got things rigged so that I can let her lie down on the floor later," Kennrick assured me. "It's going to be a little hard on her back, but there's only one bed in here. Unless she wants to share?"

"I don't think so," I said, sternly forcing back a sudden surge of rage. If he so much as touched her . . . "Let me go get her a pillow and blanket."

"From your compartment?" he countered. "Sorry. I'm not letting you go pick through whatever other goodies you've got back there and try to smuggle something in. Before you leave, you can grab a pillow and blanket from right there behind you and stuff them through the gap."

"Good enough," I said. Not that I had anything in my compartment that would help Bayta anyway. "What about food?"

"Not a problem," he said. "I have enough ration bars to last me to Venidra Carvo." He raised his eyebrows. "Sorry—did you mean food for *her*?"

I took a deep breath, again forcing down my anger. He was taunting me, I knew, trying to see how far he could push before I lost it.

He could just keep pushing. I wasn't going to give him the satisfaction. More to the point, I wasn't going to let anger crowd out brainpower that would be better used for tactical thinking. "We've got plenty of other ration bars aboard," I said. "Let me get her some."

"In a bit," Kennrick said. "My turn now?"

I swallowed. "Go ahead."

"Okay," he said. "First of all, obviously, no one is to attempt to come in here. Not you, not the Spiders, not anyone."

"Don't worry," I said, eyeing the glinting wires wrapped around Bayta's throat. "How the hell did you get all that wire past the Spiders' sensors, anyway?"

"Ah, ah—*my* turn," Kennrick said firmly. "When we get to Venidra Carvo, I get to walk free and clear without interference. Sorry—*we* get to walk free and clear."

I saw the muscles in Bayta's throat tighten, a sudden stricken look in her eyes. Apparently, she hadn't thought past our arrival at Venidra Carvo. "You planning to take her along all the way back to Earth?" I asked Kennrick.

"Why not?" Kennrick said blandly, letting his eyes run up and down Bayta's body. "I'm sure she's very pleasant company." He looked back at me and gave me a faint smile. "Relax, Compton. She stays with me only until I feel safe. At that point, I turn her loose. I promise."

As if the promise of a murderer was worth a damn. "Fine," I said. "Anything else?"

"Yes; the accommodations," he said. "Rather, everyone else's accommodations. I'm sure you've already made plans to isolate me by moving everyone else out of this car?"

"We thought it would help keep down the noise," I said. "You know how neighbors can be."

"Oh, there's no need to convince me," he said. "I agree completely. In fact, let's go whole hog and move everyone out of all three compartment cars."

I frowned. "*All* of them?"

"Like you said, peace and quiet. You've got two hours to get everyone out of here. Including you."

"I'd like to stay, if you don't mind," I offered. "You might realize there's something else you need."

"I do mind, and I won't need anything," he said coolly. "More to the point, I want to know that any noises I hear in the night aren't coming from some clumsy Shorshian falling out of bed. This way, anything I hear after the next two hours will be unauthorized." He shifted his gaze to Bayta. "And will be dealt with accordingly."

"I already said there wouldn't be any intrusions."

"This way, I'll know you mean it," he countered. "You'd better get going—you've got a lot to do in the next two hours."

"Look, Kennrick, I understand—"

"Just go, Frank," Bayta interrupted tautly. "You heard him. Go, and start getting it done."

I frowned at her. There was a tightness around her eyes that hadn't been there a minute ago. Was she suddenly worried about Kennrick's order to move everyone out?

I didn't know. But whatever the reason, I'd clearly run dry on hospitality here. "Okay, I'm going," I said. "First let me get your bedding for you."

I crossed the room and pulled the pillow and blankets off Minnario's bed, wincing at the thought of him about to be kicked out of his compartment for the second time today. I thought about asking Kennrick if he would make an exception, decided I might as well save my breath. A four-time murderer was hardly likely to have any residual compassion for children, puppies, or cripples.

The blankets slipped easily through the gap in the divider. The much thicker pillow was trickier, but I eventually managed it. "That's good," Kennrick said. "I'll take it from here."

"What about Bayta's food?" I asked. "And are you going to want anything in the way of liquid refreshment?"

"I think we can make do with water from the sink," Kennrick said. "That way, since you'll never know who's going to be drinking next, I know you won't try poisoning it or anything."

I sighed. "You know, Kennrick, paranoids don't really live any longer than other people. It just feels like it. What about her food?"

"Come back here in two hours," he said. "Bring enough to last her the rest of the trip."

"All right," I said. "If you change your mind and want anything else—"

"Good-bye, Frank," Bayta cut me off, the intensity in her voice matched by the look in her eyes.

"Yes, good-bye, Frank," Kennrick repeated sarcastically. "See you in two hours. Don't be late."

"I'll be here." I looked at Bayta, wondering if I should try to say something soothing. But she didn't look like she was in a soothable mood. Nodding to her, I headed back across the compartment. I had just reached the door when I felt a subtle puff of air behind me, and turned to see the divider seal itself against the wall.

I swore under my breath. But it wasn't a curse of anger or frustration or even fear. The conversation with Kennrick had burned all such emotions out of my system. All that remained was the cold, detached combat mentality Westali had worked so hard to beat into me. *We'll outthink him,* I'd told Emikai. It was time I got started on that. Punching the door release, I stepped out into the corridor.

And came to an abrupt halt. Standing motionlessly in the corridor between me and the car's rear door were two conductor Spiders. "What?" I demanded.

Neither of them answered. I opened my mouth to ask the question again . . . and then belatedly, my brain caught up with me, and I took a second, closer look.

Because they weren't conductors. They were larger, with the pattern of white dots that usually denoted a stationmaster.

I'd almost forgotten about the message we'd tried to send as we'd blown past the hidden siding a few days ago. Apparently, the gamble had paid off.

No wonder Bayta had been so anxious for me to cut short the conversation and get out here.

"Frank Compton?" one of the Spiders said in the flat voice all Spiders seemed to have.

"Yes." I took a deep breath, a cold chill shivering across my skin. "Welcome, defenders. And may I say, it's about damn time."

I'd expected to have to spend at least the first hour helping get all the compartment cars emptied of passengers. But either Bayta or the defenders had already given the orders, and I quickly discovered that the conductors had the procedure under way. Leaving that task to them, I took the defenders back to my compartment for a quick tactical session.

"Let's start with you," I said as I closed the door behind me. "How many of you are there, and where's your tender?"

"We are two," one of the defenders said. His particular white-dot pattern reminded me of a military chevron lying on its side; privately, I dubbed him Sarge. "Our tender currently travels behind this train."

"Which I assume means you came aboard from the rear through the baggage cars," I said. "Did you bring any specialized equipment?"

"What sort of equipment?"

"Anything besides standard Spider tools and replacement parts," I said. "Weapons, another *kwi*, burglar tools—anything?"

The Spiders were silent for a moment, probably discussing the matter between themselves. "No weapons or tools," Sarge said at last. "But the tender is equipped with a side-extendable sealable passageway."

I frowned. "You mean like a portable airlock?"

"Yes," Sarge confirmed.

"Good," I said. "Let's get whatever you do have within a bit easier reach. Can you bring the tender up the auxiliary service tracks alongside the right-hand side of the train?"

"We require a crosshatch to change tracks," Sarge said.

"Yes, I know," I said. A crosshatch was a section of spiral-laid tracks that allowed a Quadrail to quickly switch from one track to another without having to first get to a station. "Are there any coming up?"

Another pause as they again communed with each other. If defenders were the Chahwyn's attempt to create Spiders with quick minds and the ability to take the initiative, I reflected, they still had a long way to go. "The nearest is three hours away," Sarge reported.

"That should do," I said. "When we hit the crosshatch, bring the tender up alongside—let's see—alongside the door into the center compartment car. Kennrick's compartment is on the opposite side, so he won't spot it."

"Other passengers may notice its passage," Sarge warned.

"Not if they're all watching dit rec dramas at the time," I said. "But you're right. We'll have the conductors opaque any open display windows before you move the tender, just to be on the safe side." I braced myself. "Now we need an update from the inside. Can you get in contact with Bayta?"

Sarge seemed to straighten a little on his metallic legs. "Frank?" Bayta's voice came.

I jumped. I'd never even heard of Spiders being able to do *that*. Something new the Chahwyn had come up with for their defenders? "Bayta? Is that you?" I called.

"Yes," Sarge said, still in Bayta's voice. "I hope things look better out there than they do in here."

"I'm working on it," I assured her. "Can you see where the other ends of your nooses are connected?"

"One's attached to the door, the other to the curve couch," she reported. "Both are running through pulley systems, so that if the door opens or the couch collapses into the divider . . ." She left the sentence unfinished.

"Understood," I said quickly. I didn't want to dwell on the consequences, either. "Is there any way to get to the wires from outside the room? Maybe open the door or divider just far enough to send in a mite with wire cutters?"

"No," the response came immediately. "Opening the door at all will kill me. And the divider can only be opened about as far as it was earlier."

Which hadn't left enough of a gap for a mite to squeeze through. I wondered briefly about the even smaller twitters, but quickly abandoned the thought. Twitters were delicate creatures, designed for electronics repair and assembly, and I doubted they would have the strength to carry and operate something as big and heavy as wire cutters. "How about the ceiling?" I asked. "We've still got almost two hours' worth of Spiders and moving passengers thudding around. Could the mites disassemble their way through enough of the ceiling so that they could get the rest of the way through later tonight while Kennrick's asleep?"

"Two hours wouldn't be nearly enough time," Bayta said. "Besides, I think he's put sensors up there. There are six lumps of what looks like clay attached to parts of the ceiling and wired into his reader."

"Gray-colored clay?"

"Dark gray, yes."

"They're sensors, all right," I confirmed. "Certainly audio, possibly motion, too. There are six, you say?"

"Yes, with four more lined up by the door," Bayta said. "From the lengths of their wires, I'd guess he's planning to put them out into the corridor after everyone's left."

I grimaced. The man had definitely thought this through. "Anything else?"

"He's been stretching more wires like the ones around my neck over the floor," she said. "I think they're all just fastened to the walls, but I can't be completely sure."

"Probably just window dressing," I told her. "The more wires he loads the room with, the harder it'll be for us to know which ones we have to cut. Anything else?"

"I don't know what it means," Bayta said slowly, "but he's brought in the oxygen repressurization tank from our car."

I frowned. Every Quadrail car came equipped with a self-contained and self-controlled supply/scrubber/regulator system as an emergency backstop against a sudden loss of air pressure. Bayta and I had used them ourselves on occasion. "What's he thinking, that we're going to try to gas him?"

"I don't know," Bayta said. "He also spent a few minutes earlier cutting into the end of his ticket. Not the key end, but the other end—"

"You talking to Compton?" Sarge interrupted himself.

Only now his voice was Kennrick's.

A shiver ran up my back. I could understand why the Chahwyn might have thought it a good idea to design their new Spiders to channel voices as well as words. But reasonable or not, it was definitely on the north end of creepy.

"If you are, be sure to tell him about the sensors on the ceiling," Kennrick's voice continued. "I don't think he'd be stupid enough to try to get those little mite Spiders digging in from that direction, but better to err on the cautious side. Oh, and ask him how the evacuation's going."

"Frank?" Bayta's voice came back anxiously. "What do I do?"

"Go ahead and tell him," I said. "He already knows you can communicate with the Spiders. *Don't* mention the defenders, though."

"All right."

Sarge's mimicry shifted tone, presumably indicating that his relay had changed from Bayta's thoughts to her verbal conversation with Kennrick. I listened with half an ear as she described how the passengers were being moved and listed how many were left to go.

"Sounds like it's under control," Kennrick said when she'd finished. "Just remind Compton that he needs to be back here in exactly—let's see—one hour and forty minutes. If he's not, the doors close and you're going to be mighty hungry by the time we get to Venidra Carvo."

"I'll tell him," Bayta's voice came back. "Frank?" she said, Sarge's tone again shifting as she switched back to telepathy. "Did you hear all that?"

"Yes, thanks," I told her. "Overconfident SOB, isn't he?"

"What do you want me to do?"

"For now, just try to relax," I said. "And keep me informed as to what he's doing."

"All right." There was a brief pause. "Frank . . . if it doesn't look like it's going to work out . . ."

"It's going to work out," I interrupted. "You just relax, okay? I'll come up with something."

"I'll try," she said. "Thank you."

Sarge fell silent. As he did so, the other defender stirred.

"One of the conductors has been asked how long the passengers will need to remain out of their compartments," he relayed.

I stared out my compartment's display window at the dull landscape of the Tube racing past, illuminated only by the coruscating glow of the Coreline above us and the faint light from our train's own windows. Over two weeks to go before we reached Venidra Carvo. Over two weeks for Bayta to be trapped with a murderer.

I looked back at the defenders. Their white-dotted silver globes didn't carry the faintest hint of an expression, but there was something about the way they were standing, something in their stance and stillness, that conveyed an unpleasant mixture of determination and ruthlessness.

The defenders weren't going to let Bayta spend two weeks as Kennrick's prisoner, either. The only question was whether I would come up with a plan to free her, or they would.

And which of our plans would get her through this alive.

"Compton?" Sarge prompted.

I took a deep breath. "Tell them six hours," I said. "One way or another, they'll be back in their compartments in six hours."

TWENTY-ONE :

Precisely two hours after being dismissed from Minnario's compartment, I was back.

"Right on time," Kennrick said approvingly as I came up to the narrow gap he'd again opened in the divider wall. "Excellent. All that Westali training, no doubt. You have your friend's rations?"

"Right here," I said, peering through the gap as I held up the package for him to see. He was back to his earlier cross-legged posture on the bed, this time with his reader propped up on the pillow beside him.

Bayta, in contrast, was now lying on her back on the floor with her feet toward me, the blanket covering her from neck to ankles, her head resting on the pillow. Her face was under control, but I could see the low-level nervousness beneath it. I also noted that there were now three loops of wire around her neck instead of two.

When Bayta had said Kennrick was stringing new lengths of wire around the room, she'd definitely been understating the case. The place was full of the damn stuff, most of it criss-crossing the room at shin height. Half a dozen of the wires ran over Bayta's torso and legs, while the rest were arranged in front of the door and divider. Even if none of them were actually attached to Bayta's neck loops, making a mad dash across the room to wring Kennrick's neck was now out of the question.

"You like the new arrangement?" Kennrick asked.

"Looks like the hobby room of a tall-ship model maker," I said. "Listen, the gap here is too small to fit the package through. Can you open it up a bit?"

"I could," he said consideringly. "But it would be a bit tricky for her to eat with a sliced throat, don't you think?"

I grimaced. "How about I open the package and send them through individually?"

"How about you do that," he agreed. "Only be careful where they land."

Tearing open the package, I started dropping the bars through the gap, making sure to miss all the wires. "I hope you're not going to try to tell me all of those are connected to Bayta."

"Some of them might be," he said. "Others might be holding back other lines, so that her throat only remains intact if you leave them alone. Just in case you were thinking about sending in some twitters with instructions to cut everything in sight."

"I wasn't," I assured him. "Look, Kennrick—"

"Hey, you have to see this," he interrupted, reaching down to the bed beside him and picking up a flat piece of dull gray metal. "Especially since you asked about it earlier. This is part of the stiffening frame for my larger carrybag. Watch."

Picking up his multitool, he used the needle-nosed pliers to get a grip on the corner of the plate. He pulled carefully to the side; and, to my amazement, a thin wire began to peel away from the metal. "Isn't that cool?" he asked, continuing to pull wire from the plate until he'd reached the full extension of his arm. "It's called knitted-metal something-or-other. The stuff's perfectly solid and perfectly innocent until you need to garrote someone." He smiled. "I'll bet Mr. Hardin didn't give *you* toys like this."

"I wouldn't have taken them if he had," I said. "Kennrick, we may have some trouble here. Another side has joined the game."

"What, *Esantra* Worrbin's making threatening noises again on behalf of the Assembly?" he asked contemptuously.

"This has nothing to do with the passengers," I said. "It has to do with the Spiders."

"The *Spiders* are making threatening noises?"

"I'm not joking," I growled. "There's a new class of Spider that's just come on line. They're called defenders, and they're like nothing you've ever seen before."

"I'll be sure to watch out for them," Kennrick promised solemnly. "Along with the ogres and hobgoblins that have also been hiding aboard since we left Homshil. Really, Compton. I was hoping for something a little more imaginative."

"Two of them came aboard an hour ago from a tender that's pulled up behind us," I went on doggedly. "Up to now, my experience with defenders has mostly consisted of being slammed up against a wall by one of them. They're strong, they're smart, they're aggressive, and they're not going to let you walk off this train. Not alive."

I shifted my eyes to Bayta. "And unlike me, they don't particularly care whether you die alone or with company."

For a long moment Kennrick studied my face. "Okay, I'll play along," he said. "Let's assume I'm sufficiently scared. What do you suggest I do next?"

"I suggest *we* get the hell off this train," I said. "I suggest you and Bayta and I get aboard that tender, turn it around, and head back toward Homshil."

"All three of us, you say?" Kennrick asked. "Interesting."

"You and I can't operate the tender," I explained. "Bayta can. But you'll need me as a hostage to guarantee her cooperation."

"As well as guaranteeing a much more exciting ride, I assume?"

"You can tie me up for the whole trip if you want," I said. "The point is that we have to get you off this train while we still can."

"I'll take it under advisement," Kennrick said. "You about done with those?"

I flipped through the last of the ration bars. "Yes."

"And the passengers are out of all three compartment cars?" he asked. "Except for you, of course."

"Yes, everyone's out."

"Good." Unfolding his legs, Kennrick got up from the bed. "See, here's what I'm more concerned about at the moment than imaginary attack Spiders: the question of what you're going to do when I close down that divider."

"I leave the car like you told me to," I said, frowning. "Why?"

"Don't be naive, Compton," he said, picking his way carefully between the wires as he walked toward me. "And don't assume I am, either."

"You can unfasten the wire from the door and watch me go," I suggested.

"You mean open the door and discover to my chagrin that you're standing right outside ready to punch me in the throat?" he countered. "No, thanks."

He came to a stop just out of arm's reach. "So let me explain how this is going to work." He held up a small object. "This is the electric motor from my shaver," he said. "I'm going to use it to rig up a device that'll automatically strangle Bayta after a preprogrammed number of seconds or minutes."

I felt my stomach tighten. "You don't need to do that," I said.

"Ah, but I do," he countered. "You see, once you've gone I'm going to go through all three cars with the infrared sensor in my reader, and it's a very *good* sensor. If I get even a hint that you or someone else is hiding in one of the compartments, I'll come straight back here and make sure Ms. Bayta regrets your stupidity."

"You kill her and you'll have lost your hostage," I warned.

"Oh, I wouldn't kill her," he assured me. "Not right away. I'd probably start by slicing off the end of a finger or two. I'm assuming she's strong enough not to succumb to shock, but of course I don't know that for sure."

I took a deep breath. "Anything else?"

"Two things." He dug into his pocket and pulled out his ticket, and I saw it was sliced about halfway through. "Point one: note the tear," he went on. "If you or anyone else tries to jump me while I'm outside my compartment, all I have to do is tear it the rest of the way through and it becomes useless as a key. You *might* be able to put it back together, but not before the automatic strangler kicks in."

"You don't have to belabor the point, Kennrick," I said. "I recognize that you've thought this whole thing through very carefully."

"Good," he said. "Point two . . ."

Without warning he turned halfway around, bringing the *kwi* on his right hand to bear on Bayta. His thumb pressed the switch, and Bayta's eyes rolled up and closed as her body went limp.

Before I could react, Kennrick had swung back to face me. "Point two is I don't want her giving you a running commentary on what I'm doing," he said conversationally. "Good-bye, Compton."

I lifted my gaze from Bayta to Kennrick's face. "Good-bye, Kennrick," I said. "Don't forget what I said about the defenders."

He was still smiling as he touched the control on the wall, closing the divider in front of me.

Sarge was waiting just inside the rear door of the last compartment car. "She is unconscious," he said in his flat Spider voice. "Why is she unconscious?"

So much for my hope that Bayta had been faking. But then, she could hardly have done anything else. There were ways of telling if someone was truly unconscious. "Because she still needs to maintain the illusion that the *kwi* works like a normal weapon," I told him. "Come on—we need to get out of here."

Reluctantly, I thought, he backed into the vestibule. "What now?" he asked as I followed him in.

"The groundwork's been laid," I told him. "Time to go to work."

We stepped into the first coach car. Many of the displaced passengers had opted to settle down there, I saw, instead of continuing on to coach cars farther back. No doubt they were hoping their proximity to the center of the action would give them a better chance of finding out what was going on.

They were going to be disappointed. "We need a base of operations," I told the defender. "Tell the conductors I need everyone cleared out of this car."

Considering the wealth and power of the travelers I was pushing around, they took the news remarkably well. Maybe the rumor mill had given a sufficiently dark cast to the situation to keep their indignation in check. Or maybe it was the look in my eyes. Either way, with a maximum of cooperation and a minimum of griping, they were soon gone. "What now?" Sarge asked when we were alone.

I checked my watch. Twenty minutes until we hit the crosshatch section, if Sarge's earlier estimate had been correct. "Is your partner ready to move the tender alongside us?" I asked.

"He is," Sarge confirmed. "You still wish it to parallel the center compartment car?"

"No, we'd better hold it back here for now," I said. "I doubt Kennrick's sensors are good enough to spot movement or heat all the way through the compartments on that side of the train, but I don't want to risk it. Make sure the conductors know to opaque all the windows on that side of the train before the tender starts moving."

"It will be done," Sarge said. "What after that?"

"There's one more preliminary job you'll need to do," I told him. "After that, we'll just have to wait until Bayta's awake again so that we'll have a real-time tap into what Kennrick's doing."

"What is this preliminary job you wish me to do?"

Spiders, even defenders, didn't exhibit a whole lot of body language. Even so, as I told him what I wanted, I had no difficulty sensing his stunned outrage. "No," he said when I'd finished, his voice even flatter than usual. "Impossible."

"Why?" I countered. "Because it's against the rules? Trust me—we're going to be breaking a *lot* of rules before this is over."

"Which other rules?"

"Rules that you're going to break so that Bayta lives and Kennrick doesn't escape with information on how to kill people aboard Quadrails," I said bluntly. "Are we all on the same page? Or will I have to go back to the Chahwyn and tell them that one of their own died because you wouldn't cooperate with me?"

"But this is—" Abruptly, he stiffened. "Frank?" he said in Bayta's voice.

"Bayta?" I said, glancing at my watch. It had been only forty minutes since Kennrick had zapped her, though a low-level *kwi* shot was normally good for at least an hour. Her unique mix of Human and Chahwyn physiologies coming into play again, no doubt. "Are you all—?"

"Something's wrong," she interrupted urgently. "The oxygen repressurization tank is gone."

I frowned at Sarge. "What do you mean, it's gone? Gone where?"

"I don't know," she said. "He must have moved it while I was unconscious."

And then, suddenly, I understood. "Damn it," I muttered, heading for the forward vestibule and the compartment cars beyond it. "Come on," I called to Sarge over my shoulder.

The rearmost compartment car was deserted. Moving as quietly as I could, I headed along the corridor to the front. Bracing myself, I touched the control to open the door to the vestibule.

Nothing happened.

I tried twice more, but it was just going through the motions. "He's got us, Bayta," I said. "Damn him. Damn me, too, for not catching on sooner."

"He vented the tank into the vestibule?" Bayta asked.

"You got it," I said bitterly. Thereby increasing the air pressure in the vestibule's confined space, thereby engaging the automatic locks on both the vestibule's doors. Now, the only way to get through into Kennrick's car would be to drill, spike, or otherwise batter our way through.

Bayta and I had used the exact same trick against the Modhri not two months ago, and yet I'd never seen this coming. I must be slipping. "At least now we know why he's got audio sensors laid out in the corridor," I said, forcing back both the anger and the self-reproach. Now was not the time. "He knows we can't batter our way through the vestibule without making a lot of noise."

"That just means we'll have to come up with a different plan," Bayta said calmly. Or maybe the calm was just an artifact of Sarge's transmission. "You have any ideas?"

I stared at the vestibule door, thinking hard. All right. We couldn't get through without making a lot of noise. The noise would trigger the sensors, which would trigger the alarm, which would alert Kennrick to start lopping off Bayta's fingers.

But only if Kennrick was able to hear the alarm . . .

"Fine," I said slowly. "He wants to play cute? We can play cute, too. Here's the plan . . ."

Sarge wasn't thrilled by the plan, for at least three separate rule-breaking reasons. Bayta didn't seem particularly enthusiastic, either, for a whole other set of reasons.

But neither of them could think of anything better. In the end, I got my way.

Our preparations took another hour. We waited another hour after that, just to give Kennrick time to settle down comfortably in the center of his new fortress of solitude.

I spent most of that final hour staring at the walls, running the plan over and over in my brain, trying to think of any alternative actions Kennrick might take that I wouldn't be ready for.

There were, unfortunately, any number of things he *might* do, any one of which would wreck everything. But I knew the man now, hopefully well enough that I could anticipate his likely responses.

We would find out soon enough if I was right.

Finally, the hour was up. "He's stretched out on the bed reading," Sarge relayed Bayta's words and voice as he and I stood at the rear of the last compartment car. "He looks calm and very much at home."

"Good," I said. "Let me know right away when that changes."

"I will," she said.

I touched Sarge's leg. "Wait here," I told him, and passed through the vestibule into the first coach car, the one I'd made into my operations base.

Krel Vevri and *Osantra* Qiddicoj were waiting there for me, both of them standing straight and tall, Qiddicoj's long Filly face still a little pale from his earlier brush with death. "Well?" Vevri asked as I emerged from the vestibule.

Or rather, the Modhri within him said it. "It's time," I confirmed, looking back and forth between the flat eyes and sagging faces.

And it occurred to me, not for the first time, that this was the riskiest part of my plan. The Modhri had promised to co-operate, but if he decided he could do better by switching sides, this whole thing would collapse into disaster and death without warning.

The two aliens nodded in unison. "Let us get on with it," Vevri said.

I shook away the unpleasant thoughts. I couldn't make this work without the Modhri playing spotter for me, and that was that. I would just have to trust him, and watch my back. "Yes, let's," I agreed. "The Spider will take the *Krel* Vevri walker through the airlock into the tender. He'll ride him up to the first compartment car—"

"You've already explained the plan," the Modhri reminded me.

I grimaced. He was right, I had. Twice. "Just remember that once you're in the compartment you'll need to stay perfectly quiet if and when Kennrick passes by," I said. "If he hears you—"

"Bayta will die," Vevri interrupted again. "I understand. Again: let us get on with it."

"Right." I nodded to the defender. "Go."

The defender didn't speak as he led the way to the car's door, but I was pretty sure I could detect some residual reluctance in his body language. Letting a passenger actually go aboard one of their tenders was bad enough. Letting a passenger aboard who was also a Modhran walker was unthinkable. Distantly, I wondered what kind of report he and Sarge would be sending back after this was all over.

They reached the car's outer door and it irised open, revealing the extendable airlock leading to the tender. Vevri and the defender went inside, and the car door closed behind them. "You ready?" I asked Qiddicoj.

"Yes," he said. "Don't worry, Compton. I've agreed to help you, and will hold to that promise."

"That makes me feel so much better," I said, trying not to be too sarcastic. "Come on."

Sarge was waiting for us in the rear compartment car by the vestibule door Kennrick had sealed. "Anything?" I asked as Qiddicoj and I came up to him.

"No," he said.

I nodded. "Let me know when your buddy's in position."

He didn't bother to answer. But then, I'd already gone over this part of the plan twice, too.

The minutes ticked by. I found myself staring at the vestibule door, tracing its edge with my eyes, trying to estimate the strength of the metal. Sarge had assured me that even with the air-pressure seal locked down tight he would have no trouble opening the thing. If he was right, we had a chance.

If he was wrong . . .

"My *Krel* Vevri Eye has entered the first compartment car," Qiddicoj murmured suddenly. "He's found the proper compartment and is unlocking the door."

The compartment at the very front of the train, the one right beside that car's emergency oxygen repressurization tank. I'd had to talk long and earnestly to the compartment's proper occupant to get him to loan me that key. "Is he in yet?"

"Yes," the Modhri confirmed. "He's sealed the door behind him."

I nodded and turned to Sarge. "Your partner ready?"

"He is in place," Sarge said.

"Tell him to go, and then connect me to Bayta," I ordered. "Bayta?"

"I'm here, Frank," her voice came from Sarge's metallic sphere. "Nothing new is happening here."

"It's about to," I assured her. "Keep the relay open."

"All right."

I listened intently, but for the first thirty seconds nothing happened. "What's happening?" I demanded at last.

"I can hear scraping," Bayta reported, her voice tight. "Coming from the edge of the display window, I think. I can't tell for sure—Mr. Kennrick has it opaqued."

"Has he noticed the sound?"

"Yes, he's looking around," Bayta said. "He doesn't look happy—wait; he's figured it out. He's clearing the window—"

"What the *hell*?" Sarge gasped, his voice abruptly switching to Kennrick's. "What the *bloody*—get the hell off my window. You—Bayta—tell it to get off my window."

"I can't," Bayta said aloud. "He's a defender—Mr. Compton told you about them. He won't listen to me."

"Tell him to get off," Kennrick snarled again. "Or by God, I *swear*—"

"He has a loop of wire twisted around her wrist," Sarge reported.

Beside me, the Modhri hissed anger. "Coward," he said contemptuously.

"Shall I order him to leave?" Sarge asked.

I squeezed my hand into a fist, emotion and logic doing a vicious tug-of-war with my soul. If this was a bluff, and I blinked, our best opportunity to nail Kennrick would be gone.

But if it *wasn't* a bluff, Bayta was about to lose a hand.

"Compton?" Sarge asked again.

Abruptly, the decision was taken from me. "No," Bayta's voice came firmly from Sarge's metal sphere. "Keep going. It's our only chance."

"Compton?" Kennrick's voice demanded. "Compton? Call him off, damn you. You hear me?"

"Keep going," Bayta said again.

"Compton? *Compton?*"

"He can't do anything," Bayta told him, her voice frightened and pleading. "Please—he can't do any—"

Abruptly, her voice went silent. "Bayta!" I barked.

"She's unhurt," Sarge said. "He has shot her with the *kwi*."

I braced myself. "What about her hand?"

"Also unhurt," Sarge assured me. "The Human has opaqued the window again."

"And?" I demanded.

"A moment."

I rubbed a layer of sweat off my forehead, willing my heartbeat to slow down as the defender hanging on to the outside of the car did whatever changes were necessary to his sensor suite to let him see through an opaqued display window. "The Human has moved to the door and is working with some of the wires connected there," Sarge reported.

"Which ones?"

"They appear to be the ones connected to Bayta's neck," Sarge said.

"It's working," the Modhri said.

"So far," I agreed cautiously. It was still way too early for us to start congratulating ourselves. "What's he doing now?"

"He has attached his reader to the motor fastened near the door," Sarge said. "The wire from the motor reaches across the compartment to loop around Bayta's neck."

The automatic strangler Kennrick had warned me about. Our quarry was about to make a sortie out of his fortress.

"He is leaving the compartment," Sarge said. "The door is closing . . . I can see no more."

I took a deep breath. It was working. It was actually working. "Tell your partner to stop scraping," I instructed Sarge. "Modhri, let me know the minute you hear movement outside Vevri's compartment."

"I will," the Modhri promised, a note of what sounded like genuine awe in his voice. "You amaze me, Compton. How did you know he would behave in precisely this manner?"

"Because I have a good idea how people like that think," I said. That, plus the fact that Kennrick had damn few options right now. If the Spider managed to break the seal around his window, his air would go rushing out into the near-vacuum of the Tube. Without keys to any of the other compartments, there was nowhere else he could relocate to, even if he was willing to leave his carefully laid defenses. Trying to camp out in the corridor wouldn't be any better.

Which left him only one real option: buy himself some time, and hope he could figure out how to get the Spider off his window. Time, in this particular case, being oxygen.

And since he'd already used the tank in his own car to block the vestibule, he was going to have to go to the next car forward and steal theirs.

"You understand him, indeed," the Modhri murmured. "My congratulations."

"Let's save the celebration until he actually gets to the tank," I warned, still refusing to allow my hopes to get too high. "He could still decide to hunker down in the corridor while he tries to think up a new—"

"There!" the Modhri cut me off. "He's outside the forward car stateroom, and has begun to unfasten the oxygen tank."

And with Kennrick a car and a half away from all his audio sensors and alarms, it was time to go. "Your turn," I said, gesturing Sarge toward the vestibule door.

The words were barely out of my mouth when two of the defender's legs lanced forward, their tips spearing hard into the edge of the door. Before my ears could recover from the sound he hit the door again, with an even harder double blow than before.

And then, through the ringing in my ears, I heard the angry hiss of escaping air. The Spider had dented the door just enough to break the seal, releasing the pressure that had kept it locked.

I stepped forward and hit the release. The door opened halfway, then faltered as the deformed metal hung up on its rollers. I grabbed the edge, and with the defender joining my effort we shoved it the rest of the way open. I crossed the vestibule, stepping over the spent oxygen cylinder Kennrick had put there earlier, and touched the control at the other end.

The door opened into a deserted corridor. I stepped inside the car and headed forward at a fast jog. "How's he doing?" I asked over my shoulder.

"The sounds of disassembly have just finished," the Modhri reported. "The sounds now are those of one hefting a large object . . . he's starting back along the corridor."

Which meant our grace period was nearly at an end. "Thanks," I said, picking up my pace. "Get back into the vestibule and make sure the door closes behind you."

I reached Minnario's compartment door, keyed it open, and slipped inside. Sarge was right behind me.

It wasn't until the door slid shut again that I discovered that Qiddicoj had followed us in. "I told you to go back," I snapped.

"You may need me," he said.

I cursed under my breath. But it was too late for him to go back now. "Just stay quiet and out of my way," I growled.

I crossed the room to where the divider sealed against the wall. Kennrick had undoubtedly locked it from his side after my last visit, and in theory I couldn't unlock it from here.

But Bayta and I had run into this problem once before, and we'd come up with an answer to it. "Ready," I said, nodding to Sarge. "Have the conductors cut power now."

For three heartbeats nothing happened. Then, the compartment around us went dark. I counted out two more heartbeats, and the light came back on.

And with that, the divider returned to its default position of being unlocked.

"The Human's footsteps have faded from my other Eye's hearing," the Modhri murmured. "Do we open the divider?"

"Not yet," I said, kneeling on the curve couch and pressing my ear against the divider. "We have to wait until Kennrick gets back and disarms the automatic strangler setup. Defender, better have your partner start his scratching again." I frowned as a sudden thought struck me. "He *can't* actually dig all the way through the seal, can he?"

"No," Sarge said. But I could hear the disapproval in his voice. Letting passengers aboard tenders was broken rule number one; even pretending to do damage to one of their own Quadrails was broken rule number two. In his place, I decided, I would probably be unhappy, too.

For almost two minutes nothing happened. I was starting to wonder if Kennrick had decided to make a camp out in the corridor after all when I half heard, half felt a faint thud. There was a short pause, another thud—

"He has returned," Sarge confirmed as he picked up the commentary from the defender hanging outside the opaqued window. "He carries the oxygen tank with him."

I started to breathe again. It was nearly over. Kennrick had jumped perfectly through every hoop I'd set in front of him. All he had to do now was disarm the automatic strangler, reconnect the door trip wires to guard against intrusion from that direction, and then take the oxygen tank to the bed and start rigging it for his use if and when the defender made it though his window seal. I pressed my ear a little harder against the divider, even though I knew I'd never pick up the subtle sound or vibration of Kennrick heaving the oxygen tank onto the bed.

Which meant I was completely unprepared for the sudden thump that bounced against the divider right beside my ear. "What was that?" I whispered urgently. "Defender? Where the hell—?"

"He has seated himself on the curve couch," Sarge reported. "He is working on the pressurization tank's valve."

I felt the blood freeze in my veins. Kennrick wasn't supposed to be on the curve couch. He was supposed to be on the bed, like he'd been every other time I'd come in here. He was supposed to be concentrating so hard on his new oxygen tank and the Spider hanging outside his window that he wouldn't notice the divider open the crucial few centimeters I needed.

But he wasn't on the bed. He was on the curve couch, which would start retracting into the divider the instant I touched the control. There was no way in hell he could possibly miss that.

The Modhri must have sensed my sudden turmoil. "What is it?" he murmured.

"I need to open the divider without him noticing," I said grimly. "*And* I need him in front of the gap where I can see him, not way off to the side the way he is now."

"I see," the Modhri said calmly. "Do you still have the bypass mimic you took from *Logra* Emikai?"

"Uh . . ." I floundered, caught off balance by the sudden change in subject. "Yes, I've got it. Why?"

"Give it to me," the Modhri said, holding out his hand.

I stared at him. What in the world was he up to? "It doesn't work on Spider locks," I said.

"I don't need it to," the Modhri said, his hand still outstretched. "You wish the Human Kennrick in front of the opening. I will make that happen."

Trusting the Modhri, the words whispered through my mind. But time was running out, and I didn't have anything better to suggest. Digging the flat gray box out of my pocket, I handed it over.

"Thank you," the Modhri said, fingering it thoughtfully.

"Stay quiet, and stand well clear." He looked at the defender. "You, too," he added.

The defender seemed to think it over. Then, with obvious reluctance, he stepped all the way back to the compartment door. I took advantage of the moment to climb off the curve couch and press myself against its end, a meter from the wall where the divider would be opening.

The Modhri waited until we were set, then stepped over to the divider control. "Stand ready," he told me, and touched the control.

The divider started sliding open. It had barely cleared the wall when I heard an explosive curse from the other side of the widening gap. "What the—? *Compton?* Compton, *damn* you—"

"Not Compton," the Modhri called hastily through to him. "I am *Osantra* Qiddicoj. I have come to make you a bargain."

"What the—how did you get in there?" Kennrick snarled, and I could hear the subtle shift in the sound of his voice as he moved away from the collapsing curve couch.

"With this," the Modhri said, poking the corner of the bypass mimic through the still-opening divider. I tensed, but almost before I could start to wonder if he'd forgotten about Bayta he touched the control again, stopping the divider at just the right position. "It's a duplicate of the locksmith's bypass mimic Compton took from *Logra* Emikai. I offer it to you as part of a—"

"What the hell are you talking about?" Kennrick demanded. "The damn thing doesn't work on Spider locks. Compton said so."

"Compton was wrong," the Modhri countered, wiggling the mimic as if to emphasize his words. "I bought this spare from *Logra* Emikai, who showed me its secret. I offer it to you now in exchange for *your* secret of bringing death aboard the Quadrail."

Abruptly, he snatched the mimic out of the gap, and I caught a glimpse of Kennrick's fingertips as he grabbed for the device. "Give it here," Kennrick snarled.

"Not until you swear to the bargain," the Modhri said firmly. "With this you can move to a different room, where the Spider attacking you cannot—"

And right in the middle of a sentence, he collapsed abruptly into a heap on the floor, the mimic clattering against the deck as it fell from suddenly nerveless fingers.

"Nice try, Compton," Kennrick called from the other side of the divider. "You really think I'm that stupid?"

I pressed harder against the divider, gesturing to Sarge to likewise keep silent and motionless. Kennrick had obviously used the *kwi* on Qiddicoj . . . but with Bayta still unconscious, I knew for a fact the *kwi* hadn't worked. Qiddicoj was faking, lying supposedly unconscious with the perfect bait lying millimeters from his hand.

"I know you're in there, Compton," Kennrick bit out, raising his voice over the scraping sound of the defender outside his window. "Come out right now, or I'm going to start cutting off your girlfriend's fingers."

I clenched my teeth, my eyes riveted on the mimic. Because it *was* the perfect bait, and Kennrick had to know that. If he could get it to work on Spider locks, then every compartment in these two cars would be open to him. He could move himself and his hostage back and forth between rooms, resetting his traps and strangle lines, keeping himself clear of whatever the defenders tried to do to pin him down or root him out.

"You hear me, Compton?" Kennrick called again. "Show yourself. *Now.*"

Only the Modhri had forgotten one crucial detail. The

rigged vestibule had been sealed by means of a purely mechanical pressure lock, with nothing that a key or bypass mimic could do anything about. If Kennrick paused long enough to wonder how Qiddicoj had gotten through that, this whole house of cards would collapse.

"Compton?" Kennrick called. The light coming through the gap shifted subtly, and I had the sense that he was now pressing his eye against the opening, trying to see as much of the room as he could. "Compton? Last chance before I start cutting her."

I took a careful breath. He was going for it, I realized with cautiously rekindled hope. He was still calling for me, but he was no longer sure I was really here. Either he hadn't thought about the vestibule question, or he didn't realize the pressure lock couldn't be triggered remotely, or he was desperate enough to take the risk.

I gathered my feet under me, ready to push off the partially collapsed curve couch the minute he made his move. I would have only one shot at this . . .

And then, without warning, Kennrick's left hand darted through the gap and grabbed the mimic.

I shoved off the couch toward him, knowing even as I did so I would be too late.

But as Kennrick had mistakenly written the Modhri out of his calculations, so had I. Even as Kennrick's fingers closed around the mimic, Qiddicoj's limp hand came suddenly to life, darting up to lock itself around Kennrick's wrist.

Kennrick gave a startled curse, twisting his arm against Qiddicoj's thumb to try to break the grip. Qiddicoj held on gamely, but Kennrick was stronger and had better leverage, and half a second later he was free.

But a half second was all I needed. I reached them as Kennrick started to pull the mimic back through the gap, locking my own fingers around the man's wrist with all the strength adrenaline-flooded muscles could manage.

Kennrick yelped in pain as I yanked his arm hard toward me, slamming his shoulder against the edge of the divider, his face contorted with rage as he glared through the gap at me. "I knew it," he spat. "Clever, Compton. Now go to hell!" Lifting his right arm over his head, he pointed the *kwi* at me and jammed his thumb against the trigger.

"Sorry, Kennrick," I gritted. "Afraid you're out of bullets."

His face twisted even more viciously as he thumbed the *kwi* again. "So now what?" he retorted as he lowered his arm. "You still can't come in here without killing her. What are you going to do, stand there holding my wrist all the way to Venidra Carvo?"

"No," I said as I reached with my left hand around to the small of my back. The worst rule-breaking of all, I reflected, a request which Sarge had nearly vetoed even with both Bayta and me pleading my case. "I'm going to dispense justice."

And with that, I brought my Beretta around to the front, the weapon that had been in a lockbox beneath the train until I'd talked Sarge into sending his partner to retrieve it. Pressing it against Kennrick's side beneath the arm I was holding, I pulled the trigger.

The blast was deafening in the enclosed space. For a second Kennrick just stared at me, his eyes wide and disbelieving. Then his legs collapsed, and he fell to the floor, landing with his torso twisted awkwardly against the wall as I continued to grip his wrist.

"It is over?" Sarge asked.

I took a deep breath and let go of Kennrick's arm. It dropped limply to his side, the impact sending a small ripple through the blood already spreading through the carpet. *Find the murderer,* Givvrac had appealed to me with his last breath. *And kill him.*

Sometimes people did indeed get what they wished for.

"Yes, it's over," I told Sarge quietly, gazing at the eyes now staring their residual astonishment at the compartment's ceiling. "Tell the mites to get busy—I want them through the ceiling as soon as possible, and never mind the mess. And you can tell the other defender he can come back inside."

I leaned forward and peered through the gap. Bayta was lying on the floor, her breathing slow and even, the loops of now useless strangling wire glittering around her neck. As I gazed at her, the scraping from the window stopped, replaced by a sort of mice-in-the-wall sound as the mites set to work on the ceiling.

Beneath my feet, I felt Qiddicoj stir. "May I?" the Modhri asked.

"Sorry," I apologized, stepping clear and offering my hand.

He ignored it, getting to his feet without assistance. "A straightforward yet effective plan," he commented, peering through the gap at Kennrick's body. "My congratulations."

"Thank you," I said. "Much as I hate to say this, I owe you."

"You know the repayment I desire," he said, his voice hardening as he gazed into my eyes. "The method of death used by the Human Kennrick must never be allowed to become public."

"It won't," I promised. "And now that we know how it was done, we should be able to tweak the Spiders' sensors to keep it from happening again."

"Good." Qiddicoj's long Filly face twitched in a wry smile. "After all, I hope someday to rule the galaxy. I can't achieve that goal if the Quadrail system is destroyed."

I felt my stomach tighten. "No, of course not," I agreed. "You'll forgive me if I don't wish you luck with that."

He inclined his head to me. "Then with your permission I'll return to my fellow passengers." He smiled again. "*Osantra* Qiddicoj will be chagrined to discover that he slept through these momentous events."

"As will *Krel* Vevri, no doubt," I agreed. "I presume he's on his way back, too?"

"Yes," Qiddicoj confirmed. "Farewell, Compton. I will most likely not speak to you again."

"Likewise," I said.

I watched as he crossed to the door and disappeared out into the corridor. "There will be repercussions from this," Sarge warned.

"There are repercussions from every action," I said. With the excitement over, I was suddenly very tired. "That's the way of things."

Sarge seemed to digest that. "I will take your weapon now."

I'd almost forgotten the Beretta still hanging loosely in my grip. "Yes, of course," I said, putting on the safety and handing it over. "Back to the lockbox, I presume?"

"Immediately," he said, taking the weapon with one leg and folding it up beneath his metal sphere. Tapping his way to the door, he left the compartment.

I turned again to the opening. Yes, there would be repercussions. Possibly very serious ones.

But we would deal with them as they arose. Right now, all I cared about was that Bayta was alive.

With one last look at Kennrick's frozen eyes, I settled down to listen to the mites working overhead, and to watch Bayta sleep.

TWENTY-TWO :

It took the mites three hours of banging, pounding, and unfastening to clear a corner of the ceiling enough for them to squeeze through. Bayta was awake for most of that time, and I spent a good deal of it bringing her up to speed on what had happened, as well as how the devil's bargain I'd made had worked out.

Even here at the payoff, I could tell she still wasn't happy about the deal. But at least she had the grace to simply thank me for my efforts, and to not argue any further about my methods.

Once the mites were through, the rest was easy. They traced all of the wires that Kennrick had laid out, confirmed that all but the obvious ones were dummies, carefully cut the ones that weren't, and Bayta was finally free.

We left the two defenders in the compartment with Kennrick's body and headed back through the deserted compartment car to announce that the crisis was over and that everyone could start heading back to their compartments. "I was only off by an hour," I commented to Bayta as we passed the jammed vestibule door that Sarge had wrecked. It wasn't going to stay wrecked long; a half-dozen mites were already working on it. "I said things would be back to normal in six hours, and it only took us seven."

"And you probably could have let them back while the mites were working on the ceiling," Bayta pointed out.

"I didn't want to risk any of them getting a look at Kennrick's body as it was dragged out dripping blood," I said. "Aside from the gruesomeness of the whole thing, I didn't want them wondering what I'd used to open up that size hole in his chest. You'll let me know when they've got him to the tender, right?"

"Yes," she said. "A shame it had to end this way. We might have learned more about Mr. Hardin's plan if we'd been able to question him."

I shook my head. "Kennrick would have been trained to hold out against all the more popular forms of interrogation," I said. "In retrospect, I'm guessing now that he *was* part of Du-Noeva's team, that spy Westali was after when we raided Shotoko Associates eleven years ago. In fact, he was probably the one who killed those Westali agents guarding the east door. How he hooked up with Hardin I can only guess."

"I imagine a man with Mr. Hardin's resources has many interesting contacts." Bayta paused. "Thank you for not arguing over the reader, by the way."

"You mean not arguing more than I did?"

"If you want to put it that way."

"No problem," I assured her, fudging the truth just a little. I'd really, really wanted a chance to go through Kennrick's reader before the defenders took it away. Larry Hardin wasn't the type to load all his oranges in one crate—the fact that he'd apparently had Kennrick already prepped and ready to take over my slot the minute I'd resigned from his payroll showed that much. I doubted this was the only plan he had in the works for taking over the Quadrail, and I wanted to see if Kennrick had taken any notes on possible future shenanigans.

But the defenders had been adamant about taking the reader and Kennrick together as a package, and I'd had enough fighting for one day. "So the plan is to load Kennrick aboard the tender, then take it back to the rear of the train and load in the other four bodies?" I asked.

Bayta nodded. "Officially, they'll be removing the bodies for direct transportation to their families. Along the way, though, they'll stop at a siding and take some tissue samples and readings."

"Sounds good," I said. Between the Spiders' readings, the samples Emikai and I had run though my analyzer the previous evening, and the data in Kennrick's reader, the Spiders and Chahwyn ought to have everything they needed to plug this new loophole in their security net.

We passed through the vestibule at the end of the third compartment car and entered the first coach car, the one I'd cleared out as my operations base.

Only it wasn't completely cleared out anymore. *Osantra* Qiddicoj, *Krel* Vevri, and Tra'ho Government Oathling Prapp, the three Modhran walkers, were standing silently a half-dozen steps in front of us, obviously waiting for us to make our appearance. Just behind them stood *Asantra* Muzzfor, the contract-team Filly who had been Kennrick's staunchest supporter and apologist. "It's over?" Muzzfor asked as Bayta and I stepped into the car. "He's dead?"

"Yes, he's dead," I confirmed, taking another, closer look at the walkers. All three were standing unnaturally stiff, their eyes looking odd in a way I'd never seen in a walker before.

And there was something else: a faint, high-pitched dog-whistle sound hovering right on the edge of my hearing. I glanced at Bayta, noting the sudden uncertainty and pain-edged tension in her face. Apparently, she could hear the sound too, possibly better even than I could.

"So then you know," Muzzfor said.

"I know lots of things," I said, frowning. Muzzfor's eyes were hard and cold, and I saw now that the oversized, gene-tically engineered throat tucked beneath his long Filly face seemed to be rapidly quivering. "Anything in particular you had in mind?"

"No matter," he said calmly. "If not now, soon enough." Without any word or signal that I could see, Prapp detached himself from the group and walked toward us. His eyes still looked odd, but as he approached I could see that there was a strangely bitter edge to his expression. "Forgive me," he said as he stepped up to us, and out of the corner of my eye I could see the other two walkers saying the same words in unison.

And then, abruptly, Prapp swung his arm at the shoulder, slapping his hand with vicious strength against the side of Bay-ta's head.

It was so unexpected that she never even had time to gasp as the blow sent her spinning to the floor. I had no time to do more than gape before Prapp turned his attack on me, his arms windmilling like a threshing machine gone berserk.

Reflexively, I gave ground, backing across the room as I blocked and deflected and dodged his blows, trying to get my brain on line. Treachery from the Modhri was nothing new, but treachery *now*? It made no sense.

Fortunately for me, Prapp was untrained and unskilled in

hand-to-hand combat. Now that I was ready for him, I was able to deflect or block most of his punches and kicks with ease, and the few that made it through were weak and ineffective. Another minute to let him wear out his reserves, I estimated, and I should be able to take him down.

But I wasn't going to get that minute. The other two walkers were moving in now, swinging wide in opposite directions to flank me. I shifted direction toward Vevri, hoping that after I took down Prapp I could similarly deal one-on-one with the Juri before Qiddicoj could reach me.

For a few seconds it looked like it was going to work. Then, over Prapp's gasping and my own somewhat less strained breathing I sensed the strange ultrasonic sound change pitch and intensity. A moment later Qiddicoj suddenly increased his pace toward me while Vevri slowed his, with the obvious mutual goal of reaching me simultaneously.

I changed direction again, ducking around behind a pair of chairs and then suddenly jumping up on one of them and kicking at Prapp's head. The blow I landed was only glancing, but it was enough to send him staggering backward out of the fight.

Just in time. I was hopping off the chair again when Vevri and Qiddicoj caught up with me.

Neither of them was any better trained than Prapp. But both were just as determined, and at two-to-one odds I found myself at a dangerous disadvantage. I kept backing and turning, using every bit of cover and blockage available, trying to work my way toward the end of the car where I could escape into the vestibule. At least there they could only come at me one at a time.

And then, out of the corner of my eye I saw the front vestibule door open. I backed a quarter circle, trying to bring the door into my direct view without having to take my eyes off my opponents. If this was another walker whom the Modhri had conveniently failed to mention, I was going to be in serious trouble.

It wasn't another walker. It was Sarge.

For the first couple of seconds no one seemed to notice his arrival. Then, abruptly, Vevri and Qiddicoj abandoned their attack on me. Turning, staggering with muscle fatigue and gasping for breath, they charged full-tilt toward the defender.

I'd seen defender Spiders in action, and Sarge should have counterattacked like a runaway freight. But to my surprise, he didn't. In fact, for those first crucial seconds he stood there, staring like a rookie at his first crime scene. By the time he stirred and lifted his three nearest legs into a sort of combat stance, it was too late. Vevri and Qiddicoj hit him like a matched pair of heat-seeking missiles, slamming into his remaining four legs and staggering him backward. Breathing hard, I shoved off the chair I had been pressed against and headed over to give him a hand.

And was suddenly shoved three meters to my left as Muzzfor slammed into my right side.

I hit the floor in a tangled mess, astonishment and exhaustion conspiring to throw off my usual hit-and-roll reflexes. I tried to get my legs under me, but before I could do so Muzzfor flung himself on top of me, nearly breaking my rib cage in the process.

And as I fought for breath, his hands closed firmly around my neck. "Foolish Human," he said, his voice abruptly deep and resonant and no longer even recognizable as Filiaelian. It made for an eerie contrast with the high-pitched background hum that seemed to be rattling even louder against the base of my skull. "I tried to avoid this," he continued. "I tried to turn you against Emikai, the Modhri—anyone except the Human Kennrick. But you would not be dissuaded." His grip tightened around my throat. "So now do you pay the cost of your cleverness."

My vision was starting to waver. But what most people didn't know, and Muzzfor almost certainly didn't, was that even with my breath cut off there was enough residual oxygen already in my muscle fibers for one good, solid, last-ditch punch.

And with his quivering, oversized throat hanging right over my face, there was only one logical target. Releasing my grip on his wrists, I curled my hands into fists and jabbed upward as hard as I could.

I had expected it to be like hitting a tube of slightly undercooked mostaccioli. To my dismay, it was more like slamming my fists into well-insulated plastic pipe. Whatever the Filly genetic engineers had done to Muzzfor's throat, they'd put some heavy-duty musculature around it.

And with that, my last reserve was gone. My hands dropped back to Muzzfor's wrists, but I had no strength left to try to tear them away from my throat. I couldn't hear the high-pitched whine anymore, and in the distance the clatter of bodies against metal as Vevri and Qiddicoj beat themselves against Sarge likewise faded into the roar of blood rushing in my ears. Muzzfor's face was an expressionless mask, the sort of face Bayta often wore. My thoughts drifted toward Bayta, wondering if Muzzfor and the others would leave her alive or if whatever I'd done to trigger the Modhri's wrath would bring her the same sentence of death.

And then, without warning, something shot into view around Muzzfor's arms and barreled full-tilt into the Filly's side, hurling him off me and ripping his hands away from my throat. Gripping my neck, gasping in great lungfuls of air, I rolled onto my side.

I found myself faced with an incredible sight. Prapp was straddling a prone Muzzfor, pounding his fists against the Filly's head and torso with the same determination he'd used in his earlier attack against me.

But even as I lay there trying to figure out what the hell was happening, Muzzfor seemed to get either his composure or his wind back. One hand slammed against Prapp's throat, snapping his head forward like the clapper of a bell. Prapp went limp, and with a surge of legs and arms Muzzfor sent the Tra'ho sailing helplessly to slam into the floor three meters away. An instant later Muzzfor was back on his feet, his cold, soulless eyes turning back to his unfinished business with me—

Just as Vevri and Qiddicoj slammed into him in a perfectly coordinated high/low double tackle.

Muzzfor gave a bellow as he hit the floor again, a deep, furious ululation that momentarily froze me where I knelt.

If Vevri and Qiddicoj were affected by the roar, it didn't show. They were all over their target, punching and clawing at him with an almost mindless fury.

I still didn't know what the hell was going on. All I knew was that Muzzfor had tried to kill me, the Modhri was no longer on his side, and I was damned if I was going to sit out the rest of this fight.

But even as I got to my feet, Vevri abruptly gave out a choked-off scream and rolled off the downed Filly. As I staggered forward Qiddicoj gave a similar scream and also fell backward, clutching at his stomach. He curled into a fetal position around himself, but not before I saw the blood spreading out across his clothing.

And then Muzzfor was on his feet again, his fingers dripping two different shades of red. He turned toward me, and as he did so his hands curved themselves into raptor talons. Something else the genetic engineers had no doubt graced him with.

For a moment we locked eyes. Then, lifting the talons to point at my stomach, he stalked toward me.

"At least tell me why you want me dead," I croaked, taking an angled step backward. He continued toward me, and I matched him step for step, walking us around in a slow circle that was taking me back toward the rear of the car. I was still breathing heavily; with luck, he would assume I was just trying to buy time. "What did I ever do to you? *Tell* me, damn it. What did I ever do to you?"

Muzzfor didn't answer, but just kept coming. I continued to back away, not daring to look behind me and see if I was about to back into a chair or some other obstacle. The Filly was getting closer, and I imagined I could see a fresh surge of bloodlust in those empty, empty eyes.

He was still coming when two of Sarge's legs stabbed like twin spears into his back.

For a moment Muzzfor just stood there, his gaze on the bloodied metal legs poking out of his chest, a disbelieving expression on his face. Very much the way Kennrick had reacted to his own unexpected defeat and death, a small, detached part of my mind noted. Then, without a sound, the Filly's eyes closed, and he sagged against the Spider legs still holding him mostly upright.

"He is dead?" Sarge asked into the silence.

"He'd damned well better be," I said. Angling in cautiously from the side, just in case, I went up to Muzzfor to check.

The examination didn't take long. Filly genetic engineers could do a lot of strange and interesting things to their clients, as Muzzfor himself had more than proved. But there were only so many places you could put the heart and lungs. "Yes, he's dead," I confirmed, stepping thankfully away from the dangling corpse. "Almost no thanks to you, I might add. What were you doing, waiting for scorecards to be passed out?"

"No," Sarge said, an odd tone to his voice. "I could not . . . it is difficult to explain. I could not think, nor could I properly react to the threat facing me."

"Compton," a voice whispered.

I swore as I stepped past Sarge and Muzzfor and hurried toward the three bodies lying crumpled on the floor. In those last tense minutes, I'd completely forgotten about the Modhri.

Prapp and Vevri weren't moving, but Qiddicoj was still breathing weakly. "Defender, get the doctors up here," I snapped as I dropped to my knees beside the wounded Filly. "*Now.* And get me that LifeGuard," I added, pointing to the orange case on the wall.

"No use," Qiddicoj murmured. Or rather, the Modhri within him murmured. "I'm sorry, Compton. Please believe this was not my doing."

"I know it wasn't," I assured him. "Lie still, now—the doctors are on their way."

The Modhri shook his head. "No use," he said again. "The other Eyes are already dead, and this one will soon join them. When that happens, I too will die."

He looked down at his blood-soaked midsection, then up at me again. "It was a call in my mind and my ears," he said. "The same as I heard two nights ago. Only this time, I was not ordered to lie, but to kill." He coughed, bringing specks of blood to his lips. The blaze on his long face, I noted, had gone deathly pale. "Even knowing it ordered me to evil, I had no power to resist."

Abruptly, a piece fell into place. "Was the compulsion tied to that high-pitched sound I kept hearing?" I asked.

"Yes," Qiddicoj confirmed. "When it ceased . . . the orders were still there, but I no longer had to obey."

And the sound had ceased right after I'd punched Muzzfor in his genetically modified throat. The damn thing hadn't been created so that he could sing high opera. It had been created as a weapon.

But a weapon against whom? The Spiders? The Modhri?

A metal leg appeared in my peripheral vision, and I looked up as Sarge handed me the LifeGuard. I set it down beside *Osantra* Qiddicoj, keying the selector for Filiaelian, and started connecting the arm cuff.

"Compton."

"Lie still," I said. I finished the cuff and leaned over him with the breather mask.

His hand lifted, brushing weakly against the mask. "No use," he said. "Compton. Remember our bargain."

"I will," I said, moving the mask around his flailing arm and pressing it over his nostrils.

"A shame it must end now," the Modhri said as I keyed the LifeGuard. His voice was so weak I could barely hear it. "We worked . . . well . . . together."

"Yes, we did," I agreed, an odd feeling trickling through me. The Modhri was my enemy . . . and yet, this particular mind segment and I had somehow been able to unite against a common threat.

There was a lesson in there somewhere, but at the moment I couldn't be bothered. The Modhri could have run away when I'd wrecked Muzzfor's Pied Piper whistle, but instead he'd sacrificed his life to protect mine. I was *not* going to just sit back and let him die.

I was still talking soothingly to him when the LifeGuard's lights went red. I punched the start button again, but it was pure, useless reflex. Qiddicoj was dead.

And then his eyelids fluttered. "Compton," he whispered.

"I'm here, Modhri," I said.

"A new bargain," he whispered. "In return for saving your life. Learn the truth of what happened here."

I nodded. "Bet on it," I said grimly.

The eyelids fluttered again and went still.

For a minute I continued to kneel over the body, until the LifeGuard's lights again went red. Taking a deep breath, wincing at the ache in my throat, I got tiredly to my feet. "You have made yet another bargain with the Modhri," Sarge said.

"Doesn't count as a bargain," I said, crossing to where Bayta was still lying unconscious. "I'd already promised that to myself."

I lowered myself to the floor beside Bayta, carefully touching the side of her neck. Her pulse was slow but strong, and her chest was moving up and down with steady breathing. There was an ugly handprint on the side of her face where Prapp had slapped her, but it didn't look like anything was broken.

"Shall I move her to one of the seats?" Sarge asked.

"I'll do it," I told him. Getting an arm under her neck, I carefully lifted her head and shoulders up off the floor.

For a long moment I gazed into her face, my eyes tracing all those familiar features. My partner, my ally, my friend . . . and I'd nearly lost her.

Thought virus, the warning whispered through my mind. Too close, and we would both be dangerously vulnerable if one of us was ever infected with a Modhran colony.

I felt my lip twist. The hell with thought viruses.

Leaning close, I kissed her.

Her lips were softer than I'd imagined they would be, probably because I'd so often seen them pursed or stiff with disapproval over something I'd said or done. Her scent was subtle and exotic, with an equally subtle taste to her lips. I got my arm around behind her and held her close, savoring the kiss even as I shivered with what had almost happened to take her away from me.

And then, suddenly, I felt a slight change in the feel of her muscles. I opened my eyes.

To find her eyes were also open. Looking straight back into mine.

I jerked back, a sudden flush of embarrassment and guilt heating my face and neck. "Uh . . ." I floundered.

"Yes," she said, and I could sense some of the same embarrassment in her own voice. "Uh . . . I think I'm all right."

"Are you sure?" I asked, trying to shift my hands to a more professional grip on her arms. This sort of thing wasn't supposed to happen. Especially since neither of us wanted it to.

"I think so," she said. For another moment, her eyes held mine. Then, she tore her gaze away.

And I felt her stiffen. "Frank," she gasped.

"Yeah," I said grimly, following her stricken eyes to the four bloodied bodies scattered around the car. "Not a pretty sight, is it?"

"What hap—?" She broke off, and I had the impression Sarge was feeding her the entire blow-by-blow.

I looked at the bodies again, perversely glad for the distraction they provided, and wondered if Bayta would want to talk later about that impulsive kiss. Part of me hoped she would. Most of me hoped she wouldn't.

"But it doesn't make sense," she said into my thoughts. "Why did *Asantra* Muzzfor do that? *How* did he do that?"

"I don't know," I said. "But I know where to start looking. You up to a little walk?"

"Of course," she said. She got a grip on my arms, which were somehow still wrapped around her, and together we got her to her feet. "Where are we going?"

"Kennrick's compartment," I said. "From the way Muzzfor was talking, I think there's something in there he assumed we'd already found. Something he thought was worth killing us for."

"Something in Mr. Kennrick's lockbox?" she suggested.

"That's the logical place to start," I agreed, tightening my grip on her arm as she wavered a bit. "Can you make it, or do you want to wait here?"

"I can make it," she said grimly. "You think we'll be able to open it?"

"Depends on how good Emikai's bypass mimic really is," I told her. "Easy, now—let's go."

Prapp's attack, plus the ordeal that had preceded it, had apparently taken more out of Bayta than she'd realized. Emikai's mimic was still only midway through its work on Kennrick's portable lockbox when she went over to the bed to lie down. By the time I pulled the lockbox lid open, she was fast asleep.

The box was well stocked, mostly with papers but also with a couple of collections of data chips. Some of the papers had belonged to Givvrac, the ones I skimmed consisting of notes and observations from the contract team's time on Earth. Other papers were Kennrick's, and I made a point of putting those aside for later study. Each of the other members of the contract team had also made donations to the stack, and I was nearly to the bottom before I found a small, sealed folder with Muzzfor's name on it.

I opened it up and carefully read through the contents. Twice. Then, sitting down on the curve couch, I stared at the bloodstained carpet and waited for Bayta to wake up.

And as I sat there, I thought distantly about the many phrases and similes and mental images we used every day without really thinking about them. Never again. Not me. I'd seen the contents of *Asantra* Muzzfor's folder.

I knew now what the Gates of Hell truly looked like.

I'd fallen into a light doze when I was jolted awake by a soft moan. I tensed; but it was only Bayta, stretching carefully on the bed across the compartment from me. "Sorry," she apologized, gingerly touching her face where Prapp had hit her. "I guess I was more tired—"

"We've got trouble," I interrupted her.

Her hand froze against her skin. "I'm listening," she said, her voice back to its usual calm.

I took a deep breath. "We were wrong," I said. "Or at least, I was. Tell me, what do the Chahwyn know about the Shonkla-raa?"

"You know most of it," Bayta said, frowning. "They were a slaver race who conquered most of the galaxy's sentient peoples almost three thousand years ago. They held that power for a thousand years, at which point their subjects staged a co-ordinated revolt and destroyed them."

"You're almost right," I said. "But there's one small detail you and everyone else has gotten wrong. *Shonkla-raa* isn't a race. It's a title. Specifically, an old *Filiaelian* title."

Her eyes widened. "The Shonkla-raa were *Filiaelians*? But then—?"

"But then why haven't they conquered everyone again?" I finished for her. "Simple. Because the Shonkla-raa was a specific Filly genetic line, and that line *was* destroyed in the revolt."

"The Filiaelian obsession with genetic engineering," Bayta said, nodding slowly. "They've been trying to re-create the Shonkla-raa."

"*Some* group of them has been, anyway," I agreed. "Only they're not trying anymore." I held up Muzzfor's folder. "They've done it."

Bayta stared at me, the blood draining from her face. "Oh, no."

"Oh, yes," I confirmed. "But it gets worse. Remember why the Modhri was created in the first place?"

"He was a weapon," Bayta said, the words coming out mechanically, her eyes staring out at a horrifying future. "A last-ditch infiltrator and saboteur."

"Which was also designed to be under Shonkla-raa control." I nodded back toward the coach car two cars behind us. "What did you think of the demo?"

She shivered. "All that because he couldn't get *Logra* Emikai to kill you earlier?"

"All that because he had to deflect me away from Kennrick," I corrected. "So that he and the others could get off the Quadrail without me ever seeing these papers." I shrugged. "And probably also because he'd figured out Kennrick was the killer and wanted to get the murder technique for himself and his buddies." I grimaced. "Remember, a few days ago, when you pointed out that the Modhri hasn't got any purpose? Well, he's got one now. The sword's on the shelf, and the swordsman's all set to pick it up again."

For a long minute neither of us spoke. "What are we going to do?" Bayta asked at last.

"I don't see that we've got much choice," I told her. "We have to take them down."

Bayta stared at me in disbelief. "Frank, it took the whole galaxy to stop the Shonkla-raa the last time. And they didn't have the Modhri to help them then."

"I didn't say it would be easy," I conceded. "But we have a couple of advantages they don't know about."

She barked out a sound that was midway between a chuckle and a sob. "Like what?"

"One: we don't have a whole galaxy's worth of them to deal with this time," I said. "With luck, they've only got a few thousand up and running."

"*Only* a few thousand?"

"*And* they don't have all the warships and weapons they had back then, either," I said. "Number two: they may be really good fighters—and they are," I added, rubbing my ribs. "But they don't know about the new defender-class Spiders. As much as you and I may disagree with the whole defender concept, it's a wild card we ultimately may be glad we've got."

Bayta shivered. "If they don't save the Quadrail only to destroy it," she murmured.

"We'll just have to make sure that doesn't happen, either," I said grimly. "And finally—" I lifted the folder again. "We know where they are."

Bayta sat up a little straighter. "Their location's in there?"

"I think so," I said. "It's clear now that it wasn't a coincidence that Aronobal and Emikai were on Earth at the same time that Givvrac's contract team was at Pellorian Medical. My guess is that the attack on Terese German and her subsequent pregnancy were already planned, and that whoever's in charge of the Shonkla-raa decided the Pellorian Medical thing would be good cover. They then maneuvered Muzzfor onto the team so that he could monitor the others while they brought Terese German to Filly space."

"But why?" Bayta asked. "What do they want with her?"

"Something disgusting, I have no doubt," I said. "But whatever the *why*, the *where* is a space station called Proteus."

Bayta frowned. "That doesn't sound like a Filiaelian name."

"It isn't," I agreed. "The station actually has thirty different names, one corresponding to each of the Twelve Empires' official languages. Apparently, it was designed to be the jewel of Filiaelian diplomatic glory and finesse." I tilted my head. "Want to take a guess as to where this multispecies crown jewel is?"

She frowned; and then, her face cleared. "The Ilat Dumar Covrey system," she said. "Where those six Modhran Filiaelians we ran into on New Tigris had come from."

"Bingo," I said. "Muzzfor had a new set of tickets and passes made out for himself, Aronobal, Emikai, and Terese. I assume he was planning to spring the package on them at Venidra Carvo."

"And we're going to follow them there?"

I turned the folder over in my hand. "Actually," I told her, "I had something a bit different in mind."

TWENTY-THREE :

We found Terese and the two Fillies waiting on the far edge of the Venidra Carvo Station, their luggage gathered in a pile around them. "Good day, Dr. Aronobal; *Logra* Emikai; Ms. German," I greeted them as Bayta and I came up. "If I may say so, you all look a little lost."

"Well, we're not," Terese spoke up, giving me one of those glares she did so well. "So go away."

"Actually, I think you are," I said. "I'm afraid the guide you're expecting won't be joining you."

"What do you mean?" Aronobal asked, frowning down her long nose at me.

"I'm sure you heard that there were four final victims of the murderer Kennrick shortly before he himself was killed a couple of weeks ago," I said.

"Yes, we heard," Aronobal said darkly. "A tragic occurrence."

"Very tragic," I agreed. "Even more so as it turns out that one of them was supposed to contact you here and give you the tickets to your final destination. Specifically, *Asantra* Muzzfor."

Aronobal jerked her head at that. "*Asantra* Muzzfor? Are you certain?"

"He told me so himself, before he died," I assured her. "Here are your tickets." I pulled out the tickets I'd gotten from Muzzfor's folder and passed them out.

Aronobal peered at the destination on her ticket. "These are for *Kuzyatru* Station."

"Never heard of it," Terese said, frowning at hers.

"In English, it's called Proteus," I told the girl. "You may have heard of it by that name."

"Well, I haven't," she growled. "No one said anything about going to a space station. I thought I was going to some big clinic on Dojussu Sefpra Major."

"That was my understanding, as well," Aronobal seconded.

"Maybe you'll be going there after you visit Proteus," I said. "All I know is that these tickets are made out in your names, and that I was asked to deliver them to you."

"You were asked by *Asantra* Muzzfor?" Emikai asked, an odd expression on his face.

"Yes," I confirmed, looking him straight in the eye. "I was with him when he died. He also asked me to accompany you to Proteus, to make sure you got there safely."

"There is no need for that," Emikai said firmly. "I will watch over them."

"I'm sure you will," I acknowledged. "And I certainly imply no slight on your capabilities. But I promised *Asantra* Muzzfor I would go with you, and I would ask that you permit me to honor that promise."

"Of course," Aronobal said distractedly, looking around. "Very well, then. Do you happen to know which track our new train will be taking?"

"Number Eighteen," I said, pointing across the station. "Just follow us."

With Bayta beside me, I started toward our new track. I'd gone only a couple of steps when I felt a soft but insistent grip on my upper arm. "Keep going," I told Bayta as I allowed the hand to slow me down. Terese and Aronobal passed me by, Aronobal giving me barely a glance, Terese ignoring me completely. As their trailing luggage rolled past me I came to a halt. "You have a question?" I asked quietly, turning to face Emikai.

For a moment he didn't speak, his hand still gripping my arm. "They will wish to know exactly how *Asantra* Muzzfor died," he said at last. "Those who now employ me."

"And I'll be glad to tell them," I assured him.

"Will you?" he countered. "Even if they assign a portion of the blame to you?"

"Why would they do that?" I asked, keeping my voice and expression calm. There was no way, after all, for Emikai to know the truth about what had happened to Muzzfor. "I had nothing to do with his death."

"You are the same species as the killer," Emikai pointed out. "That may be enough." His eyes flicked ahead to Bayta and his two companions. "There is no need for you to escort us. It would perhaps be better for you to go about your own business."

"My business is the protection of innocent people," I said. "I have an obligation to see Ms. German safely to Proteus."

Emikai's eyes bored into mine. "Very well," he said. "If you are truly determined, I will not forbid you to accompany us."

"Thank you," I said.

I started to turn away, turned back as his hand darted up again to grip my arm. "But remember," he added. "I too am a protector of my people."

"Indeed you are," I said softly. "Don't worry. I won't forget."

ABOUT THE AUTHOR

Timothy Zahn is the author of more than thirty original science fiction novels, including the popular Cobra and Blackcollar series. His recent novels include *Night Train to Rigel*, *The Third Lynx*, *Odd Girl Out*, *Angelmass*, *Manta's Gift*, *The Green and the Gray*, and the Dragonback young adult adventures *Dragon and Thief*, an A.L.A. Best Book for Young Adults, *Dragon and Soldier*, *Dragon and Slave*, *Dragon and Herdsman*, *Dragon and Judge*, and *Dragon and Liberator*. He has had many short works published in the major SF magazines, including "Cascade Point," which won the Hugo Award for best novella. Among his other works are the bestselling *Star Wars*® novel *Heir to the Empire*, The Hand of Thrawn duology, and the recent *Allegiance*, as well as other *Star Wars*® novels, and *Terminator Salvation: From the Ashes*. He currently resides in Oregon.